Creative Approach to Sex Education and Counseling

CREATIVE APPROACH

TO SEX EDUCATION
AND COUNSELING

by Patricia Schiller

ASSOCIATION PRESS   NEW YORK

International Standard Book Number: 0–8096–1862–1
Library of Congress Catalog Card Number: 73-4033

Library of Congress Cataloging in Publication Data

Schiller, Patricia.
    Creative approach to sex education and counseling.

    Bibliography: p.
    1. Sex instruction—United States. 2. Counseling. I. Title. [DNLM: 1. Counseling. 2. Sex education. HQ 56 S335c 1973]
HQ57.5.A3S34   612.6′007   73-4033
ISBN 0-8096-1862-1

To My Husband Schiller

Contents

FOREWORD by David R. Mace   11

INTRODUCTION   15

1. History of Sex Education and Counseling   19

    Roots of American Sexual Attitudes and Behavior, 19
    The Development of Divergent Tendencies, 22
    The Current Scene, 24
    Emerging Needs and Programs, 28
    Differentiation Between Sex Educator and Sex Counselor, 29

2. What Is Sex Education?   32

    Human Sexuality as Part of the Total Personality, 33
    Sexual Development, 35
    Self-Awareness and Sexual Identification, 42
    Facts and Myths in Sensitive Areas, 46
    Learning the Language of Human Sexuality, 48
    Verbal and Nonverbal Education, 50

3. What Is Sex Counseling?   52

    It Is a Process in Communication, 52
    It Deals With Relationships, 55
    Types of Problems, 56
    Group Premarital Counseling, 62
    Extramarital Problem Counseling, 63
    Marital Problems, 66

4. Adolescent Pregnancy and Parenthood   72

Problems of Adolescent Pregnancy, 72
The Webster School Experiment, 75
Recommendations to Improve Current School Programs, 78
Abortion Counseling in Adolescent Pregnancy, 79
Sex Education and Counseling of the Handicapped, 80

5. Developing Communication Skills   84

Coming to Terms With One's Own Sexuality, 84
Learning the Language, 86
Learning to Listen With the Third Ear, 88
Exercises in Sensitivity, 90
Sensitive Areas in Teaching and Counseling, 97

6. Techniques for Teaching   103

Group-Centered Approach, 104
Case Study—"Put Yourself in His Place," 111
Other Resources, 111
Role-Playing, 113
Other Teaching Aids, 119
Team Teaching, 122
Using the Expert, 125
Teaching Decision-Making, 126

7. Settings Where Teaching and Counseling Take Place   132

Home, 132
Church, 133
Peer Group, 134
Mass Media, 134
Schools, K–12, 135
Clinics, 135
Social Service Agencies, 136
Family-Planning Centers, 137
Universities and Colleges, 139
Graduate Schools, 140
Health Departments, 142

8. Model Training Programs, I   143

Preschool Training Program, 144
Training Programs for Elementary and Secondary Schools, 155

9. Model Training Programs, II   172

    College, 172
    Graduate and Professional Schools, 175
    Institutes, Seminars, and Workshops, 179
    Family-Planning Centers, 180
    Church Groups, 182
    Parent Education, 185
    Preparing the Community for Sex-Education Programs, 186
    Interpreting Sex Education and Counseling Programs to
        Parents, 189

10. Curricula for Sex Education   197

    Preschool Through Third Grade, 198
    Fourth Through Sixth Grade, 201
    Junior High School, 203
    Senior High School, 206
    Sex Education and Counseling for Adults, 209

APPENDIXES   214

    I. *Sex-Attitude Sample Inventory for Adolescents,* 214
    II. *The Training of Sex Educators,* 221
    III. *Building a Core Library in Sex Education,* 230
    IV. *Glossary,* 244

BIBLIOGRAPHY   249

INDEX   251

Foreword

In the summer of 1969, a nation-wide attack was launched on sex education in the schools of this country. It was a brutal assault led by ignorant people with closed minds, and it destroyed many excellent and promising programs. At the time, many of us interpreted this as a serious setback for a good cause. Now, looking back, we are not so sure.

The programs of classroom sex education developed at that time were motivated by panic reactions on the part of many parents and some teachers. The complexity of the task was poorly comprehended by many of the persons involved. We were simply not ready, in terms of experience gained, to put on well-planned and well-tested programs on the scale demanded.

Since then, a great deal of quiet, relatively unobtrusive work has been going on. Specialists in the field have thought deeply and exchanged opinions widely. Careful experiments have been carried out without pressure or haste. A far-reaching learning process has been taking place. We feel much more confident now that we understand what sex education really means.

How far we have progressed is not yet common knowledge. In this book Dr. Patricia Schiller tells the whole story, and brings the reader completely up to date. There are many books that discuss the philosophy of sex education or outline the ground to be covered, or indicate its importance, or explain it in a given context or for a particular group of people. I know of no other book which covers all of these, on a comprehensive basis, with such a wealth of practical detail, as does this one.

Dr. Patricia Schiller is well qualified for her task. She was trained first as a lawyer, then as an educator and marriage counselor, and is now a professor in a medical school. She has worked extensively with

children, with youth, with young adults, with adults, and with professionals in training. She has carried out important research projects under Federal Government and private auspices—particularly in the sex
education of children and of pregnant teen-age girls. She is the founder,
and currently Executive Director, of the American Association of Sex
Educators and Counselors, an inter-professional organization which is
working to establish standards for the training of men and women seeking to qualify themselves as specialists in the field of human sexuality.
To this organization she has contributed richly out of her extensive experience as a practitioner in the field.

I have known Pat Schiller personally for twenty years, and have been
closely associated with many of her professional activities. Besides being
well qualified and capable, she is a person who is ideally suited to work
in the delicate and highly controversial fields of sex education and
counseling. She is an exceedingly warm, kind, and understanding person.
She moves very easily into helping relationships with others and is
able to convey to them a clear and strong awareness that they will find
her completely trustworthy and supportive. This gift of being able to
put people at ease, to accept and respect them as persons, and quickly
to achieve meaningful two-way communication with them, has contributed greatly to her success in a variety of enterprises calling for a
high degree of skill in human relations. All this will be evident to readers
of her book. In these pages she is communicating not simply her ideas,
but herself. She is offering the philosophy she has hammered out in the
crucible of experience, in thousands of hours spent in interaction with
individuals and with groups. She has been ready to learn from a variety
of methods and procedures—from formal classroom education and
traditional psychotherapy to encounter groups and rap sessions. Out of
these she has taken what she found to be effective, and has shaped her
own working patterns, which she now shares with others who are trying to find their way in this relatively new and still highly experimental
field.

What she is saying in this book is that the subject of human sexuality,
far from being limited to a few basic facts about coitus and reproduction, covers a highly complex and extremely subtle blend of biological,
psychological, social and interpersonal aspects of the total meaning of
being either a man or a woman, and that sex education is the process
of helping men, women and children to accept, gladly and positively,
all these aspects of themselves, and to learn to take full responsibility
for their use. Sex can no longer be considered as incidental or auxiliary
to our human nature—something that can be exploited by the hedonist
or discarded by the celibate, because, as Pat Schiller herself so well

expresses it, "sexual development is at the core of personality development."

Given this fundamental concept, certain implications inevitably follow. The first is that in the field of sexuality the word "education" *must* be given its true meaning, which is "to draw out," rather than the more commonly understood (or misunderstood) pedagogic concept that teaching means "to pump in." This implies that the traditional classroom setting, in which the teacher authoritatively imparts knowledge which the students obediently assimilate, is simply an inappropriate setting for the major task which sex education involves. I am not saying that the imparting of information has no place in sex education, but this must always be secondary to the exchange of experience and opinion.

A second implication is that the major qualification of the teacher/counselor in this field is that he must have made considerable progress in his own process of sex education, and therefore can comfortably initiate a process of exchange between himself and those with whom he is working, accepting those persons where they are and being ready to communicate with them concerning any aspect of their personal experience. For this reason, Pat Schiller places central emphasis, in the training of professionals, upon the development in them of personal awareness and their learning of communication skills. Fortunately we have in recent years discovered, through our widespread experimentation with growth groups of various kinds, new and highly effective methods for achieving these goals.

Not only has Pat Schiller made extensive use of group process as a central element in training but she has concluded also that it offers the best medium for sex education itself. She has described and documented this convincingly in working with children, youth, and adults.

The new sex education, described in the book's title as the "creative approach," therefore goes back fundamentally to the manner in which any human society arrives at its values and standards in coming to terms with any new situation. The first step is to turn to the persons who appear to be coping most effectively with the situation concerned. These are personified by the individual in authority, to whom the others are ready to listen. But what he has to say soon ceases to be *authoritative* unless it is also perceived to be *authentic*. The test of this, quite simply, is evidence that the theory is working for the person who expounds it. If the judgment is that it isn't, his hearers may appear to go on listening, but in fact they will have tuned him out, and no real process of education will be taking place.

The person judged to be authentic, on the other hand, is listened to attentively. But his real effectiveness begins when he stops making pronouncements and enters into dialogue with his hearers, and most of all when he encourages them to enter into genuine dialogue with each other, and himself adopts a dual role combining that of learner with that of facilitator. In time, he will be able to provide the members of the group with enough basic understanding of the subject and enough confidence in the procedure to enable them to continue the dialogue, in this or in other groups, without the necessity of further participation on his part.

This is the manner in which our contemporary society will inevitably move ahead in the great task of coming to terms with human sexuality. And it will happen no matter what kind of sex education is officially provided, and indeed even if none at all is provided. The breaking down of our traditional sexual taboos and the great advances in our knowledge have combined to create the equivalent of a human society learning to cope with an entirely new phenomenon. We cannot prevent the process of adaptation that must inevitably follow. What we *can* do, however, is to facilitate that process, give it some guidance in the right direction, and prevent a good deal of needless suffering from being visited upon individuals caught up in the swirling tides of cultural change.

In this book, Pat Schiller shows us the way to do this. We may not agree with everything she says or advocates—she would be the first to recognize this. But I am convinced that the broad outline of what she has presented is sound, relevant, and practicable. What we have here is a good and important book, and I hope it will have the success it deserves.

DAVID R. MACE

(David R. Mace, Ph.D. is Professor of Family Sociology, Behavioral Sciences Center, Bowman Gray School of Medicine, Winston-Salem, N. C. He is a past President of SIECUS (Sex Information and Education. Council of the United States), and was for seven years Executive Director of the American Association of Marriage Counselors).

Introduction

Sex education and counseling programs are here to stay. Two Presidential Commissions within recent years have recommended massive sex education for children, youth and adults. Parents are requesting such programs, and children want them, but many classroom teachers, parents, and clinicians shy away from conducting them because they are unprepared. Materials of all kinds, in print and in preparation, are passed off as sex education and counseling. The programs themselves run the gamut from the showing of films before rigidly segregated groups of boys and girls to single sessions on contraceptive methods. And it cannot be denied that these aspects of sex education and counseling are significant and important. But more specific direction is needed.

This book began to take form as I became convinced that sex education is essentially a part of education for human relations, and to be effective requires a group-centered approach—an approach where the teacher acts as catalyst for the group, and each member feels free to sort out conflicts and concerns. I also felt that the influence of the peer group is significant in the learning process and needs to be clearly perceived by the teacher or counselor, and that skills are required to implement this approach. Through the group-centered approach schools would not have to be moralizers. The home could deal with that. But educators and counselors could be trained to help others discuss relative sexual values.

This important field needs many, many experts—experts whose knowledge crosses many disciplines—to interpret and teach, in a nonjudgmental manner, those with widely differing backgrounds.

My experience as a marriage counselor first alerted me to the importance of effective communication between sexual partners. My patients' inability to communicate their feelings of guilt, self-doubts and lack of confidence, as well as their joy in their sexuality, seemed critical to their desire for intimacy. Their inability to risk trusting each other with their sensitive feelings was often central to their problem. Somehow factual knowledge of human sexuality did not help their sexual situation. The process of effective communication became an essential part of the sex education and counseling involved in treating and working with patients.

The same need for effective communication was apparent in the pregnant adolescent girls whom I knew at the Webster School for Pregnant School-Aged Girls, in Washington, D.C., where I served as clinical psychologist. These were intelligent teenagers who had a satisfactory knowledge of the human reproductive system and birth control, and who could easily identify and correctly spell the vocabulary terms dealing with human sexuality. *But* these accomplishments had been inadequate to prevent their unwanted pregnancies. These girls were searching for opportunities openly to discuss and understand their feelings with people whom they could trust. They also wanted to know how their school friends felt about the situation that concerned them. They felt a deep need to be able to talk out their concerns and to understand the feelings of their partners so that they could make decisions that would help them cope with their sexuality.

It was these young teenagers who suggested that I carry the group-centered approach to their younger brothers and sisters, starting at the preschool level. And more important they insisted that teachers and counselors should be helped to open up to children, youth and parents in warm, accepting ways. They were turned off, they said, by teachers or counselors who lectured to them about sex in a sermonizing way. They felt this made sex sound awful and dangerous.

Since 1967 the group-centered interdisciplinary approach outlined here has been used extensively in the training of professionals working in sex education and counseling. They are trained in content, attitude and skills. This includes doctors, nurses, teachers, counselors, social workers, ministers, psychologists, sociologists, home economists, planned parenthood and family planning workers, and many other professional workers. Frequently parents are also included in these training groups. The approach has been publicized and demonstrated at professional conferences conducted by the American Association of Sex Educators and Counselors, as well as by numerous other professional organizations, and at many professional schools, including schools of medicine, social work, teacher training, and nursing.

Many excellent texts have been written about the subject of human sexuality. Others have appeared which deal exclusively with methods, techniques for training, and curriculum guides. This book focuses on the process of delivering sex education and counseling and the importance of communication to teachers, counselors, and parents. It combines, at various educational levels, knowledge about human sexuality, attitudes and skills in education and counseling. Because it is a first, it is only a beginning. Hopefully, the experiences described here will help introduce greater skill and interest in training approaches which can assist in helping sex educators and counselors enhance their competency.

What is reflected here is more than one person's training experience. This book represents the joint efforts of myself, my colleagues, and those whom we were asked to train but who actually shared with us in developing the training program, including parents, youth and children in addition to professionals. Our trainees in many ways became the trainers. My gain was both professional and personal. New attitudes, feelings, skills and facts affected both my professional and personal life.

The reference books which I have used have been written by women and men of outstanding stature. Through the years, they have influenced my thinking and given me the courage to take calculated risks in our training programs. Many of these writers have actually participated in the programs themselves as consultants or faculty.

Putting together in a book a process which has grown with me over a long span of years has caused me to experience a range of emotions which have run the gamut from euphoric moments to periods of frustration and doubt. But teaching and counseling in the realm of human sexuality often include the same wide range of emotions, for we are involved with others in deep and sensitive relations. It is my hope that the concepts, methods, techniques and illustrations set forth here will help all of us to be both comfortable and more effective.

P.S.

1

History of Sex Education
and Counseling

It comes as no surprise to those involved in sex education and counseling to be told that many Americans are self-conscious about sex. Even at a lecture concerned with sex the speaker of the evening is apt to be tense and uneven in his handling of the subject. Intelligent parents cringe with terror when their child utters a four-letter word or when that same child inadvertently rushes into their bedroom when they are half dressed or naked.

Roots of American Sexual Attitudes and Behavior

As in most areas of living, the past offers many clues to an understanding of present behavior. A detailed examination of this background would require a book in itself, but it is important to take at least an overview of the influences from the past which have affected many of our negative and positive feelings toward sex. Putting the pieces together may help us cope with the sexual hangovers that still exist. Not only do these hangovers cause personal problems for those whose lives they still rule but they also retard effective teaching and counseling of human sexuality by causing intelligent educators and counselors to fear their sexuality and, in turn, to project these fears on those who seek their help.

The two dominant forces which tower above all others appear to be the moral and legal codes surrounding sexual behavior. In the past these were often prescribed by tribal sex customs, communal folklore dealing with human sexual conduct, and by common law as well as laws that were written and often codified. Their influence touched the family and the lives of all its members.

Without question, the most significant single source of influence on sexual mores was the Bible. Its teachings permeated the sexual attitudes, values, and behavior of the entire Judeo-Christian world. Our Western culture accepted the authority of its absolutes concerning human sexual behavior. To doubt, question or behave in a manner contrary to the moral teaching of the Bible was to risk being labeled immoral or even infidel and thus incur the wrath of community and religious leaders.

Until the twentieth century this kind of controlled sexual morality dominated the American scene. The nature of the sexual relationship between men and women in and out of marriage was, and is still, greatly influenced by these religious teachings. The double standard, with all its accompanying expressions of sexism and male chauvinism, found its origin in the many Judeo-Christian doctrines concerning sex.

All too often today, writers and lecturers deal exclusively with the negative aspects of sexual teaching reflected in moral law and the Bible. They emphasize the repressive and punitive injunctions which they claim have developed unhealthy attitudes of guilt and fear in people. These attitudes are justified in many instances. The harsh tone reflected in many of the Biblical pronouncements also needs to be examined in the light of the customs and life-styles of the period.

The leading moral sexual teachings reflected in the Bible, however, have also had a profoundly positive impact, and this must be kept clearly in mind if we are to understand its influences—both negative and positive—on past and current sexual behavior and family-life practices.

The Bible leaves no question but that our forefathers believed sexuality to be deeply embedded in the human personality. In the Old Testament, sex is regarded as a gift of God. Genesis speaks of the creation of man as a sexual being, male and female. And the comment on the endowments of man and woman, "It is good," implicitly includes their sexuality.

The Old Testament frequently makes reference, with sensitivity and understanding, to the male-female sexual relationship, and the physical desire and love that exists between wife and husband.

The sensuous poetic passages in the Song of Solomon are sheer erotic ecstasy and can hold their own with modern aesthetic expressions of sexuality. In many instances the New Testament reinforces the positive accepting view toward human sexuality as being at the core of our personality.

How can we reconcile this healthy positive approach with the negative idea that "sex is sinful" which appears to permeate the early teachings of the church?

The protagonists of "sex is sin" came into prominence during the second century A.D. Many modern scholars believe that Paul was quoted out of context. "It is well for a man not to touch a woman" they said, and followed through with the thesis that sexual intercourse is the "original sin." Asceticism, virginity, and self-denial were widely regarded as the religious routes to God. These ideas found considerable support in the writings of Augustine.

Medieval Christianity, strongly influenced by Augustine, came to regard celibacy as higher and more spiritual, and of greater value than carnal marriage. Here are the roots of one form of the double standard: celibacy for the clergy or monks who lived apart from the people; matrimony for the ordinary people who needed to get married because of their passions and weaknesses.

The Reformation movement headed by Martin Luther rejected the double moral standard of the Middle Ages. As Luther saw it, marriage was an order of creation. However, John Calvin remained closer to the Augustinian understanding of sexuality and sin. And it was the Calvinistic influence which was carried to America by the Puritans. For the Puritans, the sole purpose of sex was procreation within marriage, and even in marriage sexual relations were thought to be base. Loyalty to God was consistent with a negative attitude toward human sexuality. Many Puritans shunned the pleasures of the world, and, within marriage, the pleasures of sex.

What were men to do with these allegedly base drives that were within them? The admonishment for chastity preached to boys was rarely given or taken seriously. A leading sociologist refers to this double standard as "an orthodox double standard." Since men needed women in order to enjoy their half-forbidden pleasures they felt morally free to do so with "bad women." By marrying a virgin from among the "good women," men believed, they would not fall from the grace of God when they entered the marriage relationship and confronted the realm of sex.

The Puritanical moral code set the legislative pattern for many of our Colonial laws and later appeared in many statute books throughout the United States. This code was reinforced by a dominant theme from one strand of the secular heritage from ancient Greece. The Greeks had set a high tone in philosophy, but a low tone with respect to femininity and heterosexuality. There were Greeks for whom friendship among members of the same sex was regarded more highly than was marital love. In the process of history, this dominant theme received curious support from a minor current which held that liberation of the spirit from sensuality could be accomplished only through the rigors of asceticism.

The famous "Comstock laws" of 1873 reflect the current moral teachings about sex both within the church and within the secular community at that time. To Anthony Comstock, secretary of the New York Society for the Suppression of Vice, obscenity was a "poison to soul and body, and anything remotely touching upon sex was to his mind obscene." The Act of 1873, which embodied anti-contraceptive and anti-obscenity laws, took its name from him. A year before his death in 1915, he had Margaret Sanger indicted because of articles on contraception that had appeared in her newspaper, *The Woman Rebel.*

The basic antipathy to public knowledge and family teaching of human sexuality was not due to ignorance of sex. Medical knowledge was sufficiently adequate to provide an educational base for systematic learning. Rather the barriers were inherent in the cultural frame.

The Development of Divergent Tendencies*

Although this biblical ethic, particularly in its Protestant versions, has long dominated American sexual mores, the successive waves of immigrants in the nineteenth century brought a variety of new cultural and religious attitudes toward human sexuality. The precise moment when these forces from the melting pot began to have an impact on American sexuality is not easy to pinpoint, although in retrospect it is not difficult to see that they have had a considerable role in enhancing and enriching American sexual conduct. To a lesser extent this conduct had been influenced even earlier by the emancipation of the black people, although only now are their sexual customs having a pronounced effect on the mainstream of American life. This variety of religious and cultural influences is reflected today in the differences that exist in premarital sexual behavior, marital sexual relations, and in the process and content of sex education and sex counseling.

The beginning of World War I is usually identified as the time when new attitudes and patterns of behavior began to emerge in a significant degree. The war was destructive on many levels, but offered a helping hand to moral freedom of the individual. For example, the U.S. Army recognized venereal disease as a reality and prostitution as a much-sought-after pleasure by the fighting men. Reform included education on venereal disease, keeping the troops occupied by large-scale recreation programs, and removing them from large cities. It has been noted by a sociologist that most of the soldiers stationed near Paris never saw it at all.

The "Roaring Twenties" reflect the dramatic swing away from the older sexual attitudes and public expressions of sexuality. Women's

---

* These views were expressed by Robert S. Pickett in a paper "Sanger to the Seventies" which he delivered at the 4th annual meeting of AASEC, April 16, 1971.

clothes, popular music and dance, bobbed hair—all represented the freedom of the flapper, and the emergence into respectability of the working woman. The Federal Council of Churches accelerated the movement toward greater moral freedom by putting forth the view that sex is a positive and stimulating force for good.

Robert S. and Helen Merrell Lynd, famous sociologists, chose Middle America to test out their assumptions about American mores, values and beliefs. Their studies included the period 1920 to 1930. Evidence of the new sexuality was reflected in the films, in the necking and petting in the dark movie houses, in the naming of the automobile as the "passion wagon" by many, and by the increase in premarital sex, divorce, and children born outside wedlock. Contraception information was available and obtainable for men. Freudian findings concerning the inherent biological determinants of the psycho-sexual development of each person surely buttressed the desire for greater sexual understanding and freedom.

The writings of Havelock Ellis, along with those of Sigmund Freud, initially were of interest and available only to the intellectual and bohemian segment of our population at the turn of the century. Later, however, with the introduction of the paperbacks and popular magazines, these newer understandings of the topic of sex became easily accessible to a broader spectrum of the population. The "naughty but nice" notion of sex continued in America through the fifties, however.

Beginning in the late forties, Alfred Kinsey and his colleagues documented mountains of data which helped our people communicate and share both sophisticated and simplistic notions about the normalcy of masturbation, the great extent to which homosexuality is practiced, the place of premarital sex play, and that to have an orgasm is the desire of most women in our country. His interviews with people from a variety of socio-economic levels helped to focus on the similarity and differences in male-female sexual needs, and the impact of cultural norms on attitudinal differences.

The Masters and Johnson research studies of the 1960's taught us much about the physiological changes involved in sexual intercourse. This famous team also highlighted for physicians and other professionals in health-related fields the impact of human feelings on the adequacy of sexual relations. The work of sex counselors and educators, who stressed that sex education is human relations education, was greatly enhanced.

For better or worse, the past is very much with us. Our hope for the present and future of sex education lies in the resources of the mass media, the greater flexibility of institutional religions toward sex, and the introduction of sex education and counseling in schools, churches and even homes. The concern of national and international groups with limiting population growth and planning families has helped to legitimize the need for more sex education and knowledge about family planning for the general public.

The Current Scene

In our pluralistic society with its diversified cultural and religious patterns a description solely of the mainstream of our population would miss the mark of reality. The presence of minority ethnic, religious, and cultural groups within our society has greatly influenced our attitudes in the past and appears to strongly influence current sexual thought and behavior. Irrespective of the difference in degree to which the various groups accept human sexuality and devote attention to its teaching, the over-all contemporary scene smacks of rapid and creative change. This applies to both individual and social acceptance of sexual behavior.

Adultery, which was once the subject of criminal sanctions, has become less reprehensible among large groups in this country. Changing divorce laws are paving the way for more compatible marital separations. Violation of long-accepted sex morality rules does not affect social and family status as it formerly did. Premarital sex relations, extramarital sex relations, unwed motherhood or fatherhood, abortion and divorce— no longer are any of these a barrier to marriages of choice and family living. Among our youth those contemplating marriage view the other as a total personality as they interact and complement each other in the here and now. Past experiences and past mistakes are generally viewed as part of the fabric of individual growth and development.

Throughout the United States today, leaders in various cultural and religious groups are rethinking long-accepted views concerning human sexuality and personality development. They are searching for legitimate and socially acceptable ways to free individuals from persistent feeling of guilt, anxiety and resentment toward their sexuality while, at the same time, seeking ways of establishing and maintaining social order and group living.

A small but vocal segment who are disturbed by the present social situation feel society can be saved from its alleged immorality by restoring traditional legal and moral codes. They conceive a stable society as one based upon fear and force and the strong implementation of legal and religious authority to uphold the punitive sanctions and guard the social order from change.

The development of safe and convenient methods of contraception resulting in the elimination of fear of pregnancy is considered by many authorities to be the most significant factor in the current sex revolution and expansion of sex education. Not only does relief from fear of un-wanted children change the size and complexion of the family but, more important, it changes the psychological attitude of women toward them-selves. The advent of the automobile and the pill, the two World Wars, the increase in cross-cultural communication through mass media, the increase in higher education for the masses, and the influence of the behavioral and social sciences have all been catalysts in propelling and precipitating change in sexual practices in the America of today.

Major problems exist, however, in effecting implementation of sex-education programs in public schools. Lack of adequate teacher training appears to head the list of problems. Lack of Government funds to sup-port teacher training is another problem. Pressure groups opposed to sex education exercised a strong influence during the 1960's against expand-ing programs and, in fact, shut down many effective programs. The Anaheim School Districts' program in Anaheim, California, is a case in point.

A survey of teacher-preparation institutions conducted by Professor James L. Malfetti of Teachers College and reported in "Sex Education: Who Is Teaching the Teachers?" found that only 21 per cent of the 250 institutions which responded to the questionnaire offered a specific course or courses designed to prepare teachers to teach sex education. Professor Malfetti noted that it is "also discomforting to find that in responding institutions only an estimated 10 per cent of graduates are prepared to teach sex education in the opinion of the administrators." He suggests, among other things, that "teachers who might be assigned specifically to sex education programs should receive special training in content, meth-ods and evaluation in the teaching of sex education appropriate to the age levels of students. Curriculum aids should be called to their atten-tion. Less than 15 per cent of our colleges and universities offer any training, and such training is frequently limited to summer workshops."

The situation is not strikingly different in private schools, clinics, and family-planning centers, where professionals and paraprofessionals with-out any formal training are teaching and counseling in the field of human sexuality. They are using books, pamphlets, and films while relying on their own experience and background to teach and counsel.

Until the 1960's the family-planning and sex-education movements developed as essentially separate entities. Family planning meant con-traception, while sex education meant teaching human sexuality, with the subject of contraception avoided as possibly inciting increased sexual encounters among the students. Recently, however, several important developments have led to the realization that sex education and family planning are interdependent. At the White House Conference for Children in 1970, the members of the Forum on Family Planning and Family Economics accepted in substance, a Report, some of the salient features of which many other national and state groups have considered and supported. The preamble stated:

The family, within its own cultural setting, is the basic unit of our society and a fundamental agency for the development of moral responsibility to help individuals and families develop their fullest potential. We urge all community agencies and institutions to provide comprehensive community programs of family-life education.

Some of the reasons mentioned in the Report for the fusion of family planning and sex education are:

1. Increased recognition and understanding of the complex physical, psychological, and social dimensions of human sexuality.

2. Development of sex-education models which include an understanding of family planning within a context of responsible behavior.

3. The realization that availability of contraception alone does not ensure utilization, especially where pregnancy planning is most crucial. Family planning has been realized in its broadest sense only where linked to an understanding of particular people's life priorities and mediated through an appropriate education system.

4. The sexual climate in which concepts related to actual behavior can be expressed openly and reflected in education services and/or laws.

It is generally agreed that family planning is one of the subjects most often asked about by students in the reproductive age group. Family-planning education and counseling can have an important effect upon men and women in their day-to-day expression of sexuality. For example, many young people of high-school and college age, not prevented by social or moral structures from having sexual intercourse, rarely practice birth control. But when family planning and sexual responsibility have been built into a sex-education program, sexual exposure with contraception soon becomes the norm.

Both private and public schools are now providing sex-education programs from kindergarten through twelfth grade. At the college level, courses and institutes on family planning and sex counseling are being offered. The University Student Health Services appears to be a center for much that is going on at this level. At the professional and graduate level, a recent survey indicated that two thirds of this country's medical schools offer programs in human sexuality. As mentioned earlier 15 per cent of teacher-training schools offer some programs, as do a number of schools of social work, law, divinity and nursing.

The churches are playing a significant role in developing and supporting sex education and counseling programs. Several national church
groups formally advocate responsible sex education and counseling as a
means of building effective family life.

A number of organizations are concerned with sex education, family
planning and counseling either directly or indirectly. Some, in particular,
have been formed solely for the purpose of giving sex education and
training to professionals and others in order to develop competency in
this field. The American Association of Sex Educators and Counselors,
a professional organization, is the single national membership organization whose primary function is the training of professionals and others
in both sex education and sex counseling. SIECUS (Sex Information
and Education Council of the United States) is concerned with promoting human sexuality as a healthy aspect of human personality. It has
been an important catalyst in awakening America to the reality of
sexuality. Its publications are well considered and widely used.*

During the past thirty years, the role of the Federal Government has
not been a consistent one. The Office of Education, Department of
Health, Education and Welfare, has issued many statements of policy
which appear to remain active for a short period of time. Under Title III
of the Elementary and Secondary Education Act (ESEA) passed by
Congress in 1965, however, many family-life and sex-education programs were funded by the Federal Government. Title III, incidentally,
primarily supports innovative and experimental programs at all levels of
education.

In personal conversation with various members of the Office of Education in the early 1960's the author gained the impression that the
following would appear to reflect official policy at that time:

Guided by the conviction that each community must determine the role
which its schools should play in family-life and sex education; that only the
community itself can know what is desirable, what is possible, and what is
wise:
The Office of Education will encourage and support family-life and sex

---

* Other organizations which are making significant contributions to the field are:

American Academy of Pediatrics	Interfaith Commission on Marriage and
American Association of Marriage and	the Family
Family Counselors	National Conference of Catholic
American College of Obstetrics & Gyn-	Churches
ecology	National Council of Churches
American Home Economics Association	National Council of Family Relations
American Medical Association	National Education Association
American Public Health Association	National Medical Association
American Social Health Association	Planned Parenthood–World Population

education as an integral part of the curriculum from the preschool to the college and adult levels; encourage and support training for teachers and health and guidance personnel at all levels of instruction; and encourage and support research in family-life and sex education.

The Office policy is directed toward supporting the schools in their vital role, which supplements that of the family, of educating the child for a healthy, meaningful, and responsible role as an individual and a member of a family.

We share the growing conviction of educators and citizens, that family life and sex education should focus on psychological, sociological, economic and social factors which affect personality and the individual's adjustment in the family and society, as well as on human reproduction. We encourage inclusion of family-life and sex education as an integral part of subjects ranging from health education and home economics to social studies, science, and literature; and the development of separate units in family-life and sex education when appropriate. We advocate preparation in this area for teachers and prospective teachers as essential to any meaningful program in the schools. We endorse the provision that family life and sex education be included in adult-education programs. We encourage the leadership of parents and community in the development of programs of family-life and sex education for children, youth, and adults, and for parents, tied in to what their children are learning in the schools.

During July of 1969, President Richard M. Nixon reaffirmed as national policy the right of all Americans to plan the number and timing of their children. He also established as a national goal the provision of adequate voluntary family-planning services by 1974 to all who desire such services.

National fertility surveys of the United States taken in 1955, 1960, and 1965 have documented the fact that despite legal and religious restrictions, the American people are using contraception extensively. In 1970, the Family Planning Service and Population Research Act was enacted. This Act authorized $352 million over three years to expand research capacity, training facilities and service activities within the United States.

Emerging Needs and Programs

A cursory look at the overwhelming disorganization in family and social life reflected in *a*) massive personal complaints concerning sexism and identity crises, *b*) dramatic increase in the number of unwanted children, *c*) commercial use of sexuality by the mass media, *d*) fears arising from the population explosion and the emerging changes taking place in styles in marriage, *e*) sexual relations between consenting partners of the same and of opposite sex, *f*) increase in marital breakdown, and *g*) legalization of abortion, emphasizes the need for realistic sex education and counseling for children, youth and even adults. Parents particularly are bewildered by the rapid change in morality and life-styles as they compare their own with those of their children. Guidance and instruction become difficult, and they need help from professional advisors.

Shocking statistics show that one third of all deliveries of babies in the United States are to mothers 19 years of age and under, and that increasing numbers of mothers are in the age group of 15 years and under. During 1971, it is estimated, 200,000 children were born to mothers between the ages of 15 and 19 years. Of these 60 per cent were white, 40 per cent black.

In the United States much concern is being expressed concerning population growth. Quality of life rather than quantity is the barometer for judging the population problem in the United States. The Federal Government urges that we achieve an early stability in population in order to make possible the quality of living that our huge resources can provide. Implicit in this attitude is the assumption that the birth rate shall be subject to some kind of control. A stationary population, or zero population growth, means that the birth rate equals the death rate and that net migration is zero. If all births occurred in marriage, population stabilization in the United States would mean an average of 2.4 live births per married woman.

Today half of the nation's mothers with school-age children are working at least part time, a third with children under six years. Implicit in the general question of adequate day care for children is the provision for adequate education and training in family-life and sex education for both parents and their children.

The liberalization of abortion laws and the repeal or invalidation of punitive laws is all to the good. However, the gap leaves much room for sex education and counseling, so that contraceptive failure and the need for abortion will no longer exist in the future. For the present, sex education and counseling appear essential for effective support to those seeking abortion.

With the changing attitudes toward homosexuality, greater knowledge of human sexual development is needed to enhance better understanding of the social-psychological factors involved.

Differentiation Between Sex Educator and Sex Counselor

The changes taking place during the current decade will be many, and the training need for sex educators and counselors will become more essential than ever before. It seems likely that in the future the training of professionals in these fields will reflect the strong element of interdependence now being increasingly recognized. Certainly it is clear that they share the need for similar basic training in such subjects as the process of reproduction, sexual development, sexual functioning, sexual behavior, sex and gender, marriage, family and interpersonal relationships, sex and health, and the historical study of sex. Both sex educators and counselors require training in personal attitudes and in professional behavior. This involves the development of a healthy and mature attitude toward themselves as persons, to their own sexuality, and to their respective roles. At present, however, it is possible to distinguish their activities rather clearly, and it seems likely this will remain true, at least in the immediate future.

ACTIVITIES OF THE SEX EDUCATOR

1. Prepare the way for the effective introduction of a sex education program into a school, agency or community institution.
2. Teach sex education in a classroom, seminar or workshop setting.
3. Develop a curriculum at various levels, with appropriate use of bibliography, and teaching materials including audiovisual aids.
4. Use the various methodologies of classroom teaching, i.e., lecture, small group discussions, role playing, etc.
5. Objectively evaluate programs through reliable assessment instruments and research techniques.
6. Lead groups which require basic counseling and referral skills.
7. Teach parent groups.
8. Serve as a sex-education co-ordinator on a college campus or in a particular geographic area which includes a school district or a group of religious or health institutions or agencies.

ACTIVITIES OF THE SEX COUNSELOR

1. Clinical counseling with individuals involving sexual dysfunctioning.
2. Clinical counseling in group settings which deal with sexual dysfunctioning.
3. Clinical counseling with marital couples or partners where the presenting problems involve human sexuality.
4. Participating as a team member in case studies involving sexual problems.
5. Functioning for sex educators and others as an advisor or referral

source concerning specific problems which go beyond the limits of educational expertise.

6. Dealing with the following types of specific problems in private, agency, clinical, classroom, or hospital settings:

Abortion counseling.

Problem-pregnancy counseling.

Sexual dysfunctioning—frigidity, impotence, premature ejaculation and others.

Family-planning counseling.

In all probability, though the sex educator and the sex counselor will continue to represent two distinct professional specialties, it is likely that many persons who plan to work in the field of human sexuality will want to possess the qualifications of both and will find themselves increasingly functioning in both areas. This is certainly desirable, for each role complements and enhances the other.

2

What Is Sex Education?

Many questions concerning the goals, the process, and the content of sex education are being asked by teachers, counselors and students. The training, educational background, and personality of the teacher are implicitly involved in this formulation of what education about sex is all about. For example, the physician who believes that giving his adolescent female patient just the facts about her reproductive system, its anatomy and physiology, including menstruation and conception, is viewing sex education essentially as the imparting of factual information. The nurse who discusses methods of birth control carefully with her male and female patients in a family-planning center on the basis of a checklist which her patients can repeat verbatim, and from which they choose a method of contraception which pleases them, thinks that she is teaching and that her patients are learning *effective* birth control and family planning.

A school principal bedeviled by angry parents feels threatened by their complaints about the moral tone of his school because one eighth-grade student developed a venereal disease and a ninth-grade student became pregnant. He calls in a nationally known sex-education expert for a day's workshop with the faculty on venereal disease and adolescent pregnancy. He also fits into the workshop two assembly sessions with the entire student body of eight hundred. Each of these assembly periods lasts one hour, during which time the expert talks about the sexual revolution, the pill, and the need for young people to be concerned about the rising rate of venereal disease. A number of students raise intelligent questions: "How far do you go on a date?" . . . "What is love?" . . . "Do boys feel differently about sex than do girls?" . . . "Does venereal disease prevent a woman from being able to have a child?" The expert answers as many questions as she has time for and recommends an ongoing dialogue and program from preschool through the twelfth grade, to include the biological, social, psychological and interpersonal aspects.

The principal feels satisfied with the day's work as he sees it. At last this dreaded subject has been opened up and one day was spent in talking about it. He doesn't feel the need to change his already overcrowded curriculum to include sex education, and especially since his teachers need more time to teach Reading and Math.

Obviously, the above examples fall within a lengthy list of sex-education programs that are inadequate. They hardly touch on the essence of human sexuality. At first blush they may appear to be adequate. Scientific facts and information are obviously essential to our understanding of human sexuality. But facts alone cannot assist us in developing attitudes and behavior patterns which prepare us to cope with the day-to-day concerns, conflicts and pleasures arising from our sexuality.

The truth is that the serious issue raised by teachers and others about a valid formula for sex education, as though one were readily at hand, arises from the contemporary problems, concerns and anxieties which young and old in America face. Concerned citizens are not able to turn their backs on the mounting incidents of unwanted adolescent pregnancy, epidemic percentages of venereal disease amongst our people, sexual causes of marital and family breakdowns, and many other symptoms which arise out of some degree of failure in sexual relations.

Human Sexuality as Part of the Total Personality

Some educators refer to sex education as just that, others prefer to use the phrase "education for human sexuality." It is really in this broader context that any significant discussion of sex education must take place.

Sex is a fundamental dimension of human awareness and development. It is involved with the ever-present desire for personal satisfaction and happiness, and as a consequence involves man's need to establish fulfilling relationships with others. The life-style of each individual will reflect the manner in which he accomplishes this goal, as will the development stage at which he is functioning. Sex education should be realistic and take into consideration that our sex is at the very core of our personality identity. It identifies our gender, our anatomy and physiology. It is personally important to the growing child as he becomes aware of himself, his parental figures, and members of his peer group. Sexual identity is at the base of our self-image. The mirror is ever present to remind us daily of our body shape, form, and gender. The feedback we receive from friends and colleagues sends significant messages.

Sex education begins with parents. It begins as soon as the male or female baby is born and perhaps before that when they are name choosing, doing up the baby's room, buying the layette and so on, from the time they are told that a pregnancy exists.

Sex involves the name we are given at birth, and the toys and activities we enjoy as children. Often this is conditioned by parental figures who tend to stereotype boy and girl roles and identity—all to the disadvantage of the child.

The home is a continuous school for sex. Public or private schools, and peers merely supplement the sex attitudes daily learned in the family circle. The church too is an influence. Many of our churches have formal sex-education programs for both adults and children. Others have incorporated sex education into the religious school programs.

The clothes we wear and the way we wear them reflects our sex. Even unisex clothing, identical outfits worn both by male and female, takes on a unique look for each, whether due to the difference in the manner of walking, the movement of the shoulder, or the smoothness and shape of the throat. No matter if the differences are slight or substantial, they reveal themselves in both subtle and obvious ways which are immediately recognizable. Our sex affects the friends we choose, and our recreational interests, from bricklaying to needle point, from basketball to skiing. Our roles and responsibilities in our families are influenced by sex. The many ways we satisfy and cope with our sexual needs and urges as responsible and committed human beings is based on our sexual perception of ourselves.

Developing the ability of children, youth and adults to cope with their individual sexuality thus becomes the task and scope of sex education. Lester A. Kirkendall, in his SIECUS Study Guide No. 1 on "Sex Education" notes: "Most people assume that in the absence of direct instruction, no sex education takes place. . . . Avoidance, repression, rejection, suppression, embarrassment and shock are negative forms of sex education."

As a matter of fact, many national surveys support the proposition that the strongest influence on the youth is their own peer group. This view is supported by the report of the President's Commission on Obscenity and Pornography which undertook a national survey. A similar view is held by professionals who are members of the American Association of Sex Educators and Counselors, the national professional membership organization in the United States.

Other important factors are the mass media, including TV, with its sexual themes in stories and commercials, radio and the movies, especially the "skin flicks" which appear naughty but nice to our youth and young adults. Not to be overlooked is the tremendous influence of the recorded music of rock 'n' roll, soul and the blues. Our young are conscientious consumers of this audio pastime. The lyrics are loaded with direct explicit sexual expressions which are repeated over and over again. This influence cannot be overlooked as significant in the education of youth. Pornography is found in many forms, i.e., books, comic strips, magazines, gadgets, and underground newspapers. Its repertoire is wide, and it forms part of our total sex education.

Sexual Development

It would be more in keeping with our philosophy to discuss the development of the sexual self in a single fashion. However, some fragmentation through labeling the physical, psychological, social and interpersonal aspects can be helpful, provided we understand that this division is artificial. Growth and development are interdependent and interrelated. We ought not to forget that they are man-made and not in harmony with nature's design unless put together in a coordinating whole.

Biological. The teaching of anatomy and physiology can degenerate into a dehumanizing process in which the educator relies exclusively on charts, illustrations, plastic models, photographs, and slides or films to teach. Many texts and many teachers approach the biology of human sexuality in a machinelike manner so that the learner finds it difficult to determine whether the teacher or text is dealing with the biology of a chicken, a chimpanzee, or a human child. Biology is certainly not the most exciting part of human sexuality, but through a teacher's warm and open enthusiasm, the biological material can be learned in a way that will satisfy curiosity and yet be full of new findings and discoveries.

Although emphasis should be given to understanding the anatomy and physiology of the reproductive process from infancy through maturity, and the universality of the biological system, it is important to connect these facts with their relationship to body functioning, to human sexual feelings, urges, and behavior, and to self-image as a male or female. In addition the teaching of human reproduction needs to include genetics and eugenics. Today, the importance of ongoing research in sickle cell anemia, severe retardation, the effect of VD on the prenatal child, and the drug addiction of newborn babies mothered by drug addicts calls for their inclusion in sex-education programs.

Education in biological sexual development aspects, suitably graded according to the age levels of students, ought to include the following:

1. Development of the male and female genitalia—similarity and difference.
2. Sex determinants—hereditary factors.
3. Process of fertilization.
4. Endocrine system in sexual differentiation.
5. The male reproductive system.
6. The female reproductive system.
7. Menstruation and the climacteric.
8. Prenatal development.
9. Parturition (process of childbirth).
10. Breast development and feeding (lactation).
11. Orgasm—male and female sexual responses.
12. Venereal diseases.
13. Sexual disorders.

Psychological. People need to accept the fact that healthy human beings of all ages are sexual and that they have sexual needs. For many, these needs are satisfied directly. Others, for a variety of cultural or religious reasons, rechannel these needs in many positive and constructive directions through the process of sublimation. Sex education needs to include an understanding of the enhancement of human growth and personality through the fulfillment of human sexuality.

In sex education it is essential to point out that an important fact of selfhood is a child's awareness of being a boy or a girl. By the end of the third year, children are likely to recognize anatomical differences between the sexes. Building pride in the child's sexuality is a parental responsibility. Parents are models and need to communicate that they value their male and female children alike.

Attitudes during adolescence which relate to sexual development arise from the fact that girls mature sexually at an earlier age than boys. This influences their choice of boy friends, their clothes, social interests, and self-image. With the beginning of puberty, the average boy catches up in sexual maturity and grows in height and general physique.

In sex-functioning, the boy is more active. It is generally accepted among sex experts that this propensity is influenced by cultural standards which have been maintained over hundreds of years.

Kinsey's findings suggest, however, that even in the absence of prohibitions, girls are less active sexually during these formative years. The adolescent girl is primarily interested in the social relationship that puberty brings.

Male and female appear to differ in their reactions to sexual stimuli.

The males appear to respond to pictures of nude women, sex jokes, erotic stories and music. Since their sex drive is less inhibited, it is not surprising that they react easily to visual and auditory stimulation. It appears that women react to the "romantic scenes" in movies, love stories and poetry, and an atmosphere of soft lights and sweet music—all of which reflect a feeling of personal interest and love rather than a primary interest in sex play. A certain percentage of females show a greater interest in sexual activity at certain times of the month. Typically this occurs just before the menstrual period. It may be related to the engorgement of the genital organs commonly found just prior to menstruation.

Males tend to participate in sexual fantasy more frequently than do females. This is particularly true when masturbating, and also, with some males, during sexual intercourse. This difference is further reflected in the greater frequency of sex dreams for males.

Men also appear to have a greater tendency toward sexual deviations such as sadomasochism, fetishism, transvestism, voyeurism and exhibitionism. According to Drs. Wardell B. Pomeroy and Cornelia V. Christenson, two nationally known researchers in human sexuality, two reasons have been advanced for the male's greater tendency toward deviant sexual behavior.

First, it has been suggested that their stronger sex drive, especially during early adolescence, makes young males more easily conditioned to these experiences. Second, males in general are more inclined toward variety in sex than are females, both in regard to sexual techniques and in desire for change of sexual partners. For example, males are usually the ones who initiate variations in petting and in coital positions and mouth-genital contact. Investigation reveals that among homosexual males where the institution of marriage is not a restrictive factor, the number of different sexual partners often reaches several hundred. In the female homosexual, or lesbian, this search for wide variety is almost unknown.

Furthermore, basic differences related to the ability to do without sexual activity for long intervals have been observed. For example when male partners leave for Army service or for trips abroad, sometimes lasting a number of years, females can tolerate this situation with a satisfactory adjustment, whereas total abstinence for the male is a rarity.

*Social.** Social aspects of human sexuality are interwoven in a network of individual sexual behavior and need to be included in sex education from infancy through maturity. As soon as a child is born, the

---

* Some of these views are expressed by sociologist Dr. Robert H. Coombs in Chapter 13 of *Human Sexuality in Medical Education and Practice* (Springfield, Ill.: Charles C. Thomas, 1968).

stage is set for him to learn. He learns from his mother and other adult figures who feed, play with and care for him that they like him and enjoy his company. He learns how they feel about his anger, fears and affection. He learns that he is a boy or a girl and whether those who care for him are pleased with his sex identity. The child's sense of his own sexuality (and his sexual behavior) is profoundly influenced by "significant persons, particularly his parents." This view has been especially emphasized by Dr. Harry Stack Sullivan, the eminent psychiatrist, who claimed that a young child's "self system" comes into being through a process of "reflected appraisals." So the parent who feels that her child is a wanted beautiful baby girl will reflect this in her voice, language, the manner in which she holds and feeds her baby, and the pride she feels in mothering.

A rejecting parent sends many rejecting signals to her child. Inattention to the child's cry for help, feeding the child without holding him, pushing the child's hand when he is playing with his penis, little verbal communication between parent and child, inappropriate toys that frustrate the child, lack of an affectionate relationship—all add up to a socialization process which negates the concept that human sexuality is healthy and desirable.

During the entire socialization process a child's self-evaluation is significantly influenced by his parents. Thus if they disapprove of his sex identity or his sexual behavior, he, in turn, will find it difficult to view himself in a favorable light. A child who is loved as a boy or girl child will find it easy to love himself as a sexual person. A parent can reject a boy child by comparing him unfavorably with his sisters, or by comparing him with a husband whom she dislikes or who has deserted the home.

Frequently in one-parent homes run by mothers where the father is never present in a parental role (or where he is passive or has little to do with family affairs, and the mother is downgrading him to the children), the mother may implicitly or explicitly develop a sense of inadequacy and guilt in her male children. Also, she may be robbing her daughters of an adequate model of the opposite sex with whom they can relate. Children need to understand and become comfortable with members of both sexes. Where this is accomplished in a stable home environment, the road for further socialization and completion of developmental tasks during adolescence is made easier.

Often romantic stereotypes of "male" and "female" become status symbols in the eyes of parents, who attempt to impose these on their children. Concepts of maleness and femaleness develop first in the home and then among one's peer group. Children learn both creative and stereotyping of roles. They learn about girl clothes, talk, games, personality characteristics ("Girls cry, boys don't" . . . "Girls get into less trouble than boys" . . . "Girls are less noisy and dirty than boys" . . . "Girls need to learn how to cook, sew and take care of children"). These images can lead to artificial expectations and sexism. In this vein boys are taught that they need to become protectors, adventurers, and in general people of great responsibility. In addition boys are taught during this socialization process that they need to learn to fix things, to be strong and make decisions, and to take care of the weaker sex and young people. All of this responsible learning is for the good if it also includes females who feel inclined to learn similar tasks. A child's temperament, talent, intelligence and motivation ought to be the determining factor as to what, when and how the child is learning skills and attitudes about himself and members of the opposite sex.

Research findings indicate a tendency for children to imitate the parent of their own sex in preference to the parent of the opposite sex. When the child enters school, however, his sphere of socialization grows and he is provided with an increasing number of models concerning appropriate sex-linked role behavior. His peer group increases (both male and female), which enriches his choice of sex-linked behavior. His association with companions of the same sex also helps to clarify and make more secure his self-emerging concept.

It appears that parents bring more pressures on their sons not to behave as girls than they bring on their daughters not to behave as boys. According to Dr. Robert H. Coombs in his chapter in *Human Sexuality in Medical Education and Practice:* "One never says to a young girl, 'Buck up and get in there and be a woman,' or 'Screw up your courage and act like a real woman.' Neither does the Army promise to make a woman out of you. But a boy is not considered to be a real *boy* unless he can prove that he has 'guts' and is not 'chicken.'"

It seems from a number of studies that, in a one-parent home, the absence of the father is more damaging to a boy's sex-role development than to a girl's, since the girl has a parent of the same sex with whom to identify.

However, the findings of P. Mussero and E. Rutherford reported in *Child Development* 34: 589–607, 1963, support the view that the father's personality and behavior are important factors in the daughter's development of femininity. They speculate that highly masculine fathers tend to foster in their daughters the development of appropriate sex-role preferences.

In the absence of daily interaction with a parent or surrogate figure of the same sex, young people tend to look for idealized figures from the world of sports, theater or music with whom to identify. These idealized figures may create unrealistic expectations and aspirations, especially when the growing child is locked into a situation due to poor health, education, or financial circumstances which precludes his attaining the standards he perceives are characteristic of his ideal person.

Interpersonal aspects. Interpersonal dynamics which relate to human sexuality include changing sex roles during the psycho-sexual development of the individual, and an understanding of the changing mores and attitudes of people in our pluralistic society. This area in sex education should help each individual to understand, to accept changing and evolving sex roles of the same and opposite sex, and to develop attitudes and behavior which are associated with warm intimate relationships with other individuals. Self-respect is basic to respectful interpersonal relations with others. This will aid men and women to accept and genuinely interact with persons whose sexual life-styles differ from their own.

In our interpersonal relations we cannot teach specific norms concerning behavior because of the variations of attitudes and practices among many groups in our culture. Jersild, in his *Child Psychology,* discusses children and their parents in Israel. Following A. I. Rabin, an Israeli researcher on kibbutz life, he states that the Israeli kibbutz viewed from the American traditional standard of family life, offers the child an environment that could be considered unfavorable by some. The mother is with her child for only a few hours each day. There is multiple mothering during most of the day, with the mother's place being taken by substitutes. The studies indicate unevenness in the early development period, but by the age of late adolescence most such children seem to have become well-balanced individuals with concern for the social good, less pressured by long-term ambitious goals and by conflict with regard to sex. Some studies indicate that the classical Freudian Oedipus triangle is not brought into full focus in the kibbutz. It appears that boys and girls who share the same sleeping quarters and bathroom facilities to the age of about eighteen do not necessarily become promiscuous. Strict taboos on sexual intimacy, combined with a degree of modesty and desire for privacy among girls, apparently makes this situation less provocative than it might be under other circumstances.

Dr. Robert Staples, a black sociologist currently teaching at Howard University, presents a well-researched and insightful understanding of family interaction and its outcome on human sexuality among black Americans. He dismisses as myths and stereotypes the research findings which produce in the public mind the image of black families as a pathological social unit ("a system incapable of rearing individuals who can adjust to the demands of a civilized society"). Instead he finds that since most sociological studies of black family interaction have been made by whites using white models as their norms, the consequences of black sexual behavior have been judged on the basis of white middle-class values and norms. Dr. Staples, who is currently concerned with studies of black families, believes that black families are different and that one must understand the way in which they live and their values and standards before one judges them. A wide range of studies indicate, for instance, that the adolescent black community is more sexually permissive than is the white community. This often reflects the absence of a double standard of sexual behavior between male and female. White women lack the same sexual freedom that white men have because of a more rigid double standard in the white community.

We would be missing an opportunity for stressing interpersonal aspects essential for individual development of sexually mature people living in a democratic society if we did not enumerate here the personality factors which are essential for maturing loving people: respect, understanding, acceptance, responsibility, affection, and loving concern. These characteristics need to be self-perceived and then become centered in the interacting person. Where sexual interaction and relationships are built on these values they tend to be self-actualizing.

As a result of their single standard, as mentioned above, sex relations both before and after marriage are more meaningful to the black partners. Out-of-wedlock children are proportionately more numerous among blacks than among whites. This is inadequately explained by some researchers as a reflection of greater sexual freedom. Many significant factors related to social and personal deprivation need to be considered. Among poor blacks, the expectation exists that their children will engage in premarital sex relations. This, in turn, causes them to anticipate the possibility that an illegitimate child may be born. The anticipation doesn't lessen the anxiety and concern that they as parents have. Blacks are troubled by illegitimacy. But they accept and value the child born out of wedlock on the same basis as legitimate children in their family.

According to Dr. Lee Rainwater, eminent sociologist, attitudes toward sexual relations are highly competitive among poor black males and exploitive toward those of the opposite sex. The girls speak of the "sweet talk" of the boys. Black adolescent girls don't seem to find any particular sexual gratification in sexual intercourse. Rather, they engage in it as a test and symbol of their maturity as women and to be part of the crowd. The competitiveness and exploitation is a constant source of concern which tends to detract from the pleasure of "doing sex."

Poverty seems to be a precipitating factor, among many others, for extramarital relations and marital disorganization among lower-income blacks and whites. The most common reason for such disorganization given by the couples involves sexual infidelity, yet the underlying reason often involves the husband's inability to earn the funds necessary to maintain the family.

On the one hand, as the economic status of black families improves, family cohesiveness increases, illegitimacy decreases, sexual promiscuity wanes, and sexual satisfaction and intimacy improves. On the other hand, there is ample evidence to support the findings that in the black ghetto illegitimacy, venereal disease, and drug-encouraged prostitution are increasing.

Because of the destructive effects of poverty it is necessary to improve the financial status of poor blacks and whites in order to bring satisfaction to their sexual interpersonal relationships and to their family relationships. There is an abundance of evidence to bolster the belief that poverty is an integral part of cases of sexual infidelity, excessive drinking, fighting, and desertion.

The interaction of the biological, psychological, social and interpersonal aspects of our sexual development reinforces the concept that sexual development is at the core of personality development. However, leading researchers have helped us appreciate the significance of social and subcultural norms in molding our self-image in both positive and negative ways.

Self-Awareness and Sexual Identification

Self-awareness of being a boy, a girl, a man or a woman begins in infancy. A child learns very early that he has a body because of pleasurable or unpleasurable sensations from touching, tasting, dressing, excreting and various other body actions, reactions and stimuli that come from within and from the external physical and personal environment. A child learns early when he is held close and addressed by his mother or another loving adult that he is loved and that he is a darling baby. He discovers for himself his body form, shape and sensations. And his curiosity impels him to wonder, to ask what his physical self is called. Positive and supportive concern from those he loves helps him to reinforce healthy attitudes about his being a boy (or, in the case of a girl, about her being a girl) and about his physical design, shape and feelings.

A fearful parent, or one wanting a child of the opposite sex, can send many negative verbal and nonverbal signals to the developing child as he grows from infancy. Verbalizations are often heard, such as "You were an accident" or "Dad and I were hoping you would be a boy because we already have two girls" or "You have your Dad's features; for a man that's O.K., but for a girl it doesn't really fit together." These careless words and the feelings of rejection and disappointment they convey may create identification problems along with self-pity and loss of self-respect on the part of a growing child. Often, when parents are merely letting off steam and getting feelings of frustration off their chest they may resort to temporary self or spouse depreciation which the listening child may perceive as being deeply ingrained in parental attitudes: "I wish I were a man, they have all the fun" . . . "This is a man's world," or "All men are no good, they are out for what they can get and when you grow up, you'll probably be like your father."

The picture children and adults have of themselves comes mainly from how they think and feel others view them. Parents or others who care for them are strong influences in developing their self-image and sexual awareness. If they fear their sexuality and are in conflict about being male or female, the chances are that they will communicate these feelings and influences in many verbal and nonverbal ways. When the male infant discovers his penis, a mother's sigh and quick motion of her hand pushing his hand away may communicate a fearful "no-no" to the child concerning his pleasure at self-discovery. Or the young adolescent girl, experimenting with a variety of makeup from facial creams to false eyelashes, may be called a "flirt" by her mother in a derogatory tone of voice. Or the four-year-old who asks his pregnant mother how the baby is going to come out may be told to shut his dirty mouth, or even be slapped for asking the question.

Self-awareness can be reinforced through self-love. We are not equating self-love here with an exclusive egotistic type of love, but with one that can be reflected in feelings of being pleased with one's sexual self, accepting sexuality as a healthy part of self and respecting one's self as a person. Along with this feeling of self-love and self-respect comes respect for others, including the opposite sex. When mother accepts her femininity, she will give her daughter the feeling that the way she was born is desirable and right. She will also give her girl-child the feeling that being a girl is something of which to be proud. Thoughts like the following, communicated through the child's developmental period, help her to accept her femininity and reduce her anxiety: "When you grow up, you will have breasts and hair on your body just like Mommy. When you are a woman you will have a man to love you just as I have. When you marry, you and your husband will have babies too. Because you will love them and take care of them, they will be as lovely as you." Of course the same content would be important for a boy as well. Both need a strong secure sense of who they are and the fact that they are loved and desired.

The child whose mother cannot accept her girl-baby or her own feminine role, and whose father is stern, unloving and critical, may encounter problems as she matures which are avoided by the child who is accepted by parents who love and respect each other.

If the child is not emotionally accepted by either, or both, of his parents, no words of endearment the child hears will counteract the feelings he acquires through interpretation of what he sees and feels going on around him.

During adolescence sexual identification is reinforced by members of the opposite sex. The fifteen-year-old young man, whether he be fat, thin, short, or tall, feels a sense of pride in his masculinity when he sees that the young woman sitting next to him in class finds him attractive and interesting. She, in turn, feels good about herself when she is socially accepted by the opposite sex as an attractive personality.

Young girls brought up in homes where they are emotionally involved with adults of both sexes have a realistic sense of their own and the opposite sex.

Children raised in one-parent homes (whether due to divorce, separation, death or out-of-wedlock birth) would gain in pride in their sexual identity through social relationships with adults of the opposite sex. Friends, relatives, and school and church friends of the same sex as the absent parent should be encouraged to become involved in the family circle. Interpersonal and social relations in the world of work, education, family and social spheres all tend to contribute toward the social-sexual maturity of growing adolescents.

The slow acceptance by the public of equal job opportunity rights for both sexes has tended to maintain the stereotyping of roles in the world of work. Today, with the increase of job opportunities and with woman's conscious appreciation of her worth and right, young women are forging ahead toward freer choices in the world of work and in educational training programs. Men who themselves feel adequate and secure in their job roles are the first to support women's claim for the opportunity to train and work at jobs and have professional choices which suit them best. As a result of the new movement toward recognition, employers and educational institutions are opening up opportunities for both male and female on the basis of aptitude and competency. More women are being accepted and achieving in the professions of medicine, law, architecture, engineering and other fields of endeavor.

Many of the traditionally all-male secondary schools and colleges are now merging with all-girl schools, as educators have become increasingly aware of the need for both males and females to maintain normal healthy social relations during their entire formal education developmental years. Sexual identification through interpersonal relationships that are not strained but comfortable and part of day-to-day living is important for adolescents and young adults.

The daily pleasures and frustrations of living become a reality in a heterosexual educational environment. Putting off socialization of male and female until school is out or during holidays may create unrealistic solutions instead of the normal healthy interpersonal relationships necessary between young men and women. "Getting to know you" is an excellent beginning for getting to "understand" and "respect" and "like" and "love" you for what you are—man or woman.

In the family, children learn quickly how their parents value and love them as sexual people. Where parents prefer boys and treat them as superior, girls are conditioned to a stereotyping which causes rebellion, submission, repression or conflicts within themselves.

As was mentioned earlier, both male and female infants begin by learning to identify with mother. As they grow, the boys normally shift by age three to a masculine identification. The self-image of each parent or parental figure and their concept of male and female roles have a significant impact on the emerging personalities of the children. Parents, good or bad, are models whom children see and interact with on both a cognitive and emotional level.

The mother who loves to cook, clean, stay at home to take care of her family, and is not interested in activities outside the home presents a model for her daughter. Likewise, the working mother who enjoys both her family and a career, and combines them with enthusiasm and competency presents another model.

Parents need to be sensitive to the impact they have on their children in developing life-styles, and to offer children a variety of possible opportunities in family and vocational life-styles. Exposing children to choices offers them a fair and reasonable way to help them recognize positive and negative factors in various situations. Of course our life-styles will greatly influence the options we offer our children. However, if we are sensitive to our own prejudices and limitations, we can help them broaden their horizon without too much interference.

Socially, both men and women are traveling alone and in pairs in ways which would have raised suspicious eyebrows only a few years ago. The double standard in both social and sexual relationships is slowly slipping away from our social world. The single standard for both sexes is by no means the male standard. This attitude would superimpose stereotyping of both male and female. Instead it appears more reasonable and more compatible with personality and sexual development for both women and men to have the equal right and freedom of choice to develop and interact socially as suits each individual's developing life-style. Inherent in this right is the mutual respect and affection that all human beings need to have for one another. To this we hopefully look for openness and trust as realistic goals in social behavior between the sexes.

Facts and Myths in Sensitive Areas

Many difficulties involved in boy-girl, man-woman, human and sexual relations are caused through misinformation, misconceptions and myths brought about both by faulty verbal and nonverbal communication. At many levels, the peer group may reinforce ignorance and prejudice with accompanying feelings of fear, guilt and shame. On the other hand, the peer group may become a strong vehicle for enlightenment from the bigotry and myths created and maintained within the family circle.

Accurate sex information is directly related to a stable and fulfilling sex life. The scientific understanding of the biology of reproduction and the guiltless acceptance of human sexuality as a healthy joyous part of each of us will help to educate young and old without superimposing a mold of myths and fallacies. There are many myths associated with sexual functioning, sex drive, reproduction and birth control, homosexuality, sexual disorders and offenses. A book such as *Sexual Myths and Fallacies* by James McCary, a noted sexologist, can be used as a reference.

A sampling of the more commonly held myths which the sex educator and counselor may well need to deal with in training and teaching classes includes the following, which are fully documented by McCary.

1. *A large penis is important to a woman's sexual gratification, and the man with a large penis is more sexually potent than the man with a small penis.*

Young boys are quite concerned with penis size from an early age. It is the subject of jokes, and there is great embarrassment on the part of the young male who is teased about the size of his penis by his peers. Where sex educators can openly point out the fallacy of relating potency to size, whether it be penis in boys or the breasts of girls, the anxiety levels of our young people can be markedly reduced.

In reality the size of the man's penis has no relationship to his ability to satisfy a woman sexually. Sexual gratification during intercourse is closely related to the feelings that exist between the couple and the state of arousal that exists at the time of penetration. Indeed, a very long penis may put pressure on the cervix, producing pain and detracting from the woman's enjoyment.

2. *There is a difference between vaginal and clitoral orgasms.*

For many years, psychoanalysts have informed their patients and the public that only mature women have vaginal orgasms, and that orgasm through clitoral manipulation is not as fulfilling and really reflects sexual inadequacy. Today we have learned from clinical research and histories that orgasm is not necessarily different in intensity or quality because of the difference in the anatomical site. The degree of the feelings of affection and togetherness which exist between a couple is more closely related to the pleasure of orgasmic response than is the fact that it is clitoral or vaginal.

3. *Sexual intercourse should be avoided during the last trimester and six weeks after the birth of the child.*

Other than taking reasonable care against excessive pressure on the abdomen, or infection, a woman in good health can enjoy sexual intercourse until two weeks prior to giving birth, and can resume after the vaginal bleeding has stopped and any incisions have healed. Because of the variety of positions available, the couple may choose those which avoid abdominal pressure.

As the date of delivery nears, the couple will need both the psychological support and sexual satisfaction that intercourse provides. Especially after the birth of the baby, both parents may desire coitus. Of course individual needs and circumstances vary. The attending physician should be consulted in this regard.

4. *Alcohol is a sexual stimulant.*

Alcohol may initially remove self-consciousness, fear, guilt or other inhibitions which prevent physical intimacy. However, alcohol acts as a depressant on the nervous system, so that it hinders sexual performance. Taken in large doses, it can prevent a man from having an erection. Although a woman is capable of having sexual intercourse while under the influence of alcohol, her chances of achieving orgasm are greatly diminished.

5. *There is an absolutely "safe" period for sexual intercourse insofar as conception is concerned.*

If all women were consistently regular in their period of ovulation, then the rhythm method of birth control would be reasonably safe. In other words, if the date of period of ovulation could be accurately predicted, then sexual intercourse could be avoided during that time, while being safely engaged in at any other time. But, because many women have irregular periods brought on by change in climate or diet, emotional stress, or for unknown reasons, such predictions of a safe period can become highly unreliable, and frequently result in an unwanted pregnancy.

6. *Oral-genital sex between a man and a woman indicates homosexual tendencies.*

Sexual variations between heterosexual partners add to their pleasure and interest with a sharing of sexual experiences. Oral-genital sex is considered part of the repertoire of sexual positions encountered in heterosexual play. The fact that homosexual partners also enjoy oral-genital sex doesn't necessarily put this sexual situation in the category of showing homosexual tendencies.

7. *Masturbation is known to cause mental illness and skin diseases.*
The list of myths associated with masturbation is quite long. In addition to mental illness and various forms of skin disease, one hears about the liver turning white, the seed running dry, and inability to satisfy a woman. Most of these myths have religious taboos as their origin. As a matter of fact masturbation is normal and widely practiced by both males and females.

8. *Pornography and obscenity lead to sexual excess and sexual acting out.*
Obviously pornography and obscene material does stimulate and sexually arouse men and women, otherwise it would not be sold or offered commercially. Anything from centerpiece magazine spreads to artifacts depicting penises and sexual positions may fall into this category, depending upon the feelings of the individual. However, no research has found any relationship between viewing pornography and any long-term change in basic attitudes and sex patterns of the viewers.

Learning the Language of Human Sexuality

There are still many fine teachers and counselors who cannot say "penis," "vagina," "clitoris," or "orgasm" without whispering or clearing their throats. Others panic when they hear a colleague or patient relating an incident, and using such words as "fuck," "pussy," "dick," and "screw" to describe human sexuality.

Sex educators and counselors need to be familiar with a wide range of sexual expressions in order to assist their understanding of the feelings, attitudes, as well as cultural and family language patterns, of those whom they teach and counsel.

To many a child and youth the word "balls" has much more meaning than "testicles," and if we are to help him understand the function of his sex glands and the intelligent management of his sexual activity, talking to him about his "balls" can bring about more effective sex education than insisting that he refer to his sex glands as *testes*.

To many a mother and child the expression "I have to go Number One" is a reality for urinating, whereas having to learn to say "I have to urinate" is like "swallowing a big dictionary" and getting uptight about it.

Intimacy and warmth are associated with certain sexual terms by both young and old. "Naughty" and "nice" words are also learned through conditioning by people of all ages. By means of a sex education which includes an understanding of language usage and derivations, we can help our students and patients look at a variety of expressions and sort out those which are universally understood from those which are provincial or have a limited use.

It is often helpful to point out to students and patients that within the intimacy of the family or neighborhood, expressions which are understood and acceptable will probably continue to be used. However, without being judgmental, it is possible to suggest that other words are universally standard and that they ought to know about those because it aids in better understanding when communication is on an equal level.

Often teachers are thrown off balance in cases where an elementary school is having a problem because the children are "running wild with four-letter words." Expressions such as "shit," "fuck," and "mother fucker" are appearing on school walls and desks, and are used in front of teachers and staff. Before punitive action, which is generally called "disciplinary action" but which is intended to repress rather than teach, is taken, the communication channels need to be opened wide. Both children and staff need to wonder with one another concerning the situation and how they feel about it. Where openness and trust are developed during the exchange of feelings and thoughts, some of the following understandings about the use of unacceptable language may be expressed:

1. Used as a new fad to reflect being "grown up" or "tough."
2. Used because some of the leaders are upset about a particular teacher's attitude or a school regulation and are retaliating.
3. Used where anger is so intense that the child loses control of his conscious thoughts and explodes, using language he himself is not aware of at the point of anger.

When these and other insights are obtained and understood, then the encounter can turn toward finding socially acceptable and more comfortable ways of working out the cause of language abuse or misuse.

The language barriers we meet almost daily obviously arise from deeply embedded cultural, social, and religious values concerning human sexual behavior. Thus our conflicting sex attitudes are reflected in a curiosity about, and rejection of, the language of sex. It is difficult to find another area of life where such a thick barrier exists to thought, communication, research and education. The question raised by Dr. Warren K. Johnson in his book *Human Sexual Behavior and Sex Education* is again raised here: "How does one teach a subject, the language of which is forbidden or offensive—even, oftentimes, when confined to the sterile, white medical terminology of a long-dead language, Latin? Among other things, the teacher or counselor must reckon with the problem of having to communicate with people by means of words which are emotionally charged—very possibly for the teacher or counselor as well as for his audience."

Our use of the words *masculine* and *feminine* has conditioned many in in our culture to think, feel, and act in stereotyped roles. The controlling stereotypes which tend to establish a double standard of sexual attitudes and behavior are reinforced and encouraged by the mass media. Many of our popular comic strips use women as sex objects and play down the woman who does not fit the Hollywood criteria for beauty. How do the popular magazines portray masculinity? The big-chested, wide-shoulder types appear to be the heroes, whereas the "brains" are often pictured as men whom the girls find unattractive.

Polarization of personalities through using masculine and feminine descriptions subjects us to many pitfalls. Once we are aware of the tendency for sexual language to limit rather than expand our thoughts and feelings, we can then focus on the individual person or situation. We are interested in understanding and going beyond sexual descriptive words to gain an in-depth impression which has a three-dimensional meaning instead of being a one-dimensional stereotype. We must find new words and new meanings to describe men and women as sexual human beings. Some of these views have been well expressed by Dr. Johnson.

Verbal and Nonverbal Education

The verbal sector of sex education which we have delineated in earlier sections of this book is generally understood by most of us. And why not? Most of our structured training has been through the written or spoken word. But how significant is the word compared to the incredible amount of nonverbal sex education we receive daily?

Modeling is a dynamic nonverbal sex educator. Parents are models to most of us as a male and female whom we attempt to emulate. Our early values, attitudes and how we see ourselves comes from the modeling and how we feel they see us as people. The smile of approval, the screwed-up expression of scorn, the hurried gait of business, the bent shoulders of sorrow, the furrowed brow filled with anxiety—all communicate deep nonverbal impressions of how they feel about us, reflecting approval, disapproval, rejection, acceptance, love, hate, jealousy, revenge and a score of nuances of feelings.

Parental, sibling, and peer group nonverbal signals often tell us how they feel about nudity, masturbation, homosexuality, abortion, adolescent pregnancies and many other sensitive areas in human sexuality.

The look on Mary Lou's face when she says to her younger sister, "There goes your friend Alice," tells much more about how she feels about Alice, who is sixteen and pregnant, than the simple sentence she utters.

"So that's Tom!" said by a mother to her son, with raised shoulders and half-blinking eyes, when she views his homosexual classmate for the first time, is powerful in nonverbal communication.

Students in sex-education classes, and patients and clients as well, need to have raised to a conscious level the impact of the nonverbal education they receive daily, incorporate, and which they in turn communicate to others.

In addition to person-to-person nonverbal education, much in mass media that is unspoken also has a great impact on our developing attitudes and beliefs.

The Hollywood impression of beauty, male and female, is reflected in the star system in pictures, rock 'n' roll, blues singers and in many entertainers and musicians such as the Beatles, Bob Dylan, the Rolling Stones, James Taylor, Sammy Davis, Jr. and James Brown, Doris Day, and Jane Fonda. These women and men are models of femininity and masculinity respectively to many of their fans and followers. Their language, clothes, hair styles, walk, and life-styles are subject to imitation. Often the imitators have revealed to them only the public image. If they knew their idols more intimately perhaps they could sense the individuality of each and thus search for their own identity and individuality.

Nonverbal sex education can be found in dance, painting, sculpture, photography, and other forms of art. The impressions of the creative artist concerning men and women have had lasting universal appeal through the centuries. Michelangelo's David, Leonardo da Vinci's Mona Lisa, Botticelli's Venus, Rubens' Voluptuous Woman, among others, have moved many of us deeply.

Because human sexuality is universal and a common modality for every man, sex education involves an understanding of cross-cultural influences as well as the pluralistic nature of western societies. It embraces the physiological functions because the origins of human sexual behavior are rooted in our biological frame. The biological function of human sexuality is only the beginning. The manner in which we feel and behave as women or men includes our understanding of three significant segments of sex education, i.e., biological, psychological, and social. They are interdependent and relate to the dynamics of healthy personality growth.

Sex education is concerned with skills and competency on the part of the educator. Knowledge of educational content is valuable to the teacher and student only when it is shared in a trusting and open fashion by both teacher and student. The group-centered approach accelerates the process of effective teaching and learning.

3

What is Sex Counseling?

Today, sex counseling is emerging as a dynamic approach to solving sex-related problems for people of all ages. Sex counseling may involve an individual, a couple, a family of two or more, or a group of individuals or couples who work together in the group because of common concerns.

The counselor may work alone or with a co-counselor. Dr. William Masters and Ms. Virginia Johnson, eminent sex researchers and therapists, focus on the two-counselor team, male and female (with one required to be a physician).

Relationships in sex counseling include parent-child problems from infancy through adulthood, sex partners of the same or opposite sex, student-teacher and husband-wife.

It Is a Process in Communication

In sex-counseling sessions the counselor and the client engage in a process of communication which hopefully leads the client to an adequate solution. The skilled counselor combines learned skills with the art of sex counseling. A successful sex-counseling process exists where a relationship is established through mutual acceptance, understanding and trust between the sex counselor and the client. Confidentiality is an essential element in the counseling process. Where a sexual problem exists, two or more persons are usually involved. Therefore the sex counselor will find it necessary to explore with the clients their sexual attitudes and their interpersonal systems of communication with each other before attempting to define the sex problem.

It is essential for the counselor to take a social sex history of the client. This history is developed during the initial interview. Irrespective of the length of time involved in sex counseling or the gravity of the presenting problems, the following would seem to represent the minimal information needed by sex counselors in the initial interview:

A. Identifying facts
   1. Basic information (name, sex, age, schooling, marital status, employment, dates of counseling interviews).
   2. Physical appearance.
B. Statement of the problem
   1. Presenting problem (as viewed by the client).
   2. Precipitating events that created need to seek assistance.
C. Sexual relationship with partner
   1. Brief history of relationship.
   2. Dynamics of the sexual relationship.
      a. roles played besides sexual (type of interaction and communication).
      b. Childhood models for sex roles (those available at the time).
      c. Manner in which patient perceives male-female sex roles.
      d. Early identification figures and ideal personalities.
      e. Adolescent sex identification figures and idealized persons.
      f. Adolescent sex self-concept: how developed, sex values, sex goals, sex aspirations.
      g. Adolescent interaction pattern with parents, siblings and peers.
      h. Sex-role concepts in dating and partner selection processes, including the quality of the relations with persons of the opposite sex.
      i. Influence of religious, educational, social and economic factors upon sex role concepts.
      j. Specific areas of sex differences with partner.
         a. How they developed.
         b. Attempts made to correct differences.
         c. Emotional reaction to differences.
      k. Appraisal of each other as to the degree of willingness to cooperate and work with problem.
         a. Feelings of emotional support.
         b. Feelings of caring and cooperating.
         c. Feeling concerning outcome of the sex counseling.*

It is important to bear in mind that religion, socio-economic and ethnic influences have a significant impact and influence on sexual attitudes and information available to clients.

If a sex counselor considers human sexuality only in terms of his own values, he will be caught in the dilemma of attempting to impose his

---

* Salient features of Dean Johnson's outline in *Marriage Counseling: Theory and Practice* have been adopted for this outline which the author uses in her clinical interviews.

values upon his clients. Especially where the counselor identifies with the middle class and its sex mores, great care and sensitivity to the client with a lower-class point of view needs to be felt and understood if he is to help the client work out a sexual problem in a manner satisfactory to him and his life-style. The client can be helped by giving him support to express his values.

Sex counseling is never a matter of giving advice. To treat a sexual problem at this level is all too often to impose the will and value judgments of the sex counselor on the client. Thus the counselor becomes the crutch upon which the client leans. This may give the client some immediate relief. What he needs, however, is the confidence and the communication skills to understand both his own and his partner's contribution to the sex problem, along with effective ways of coping with it, so that the sexual relationship between them grows and matures. Often a change of attitude toward human sexuality is involved in the process and just giving information may fall short of helping the client to look at her sex problem a little differently. Empathy without smothering the patient with sympathy is essential.

There appears to be evolving in this new field of sex counseling the need for the sex counselor to explore with the client (during the first interview if possible) 1) her feelings and self-concept as a sexual person, 2) her feelings and sex concepts of the others involved in the relationship, 3) what she expects of herself and the others in the relationship (In other words, what are her goals, and how are they in conflict with the others?), and 4) how does she communicate her feelings and concepts? Obviously this last is significant to the problem-solving approach. Many a sex counselor is able to help the client understand the problem, but working through communication barriers is a difficult and yet essential part of sex counseling. The counselor should not rush through the interview but needs to go along at a pace which is best for the client. The goal in effective sex counseling is more than assisting the client to clarify his feelings and attitude concerning the problem. It involves helping him in a supportive way to find solutions to his sex problems with those people to whom he relates, and also to develop a clearer understanding of himself and sex partner or person involved in the problem, so that a deeper and more satisfying relationship is established.

Problems presented by clients vary widely. For our purpose in developing insights into the nature of commonly occurring sex problems, only a small number will be discussed.

It Deals With Relationships

Sex counseling is a form of relationship counseling concerned with improving feeling tone and communication between the parties involved. During the initial interview, or when convenient, all interested parties should see the counselor. This will help the sex counselor gain a reasonably clear picture of the manner in which the client and others communicate. It also provides the sex counselor with an opportunity to view how each of the parties feels about the problem and the degree of conflict that exists. It is also an opportunity to discuss with two or more people present the fact that *1*) each has a responsibility to work at the problem, *2*) each is involved in contributing to the problem (because the counselor does not view the problem from the point of view that there is always a guilty and an innocent party), and *3*) both people need to agree on what the gist of the problem is before they can begin to work toward a satisfactory solution.

The joint interview with two or more present, although deemed essential by this writer, offers many pitfalls to a sex counselor. She may be pushed by the parties into the role of referee (Who is right? Who is wrong?) or she may find herself asking them to stop shouting at each other in order to listen. When the counselor finds the joint interview difficult, she will need to see the parties separately, with the assurance that the interviews are confidential and that she is concerned with helping them solve their problem. Above all, she needs to be nonjudgmental: genuinely appearing to accept and respect them and their problem, to understand their concerns and conflicts, and in a supportive way want to help them.

After the sex counselor has a grasp or at least a tentative impression of the client's problem, it is important to understand the manner in which the client has previously endeavored to handle her problem. Perhaps she feels that others have tried to help her and have failed and that the situation is hopeless, so she keeps repeating her self-defeating behavior.

Because sex problems involve more than one person, the counselor needs to understand the client's motivation for seeking help. Is she coming because a parent, partner or professional person urged her to come, or does she really want to be helped? An open and honest discussion on this point helps clear the air, and lessens the defensiveness of the client. Often a client who is pushed by the partner or parent into a counseling situation responds with an attitude of "I dare you solve my problem," or "If you think you are so smart, go ahead, I'm not going to help" . . . or "All you are interested in is the money or your job, not me."

The sex counselor needs to be aware of the fact that sexual problems generally are fraught with emotional reactions and that her ability to work with the client depends on her awareness and sensitivity to the depth of the client's feelings. Therefore, some evaluation of the client's emotional state is necessary. This is particularly important when the counselor recognizes evidences of gross pathological reactions. Also of importance is the counselor's ability to recognize various ego defenses, including resistance. Without placing "labels" on the client's emotional level, the sex counselor is in a position through evaluation to appraise her competence and that of the client's to work with the problem, and to recognize when a referral to another or original source is necessary.

Types of Problems

What problems are most often presented by clients? The sex problems encountered by counselors relate to concerns of young and old, male and female. For purposes of brevity and illustration, typical types of problems will be outlined and illustrated.

SEXUAL IDENTITY

John at age two was frequently told by his mother that "boys are hard to handle." He was also told at seven that "girls are smarter," and when he played with his penis at eight, he was shouted at and told that his "ding-dong will surely get you into trouble." His father had left the household when John was three and his mother and older sister would repeatedly state in his presence that "men are out for what they can get" and "you will probably be like your father when you grow up."

The young boy developed difficulty in achieving a satisfactory male image. He did poorly at school and at the time of counseling he had "got a teenage girl pregnant." The two teenagers (boy and pregnant girl) and the mothers of each were involved in the clinic counseling where the pregnant girl came for prenatal care. The role of the sex counselor was to assist in building up a favorable sexual self-image for both the boy and the girl and help them mature, talk to the mothers and help them understand how their relationship with their children and their attitudes about sex had affected their children's attitudes and feelings. The counselor interviewed the foursome together, individually, and then in two's (boy and girl), (boy and mother), (girl and mother). As the relationship became more supportive and respectful, the ability of the teenagers to make appropriate plans for continuing school, for financial assistance, for baby care and medical support improved.

The need for knowing "Who am I?" as a sexual person, the need for pride in self, the need for approval and belonging—all these are essential to our ability to cope with our sexuality.

FAMILY PLANNING

Where family planning is equated with improving the quality of life in a family, without playing a population control game with the client, the sex counselor can realistically give effective support to her clients as they explore the problem. Often family-planning problems focus on *a*) birth-control method to be used, *b*) conflicts between partners over differences of opinion as to preferred method, and *c*) anxieties concerning sterilization by both partners involving physical injury and/or loss of femininity.

A fifteen-year-old girl visited our clinic recently wishing an I.U.D. (intrauterine device) because she often forgot to take the pill and constantly worried about becoming pregnant. As she was under sixteen, her mother authorized medical and sex counseling for her, but wished her also to continue on the pill. The mother feared that the IUD would cause her daughter to develop cancer. The daughter's boy friend was indifferent as to the form of birth control she was using. Both mother and daughter were seen together and the mother was also referred to the clinic physician so that he could explain the medical data on IUD and cancer to her. It developed that her neighbors had exaggerated the statistical picture concerning the relationship of cancer to IUD usage. She came away from the counseling more confident in the IUD. Her relationship with her daughter improved and she was able to talk more easily about sexual concerns. Her daughter's boy friend was invited to the clinic for a joint interview to help him appreciate both the pleasure and the responsibility involved in sexual activity, and to recognize that his partner was assuming full responsibility for birth control, but that both had a joint commitment to see that the situation was a happy and healthy one.

ABORTION

In abortion counseling, the sex counselor ought to consider the need for a post-abortion medical checkup, to follow through on any uneasiness in the patient's feelings, including depression arising from both physical and psychological adjustments, and also work with the patient on concerns which deal with her sexuality. Clients often seek help concerning birth control and ways of improving sexual pleasure after the abortion, while others tell the counselor in no uncertain terms that "they are through with sex *and men!*" The second group obviously are reacting with hostile feelings rather than with rational concern for improving their future sexual relationships.

During her first week at college Jane, a college freshman, unmarried and eighteen, away from home for the first time, meets a young man who is a fellow freshman. Both Jane and he have had previous sex relations but neither has ever used birth control. They like each other, see each other frequently and after one month begin having sexual intercourse. By midterm, Jane is pregnant. She visits the University Health Service, the doctor discovers she is ten weeks pregnant and refers her to the sex counselor. Jane wishes an abortion. She advises the sex counselor that she does not wish her mother or family to know she is pregnant. Her father and mother are divorced. She says her boy friend will scrape up the necessary money. She doesn't intend to tell her roommate or any of her friends. The counselor discusses with her the fact that a dilation and curettage (D and C) is usually performed only until the twelfth week and that after twelve weeks she will require a saline, which is far more expensive. The counselor suggests that the young man come to the clinic, but Jane refuses to get him involved in any way other than pro- viding the money. Arrangements are made with an outside clinic to have the abortion performed the following week. The counselor explores with her the subject of her friendships on campus and the possibility of having someone go with her to the clinic. The client is advised to call the clinic when she has obtained the money and to return the day before she is due to go to the clinic. On the day of her appointment, her boy friend calls and informs the counselor he can't raise the sum needed and Jane is threatening to commit suicide. The counselor visits the dormitory where Jane is living, and with the boy friend present the three try to reduce the emotional anxiety and work toward a realistic solution. After looking at the problem from several different aspects, including Jane's sexual di- lemma, her school situation, her boy friend's affection and concern for her, and her lack of financial resources, Jane is persuaded to communi- cate with her mother by phone, finds her supportive, and receives the funds she needs.

Jane and her partner both required follow-up counseling to help them gain perspective concerning short- and long-term personal goals, the current sexual needs of each, and the process of maturing in their sexual responsibilities to each other.

FRIGIDITY

In a woman, frigidity includes different degrees of inability to respond to sexual stimulation. Her partner may be of the same or opposite sex. In some patients the inability to experience orgasm gives them the impression that they are frigid. Problems of frigidity in women frequently are based on feelings of guilt concerning sexual behavior.

A female client of mine complained of a lack of interest in sexual intercourse. She told her husband she was too tired when he showed signs of passion. She was twenty-six and he was twenty-eight and both were in good health. Although she claimed fatigue she still managed to stay up later than he and watch television. When she finally got to bed, she claimed she was too tired. In the morning, she resisted sex play because she claimed she had to rush off to work after breakfast and didn't wish to tire herself. During the interview I asked her about birth control and her desire for a family. She said she used the diaphragm because the pill made her ill and filled her body with fluid. She hated using the diaphragm because she felt dirty when her hands were spreading jelly over the diaphragm and she also disliked putting her fingers into her vagina. We discussed her childhood, including her toilet training and her parents' attitude toward sex. She spoke of her mother's insistence that she be a little lady who didn't mess her clothes or dirty her room by leaving toys about. She recalled her parents' anguish because they thought it took her a long time to be toilet trained. She disliked baking because she didn't like to get her hands in the messy mixture. It was quite clear the client had developed discomfort and an attitude that sex was dirty and associated with her excretory functions.

Her husband became involved in the sex counseling to lend support and to aid in the communication of her fears and concerns. His understanding and empathy helped her to open up more comfortably. They both recognized how much they needed each other's confidence to share the problem and work together. After a number of visits, the couple learned to enjoy each other and to take pride in their sexuality.

MASTURBATION

Masturbation is generally used to describe manual stimulation of the genitals. For some it means stimulation to climax. On the other hand, when an infant of four months discovers his penis and enjoys playing with it, I would hesitate to describe his play as masturbation. There are many forms of masturbation that do not involve manual stimulation. For instance, rubbing the thighs together, or friction against an object, whether it be the mattress, cushion or any other object deemed desirable. Masturbation may be an auto-erotic act or be done by mutual consent between two or more persons of the same or opposite sexes. Male and female from infancy through advanced age have always been capable of orgasm. Prior to puberty, however, where orgasm through masturbation occurs by penile stimulation, it is not accompanied by ejaculation.

Getting to know one's body and its pleasurable resources through erotic stimulation during childhood and adolescence paves the way for pleasurable foreplay during sexual intercourse. Learning about and enjoying one's sexuality without guilt is a forerunner to satisfactory and joyful heterosexual experiences.

On the other hand masturbation may be symptomatic of many problems or conflicts which are not related to sexual freedom. It can reflect compulsive behavior. Warren P. Johnson, in SIECUS Study Guide No. 3, enumerates some of these nonsexual reasons. "Boredom, frustration, loneliness, a poor self-image, inadequate boy-girl relationship, conflict with parents, too many pressures in school, fears about one's physical health—all create tensions that the adolescent tries to relieve through masturbation. In such cases it is not the masturbation that should be treated by suitable counseling but the conflict of which it is a symptom."

A good deal of folklore and fear of physical illness foolishly surrounds masturbation. Fear of skin diseases, mental illness, liver ailments, "drying up the seed," and so on, are among the ailments caused by masturbation according to old wives' tales which are still heard and believed.

The sex educator and counselor needs to deal with these anxieties and fears. She needs to face them openly in a nonjudgmental approach, explore the origin of these myths and misinformation with patience, and present the documented opinions of authorities in the field. Open discussion by students and clients when they can reflect their feelings in the peer group helps to clear the air and accelerates the process of logically viewing the data. A supportive teacher or sex counselor is essential in helping to change or modify attitudes.

Many a teacher has asked what to say or do when a third- or fourth-grade boy or girl is masturbating and drawing the attention of the class. One of the options available to the teacher is to talk privately to the student when the class is not meeting. She can then help the student develop an awareness of the difference between behavior which is acceptable when carried on in private and behavior which arouses concern in others when carried on in public. Such behavior, when practiced in the classroom, may distract students from attending to the work at hand.

SEXUAL INTERCOURSE AND ORGASM

For many people sexual intercourse is generally the beginning and end of sex. However, sexual intercourse is more than orgasm or less than orgasm. It is a sharing relationship between two people who are engaged in a physical act, satisfying to either or both in accordance with their psychological needs. This act of intercourse is always performed in a social context. Hopefully it is performed by two consenting mature people who care for each other and find pleasure in their sexuality.

Foreplay is an essential introduction to mutually satisfying coitus. It is here that the counselor may be approached with presenting problems. "He doesn't wait until I get excited too" . . . "It hurts when he comes; because I wasn't ready" . . . "She doesn't play with me and wants me inside her before I can come" . . . "She expects me to do all the work without cooperating." Foreplay is similar to petting except that it continues on into sexual intercourse. It sets the stage for sensory arousal and heightens desire for coitus and orgasm.

A common complaint high on the list of patients and clients is reluctance to engage in oral-genital sex play. Women seem to be more reluctant to participate in oral-genital foreplay than do men. The sex counselor should discuss this situation with clients in terms of personal preference and the importance of each partner's freely consenting and enjoying the sexual activity.

Clitoral stimulation plays an important part in female arousal. The counselor needs to review tactile stimulation with both partners, so as to help free them from misconceptions and myths and help them to enjoy the pleasure of touching. Without using a checklist approach to intercourse, the counselor can share with them basic biological and psychological data calculated to encourage freedom, flexibility, and active participation by both in the sex act.

When the male fully understands the capability of the woman to enjoy multiple orgasms, clitoral and vaginal, he can enjoy his orgasm without feeling guilty about not being able to reach a climax at the same time or close to hers.

A complaint which echoes feelings ("Once he is satisfied, he turns over and goes to sleep") is not uncommon. This complaint is most frequently heard in cases where the male reaches his climax and then is unable or not desirous of having a second erection. Under these circumstances, the male needs to be encouraged to bring his partner to climax by finger or other mutually enjoyable method of stimulation.

Two leading psychosexual problems which interfere with satisfying intercourse are premature ejaculation and frigidity. The former may be due to the man's inexperience, fear of failure to satisfy his partner, or generally low self-esteem which can be "precipitated or aggravated by a nagging and dissatisfied wife. The male is only too receptive to the message that if he were more of a man, she would be happier. Building up the male ego through realistic cooperation and good feelings from his partner will help the inexperienced or anxious man." The woman needs to see herself as a possible contributor to the problem. Of course, however, more deeply rooted causal factors may require referral and intensive therapy.

Frigidity can include degrees of female inability to respond to sexual stimuli and for some patients the inability to attain orgasm. Problems of frigidity are frequently based on feelings of guilt about sex, or fear of pregnancy, or may relate to unfortunate circumstances such as a forced marriage or derogatory comments regarding the female partner's sexual activities with other partners. Misunderstandings about sexual physiology or misconceptions about anticipated performance can contribute to frigidity as well.

From the review of sexual intercourse and orgasm, the psychological implications seem to dominate the problems of sexual dysfunctioning. On the other hand, a satisfying pleasurable experience can be anticipated when both partners view their sexuality as healthy, place a value of goodness on sexual intercourse, and are involved with each other as caring open people. In the main, the sex counselor will be presented with problems of premature ejaculation, frigidity and inability to obtain orgasm. Where she is alert to the psychological factors of interpersonal relations, she can do much to help the sexual problem.

Group Premarital Counseling

Group counseling with couples about to be married is gaining in popularity and importance. For the busy counselor, it affords the best opportunity to deal with a larger number of clients. Many clients prefer a combination of group and individual sessions. During these latter, they may even raise matters which they prefer to keep confidential. In group discussions the sharing of mutual concerns and fears can reduce individual guilt and anxiety. Young couples often are seeking to test their feelings about such matters as personality, finances, in-laws, and sex, with others in their peer group.

A group session should consist of at least five couples, so that the group dynamics and interaction can be stimulating and varied. Subjects ranging from love, sex, and parenthood to effective communication can be discussed in an open and trusting manner. The counselor acts only as catalyst and leader, permitting the group as a whole to explore, question, challenge, support, and evaluate the attitudes, feelings, and information generated. When necessary, the counselor should follow through with individual counseling.

In premarital counseling, the counselor has the opportunity to educate the patient and her partner regarding sexual concepts, information, and experience to an extent which will facilitate later adjustment. Adjustment for newly-married couples may take one to two years, and sometimes longer. Involved are sexual, social, economic, religious, and psychologic factors which require individual resolution. It takes time for a person to change from an "I" to a "we" concept of living. Premarital counseling should aim not only at preparing a couple to avoid serious problems but also to recognize conflict at an incipient level. Also, it should encourage them to seek professional assistance when problems do arise.

Young couples should be encouraged to begin premarital counseling at least six weeks in advance of the marriage. Occasionally problems are encountered that cannot be resolved in less time.

Extramarital Problem Counseling

Sexual intercourse without being married is a frequent presenting problem brought to the counselor by adolescents and young adults. While all such extramarital intercourse has traditionally been defined as "premarital," it is increasingly the case that in many instances neither party has any intention of ever being married in the legal sense and the term "nonmarital" is being used to describe such situations.

Usually the woman initiates the contact with the counselor. She feels she has more risks to take, i.e., pregnancy, being dropped by her boy friend for another, and being involved with romantic feelings of love whereas her male partner usually has fewer of these risks to consider.

Although the double standard is losing its hold among the majority of younger couples, the many years that women have lived under its yoke have created hardship even for those who believe in the new freedom. Young women are still sensitive to the opinions of their parents and peer group and uncertain at times as to their reactions should the relationship be terminated by the male partner.

Mary and John were both eighteen years of age and seniors in high school. They had known each other for one year and toward the end of the year began deep petting in which John would reach orgasm and ejaculation without intromission. Mary would help him to masturbate. He in turn would help her reach a clitoral orgasm. They decided to have sexual intercourse and went ahead before visiting Planned Parenthood or a family doctor for contraception. Mary missed her menstrual period and decided to share her fear of pregnancy with her school counselor. The counselor suggested she visit a physician or clinic to find out whether she was pregnant. This was done and the doctor found that Mary was not pregnant. However, the counselor suggested that it might be wise for Mary and John to come in for an interview concerning their relationship. She also suggested that if they were continuing their sexual relations they should arrange to use a mutually acceptable form of birth control prescribed by a competent physician. Since Mary had already had her pelvic examination, she would not need go through another.

The counselor then saw both partners in a joint interview. During the course of this interview, she explored with them the meaning of their relationship and the depth of their caring for each other. She had them check out their attitudes about sexuality as compared with their parents'. She wondered how they accepted the differences in parental attitudes from theirs. She asked them to explore the possibilities of a pregnancy and how they would cope with that situation. She wondered too about future plans when both would be going to different colleges. How would they accept their separation and the pursuing of different directions without commitments?

The young couple expressed the feeling that they cared for each other and shared a deep affectionate relationship. They felt no guilt about having sexual intercourse before marriage, even though their parents considered it immoral. They were willing to accept the fact that they could not make any long-term commitments because they had not fully matured, and because of the long separations during the coming school years. They planned to write, however, and to see each other during vacation periods, but they left open the possibility that their romance might end someday.

The counselor felt they had frankly faced important issues—including the desire for abortion if Mary became pregnant—and that they had mutual confidence and trust besides caring very much for each other.

In lower socio-economic groups, commonly referred to as "the poor" (and this includes both our white and black population), sexual competition and sexual intercourse with other persons frequently continues after marriage. Various studies dealing with marital breakup in communities where the poor reside give reasons such as "running in the streets," "jealousy," and more directly, "having a girl friend," and "not coming home to see me and the kids" as causes for marital breakup.

In marriage counseling with poor people the most frequent complaint from clients is "another man (or another woman) is taking my place." Jealousy and anger appear to be very much a part of the negative feelings.

The sex counselor needs to appreciate the socio-economic pressures which these people face in order to understand the strong connection that sexual activity has with pride in self. Being wanted by women is a great comfort to a poor man, especially when he finds no ego satisfaction in work or in his family life. In spite of the economic pressures and absence of job satisfaction, many poor people find satisfaction in their relationships in which each makes the other feel important and needed.

It is generally accepted among professional investigators of ghetto life that unless there is improvement in housing, manpower training and opportunities for jobs with upward mobility, educational opportunities, comprehensive medical care, along with an improved standard of living, the situation will worsen and the ghetto dweller's sexual relations will continue to be exploitive and competitive.

Recently I interviewed a couple where the wife because of her religious beliefs would not use any artificial birth-control device. On the other hand, her policy of sexual abstinence during certain days of the month had proved unsuccessful and two of the couple's three children had not been planned for and were considered accidents. The husband had become unduly distressed when the last birth occurred because his salary could only maintain a family of four at most in relative comfort. He had urged his wife to take more secure precautions in the future. She had refused. He began drinking and lost interest in having sexual intercourse with her. His mood changed from depression to overt hostility. Six months after the birth of the last child, she found him sitting in a bar with his arms around another woman. On other occasions, he frankly informed her that he was enjoying sexual intercourse with his girl friend. During the counseling sessions, the husband brought to his wife's attention her insensitivity to his fears of poverty and his shame at being unable to adequately provide for his family whom he loved. He felt his wife lacked the understanding to appreciate that she was aggravating his feelings of inferiority by her stubbornness in refusing to discuss the family problems with her religious leader. He needed emotional support and security from a woman, and his current companion was providing that. The sexual relations between them reinforced his need for a close tender relationship.

When his wife realized how much he looked to her for approval and support which was not forthcoming, and her role in impairing his desire as a father and husband to care for the family with pride and confidence, she reconsidered her original position.

The couple visited their religious leader and put squarely before him the tremendous strain that birth-control failure was creating for each of them and for the family unit. The religious leader wisely told them that they needed to make an independent judgment as to what was best for the family and weigh that against the church's teaching. They decided on using the pill. The end of the situation can be readily surmised. The marriage was saved and once again there is tranquillity in their home.

In dealing with extramarital relations, regardless of whether the clients are rich or poor, the presenting problem reflects a dissatisfaction with the ongoing relationship between man and woman. With many new life-styles emerging, the term "extramarital" must be understood to include sexual relationships outside the marriage or an arrangement whereby the heterosexual partners are living as a couple under one roof. This could include common-law marriages, communal living, or a pair living together without having undergone a legal marriage ceremony. The sex counselor should be alert to various factors involved in these situations which may not be based on mutual consent.

Marital Problems

In spite of new sexual life-styles in marriage—group sex, "open marriage" and a greater acceptance of extramarital relations—approximately 50 per cent of married couples experience problems dealing with human sexuality. In many instances when a child is having difficulty in school and a parent is asked to come in for a conference, the staff member is brought to the realization that a marital problem in the home has created anxieties in the school child which he has carried with him to school.

A list prepared by Drs. Walter Stokes and Robert A. Harper, two prominent counselors, of the more frequently discussed marital problems which have created conflicts between spouses includes:

1. Conflict as to who should be sterilized—husband or wife?
2. Form or method of birth control to be used—medical and/or religious differences.
3. Inability to communicate effectively with each other in sexual and other matters.
4. Excessive sensitivity on the part of one or the other to real or imagined injury to self-esteem.
5. Chronic nagging.
6. Lack of tenderness and affection.
7. Few common interests.
8. Attitude of martyrdom about the marital relationship.
9. Severe quarrels over management of children.
10. Poor management of family money.
11. Jealousy.
12. Sexual impotence, frigidity, and lack of orgasm.

13. Differences between the spouses as to frequency of sexual encounters.

14. Pornographic attitude toward sex on the part of one spouse.

15. Refusal to practice sexual variations.

16. Extramarital love interest of one spouse.

17. Psychosomatic symptoms related to marital unhappiness.

18. Abortion counseling.

19. Onset of menopause.

Other problems underlying the complaint of sexual conflict may be lack of respect and loving concern for the partner, rigidity and the tendency to dominate and control, or projection of one's feelings of inadequacy upon the other. Inability to share and to agree on important decisions may predispose the couple to both fiscal and sexual conflicts.

It is important for the counselor to appreciate important aspects of the relationship, other than sexual, that bring satisfaction to the couple. If sexual interaction is viewed as one major form of satisfaction among others available to the couple for gaining respect, understanding, ego support, and physical pleasure, the area of sex can be considered with greater clarity and perspective.

There is a tendency for the inexperienced counselor to place labels on his clients and then proceed to establish the validity of the labels. This can only be destructive to the well-being of the patient and the purposes of the counseling.

Where it is obvious to the counselor that the patient needs the services of a lawyer, a minister, a psychiatrist, or other specialist, she should make the referral promptly. The reason for the referral should be shared with the patient, so that a sense of rejection by, or lack of interest on the part of, the counselor is not imparted inadvertently.

PARENTAL ATTITUDE TOWARD SEX OF CHILDREN

A parent may come to the sex counselor with a problem involving the fact that her husband and she are disappointed because their baby is a girl. This complaint is heard frequently from the mother while she is still in the hospital, a day or two after she has given birth. During the preadolescent stage as the child grows, such remarks as "My wife is making a sissy out of John, because she wanted a girl," or "Mary is a real tomboy, she acts and walks just like the fellows and hangs around them all the time" are spoken and discussed in the presence of the child.

Obviously, pretending a child is of the sex other than nature intended is confusing both to the child and to her peer group. She needs to feel pride in who she is. She needs to feel that her ways and feelings are accepted and normal and that her friends approve. As she develops toward adolescence, having someone of the same sex with whom she can identify will propel her toward sexual maturity with greater ease than if she is floundering. Ambivalence and confusion can be avoided by helping parents understand the importance of sexual identification in each child's development. Where parents lack the maturity of emotional stability to work with the situation, they may need referral for psychiatric assistance. Clothes, toys, activities, stereotyping—all play a significant role in helping children define their sexual identity.

DISCUSSING SEX WITH CHILDREN

Menstruation is more easily discussed these days. Fifteen years ago it was a favorite subject for a Girl Scout leader or the school nurse to tackle with female adolescents because home, school and church wouldn't touch the subject. Mothers considered themselves too embarrassed or too ignorant to know either *how, what,* or *when* to tell their growing daughters on the threshold of physical maturity the "facts of life."

Today, many mothers, and more fathers are still fearful of discussing the physical changes and expectations of puberty with their children. However, more are willing to risk sharing their knowledge and ignorance with their children. Also, major changes have taken place in the schools, so that many of our young people are learning about their sexuality from teachers and others in the classroom.

Since parents are models, a mother's attitude toward her daughter's first menstrual period ought to include comments about the joys of being a young woman—a new figure, new attractiveness, new ways of socializing and companionship with boys. Also, the mother should speak of the new kinds of clothes and the expectations of the future—marriage, motherhood, family life, the joy of loving and being loved. Whatever may pass during these moments of talk and assistance between mother and daughter—the outcome ought to be one of "feeling happy at the thought of being a woman," and liking the idea that there are males in this world, who are no better or worse than females.

Boys, too, ought not to be deprived of the "serious talk" that rarely comes off. Father is too busy or really too embarrassed to know what to say and often wishes his son would approach him, instead, with that first question. In most cases the first question never comes and so the young adolescent must needs shift for himself. Suggest to those you counsel that if father and son, or the son and another male whom he trusts and likes, could casually get together, it would be possible to intelligently discuss the topic.

Here, again, more is needed than explaining the biological facts of reproduction. To discuss with the boy the pride of being a parent, and how much you admire and respect him, will help him exercise sound judgment as to how he behaves in his sexual encounters. Discussing exploitation and using girls can help, along with stressing the desirability of the boy's finding out the girl's attitude toward sexuality before rushing into sexual activities.

Teaching both adolescent boys and girls about birth control is important. It doesn't necessarily imply that parents are in favor of adolescent sexual intercourse. It does imply that this-and-such can happen and that helping one's child to understand how to avoid an unwanted pregnancy is a responsibility every parent ought to assume.

Nocturnal emissions are worrisome to many young boys. They feel ashamed when they wake and find their sheets spotted. Rushing to the bathroom to wash the spot out or covering it up with a towel still leaves the situation confusing and the boy often guilt-ridden, especially when the dream that night was erotic and culturally forbidden. Many a young man needs a helpful father, older brother or friend to discuss the normalcy of nocturnal emissions ("wet dreams"). How much easier to face the knowledge that one is growing and changing and that growing pains need not be agonizing ones.

NUDITY

Cultural norms regarding nudity vary in this country. Most of us accept a bikini on the beach, then blush at the sight of a miniskirt. Now that men have taken to posing naked for centerpages in popular magazines, attitudes toward nakedness for both sexes may take a dramatic turn during the next few years. Few will deny the beauty and grace of the human body. I need not delineate, for fear of being boring, the various art forms which have glorified and exalted the naked bodies of both men and women. Yet in our culture we wish to exercise a free choice as to the extent to which we reveal our bodies. For most of us have been taught—and we, in turn, teach our children—the differences between private and public behavior.

Swimming in the nude is fine for those who like it and where it is permitted. Young adolescent girls and boys whom I have counseled tell me that where they are accustomed to swim naked, and have been doing so since childhood, they do not feel any erotic overtones associated with the nudity.

On the other hand, even professional men and women who visited a cove on an island where swimming in the nude was permitted came away upset and anxious about the situation. In counseling, they gained insight concerning their guilt feelings about nudity and their need to control the situation. They were wanting others to conform to their point of view. They also came to understand the strong impact their early training had on their attitudes toward nudity.

Through counseling one can help children and their parents to express their attitudes toward nudity, the situations they find congenial and those they find threatening, and then help them work out reasonable solutions.

A parent recently asked whether appearing in the nude in front of her children at home would help to free them from inhibitions about nudity and sex in general. For some children casual nudity may be an acceptable pattern in the home, but it may create real difficulties when the child learns that his friends' parents do not accept this form of socializing. Some children react with curiosity and possibly some anxiety when they view the adult naked body. There are differences in the size of the breasts and penis, and the pubic hair makes an impression on some. It would seem that any natural and spontaneous need for being naked within the home or at a place where it is an acceptable occurrence can be learned by children as part of living. Nakedness in the bathroom, bedroom, and private areas of the household seems reasonable. Children, of course, enjoy and love to run about the house naked, especially in warm weather, until they are about three or four years old. What is more important than age or place, is the attitude of parents toward nudity and their sensitivity to the attitudes of those with whom they live intimately in the home.

HOMOSEXUALITY

For many years the psychology and psycho-analytic community looked upon homosexuality as a personality disorder. The literature is thick with Freudian and neo-Freudian analysis supporting this point of view.

Within recent times, both the public and the therapeutic sectors are re-examining old concepts. With the new openness in which sexual lifestyles are viewed on film and in literary works, the public is stretching its psychological muscles and becoming amazingly flexible. So, too, the counselor and educator often hear their students and clients talk about their desire to explore and participate in erotic or sexual experiences with members of the same sex and/or opposite sex. Many of our more vocal citizens denounce the conception that all human beings are either heterosexual or homosexual. Kinsey was one of many investigators who found that a certain percentage of the population have had between adolescence and old age some overt homosexual experience to the point of orgasm. Actually, national surveys indicate that about 44 per cent of white males and 3 per cent of white females appear to be almost exclusively homosexual over a long period of their lives.

The psychiatric studies of homosexual patients present a dominant theme of disturbed relationships between the child and his parents, and also between the child's mother and father. The stereotype of the mother pictures her as possessive, domineering, overprotective, demasculinizing and seductive. The stereotype of the father pictures him as distant, and ineffectual in dealing with his domineering and frigid wife. The male child, it is said, finds it difficult to establish a masculine identity. His fuzzy ambivalent picture of his gender is further hurt if his peer group has difficulty in accepting him.

It may well be that the attitude of other people toward the homosexual creates the anxiety-producing condition. Where hostility appears in the form of avoidance, ridicule or patronizing behavior toward the homosexual, it can be damaging. This may be similar to the feelings engendered in blacks by white racists.

Supportive help during these early maturing years by an accepting counselor can help these young people maintain the gender identity they desire without fear or emotional stress. Occasional variations in sex play can then be viewed as healthy rather than as perversions or sick behavior.

Many sex problems involve conflicts over problem pregnancies, frigidity, premature ejaculation, sexual identity crisis, homosexuality, masturbation, nudity, and unmarried parenthood. Both males and females seek assistance from early adolescence to the golden years. Sex counseling is performed in many settings and takes place on both an individual basis and in groups. Since the advent of the pill has brought into focus a greater frankness about sexuality, many people are now openly seeking help for their sexual problems.

4

Adolescent Pregnancy and Parenthood

The Office of Child Development of the Department of Health, Education and Welfare considers the various problems associated with adolescent pregnancy and parenthood to be of major concern. Programs geared toward alleviating these problems are given a high priority in our Government's national domestic programs. This is certainly as it should be, considering the appalling statistics and the problem of the neglected young people involved in unwed parenthood. During 1971, one out of every four babies was born to a mother under twenty. One out of every eight thirteen-year-old girls will become pregnant out of wedlock before she reaches the age of twenty. Also one out of every four eighteen-year-old girls is currently married. Out-of-wedlock births mothered by adolescent girls during 1972 are estimated at 200,000 in the United States; 60 per cent of these girls are white and 40 per cent are black.

Problems of Adolescent Pregnancy

After the collection of massive data, the evidence concerning the outcome of these early pregnancies generally reflects the calculated guesses that those who work with adolescents have been making in their day-to-day counseling and educational experiences. These findings support the assumptions that

—adolescent family life is linked to unwanted children who were "accidentally born,"

—family life is fraught with financial, social and interpersonal problems,

—unfinished secondary (or sometimes elementary) education is common,

—poor health is present or anticipated for mother and infants,

—there is a high incidence of separated families and divorce,

—welfare dependency is widespread,

—work potential is reduced because of lack of skills due to the failure to complete educational and/or technical training,

—general frustration at the inability to achieve long-held aspirations and desired life goals.

In addition to helping the unwed mother and assisting her family in understanding her plight, so too the family of the involved adolescent boy needs guidance to help him mature and cope with the problems he faces.

The frustrations and anxieties of our young people appear to be aggravated because they cannot cope with the stresses and pressures from family, school, and the social environment. Society, instead of being supportive and helpful, has generally behaved in a punitive fashion.

Because of the poor planning on the part of educators relevant curriculum for educating both boys and girls is neglected to a degree which smacks of social irresponsibility. In addition to the education of children, however, parent education also is essential. The parent in the home is the most consistent and long-term educator for better or for worse, and most young parents need guidance and training.

SCHOOL INADEQUACIES

The shortcomings generally found in our educational systems for adolescents are as follows:

1. Sex-education programs from preschool through grade twelve usually do not include family relations, parental roles, the responsibilities of being a parent or child, health care, early childhood development, the economics of family living, and family planning for quality living. They often concentrate on reproductive biology to the exclusion of the more comprehensive context of human relations.

2. Both pregnant girls and their male partners are forced to submit to punitively rigid policies which force them out of school. Frequently school officials call on the juvenile court and its procedures, placing the young father in the category of juvenile delinquent, often to the detriment of his future job or educational opportunities.

Many of our school systems offer homebound studies which tend to isolate the young women from their peer group and thus enhance their feelings of personal inadequacy. After pregnancy, especially where they have been given little or no opportunity to continue their education, many young mothers do not return to school for fear of further failure, criticism or rejection by their teachers and peers.

3. Even though some school systems provide for continuing education of the unwed parents during the pregnancy period, little or nothing in the way of social services or counseling is available during the transitional period of returning to the normal school situation. Day-care services, health care for both infant and mother, adjustments in day-to-day social-sexual relations combined with educational responsibilities are immediate and vital concerns which require professional help and guidance. Many of the young men and women who drop out of school do so because one or more of these vital concerns have not been met.

During the sixties, the social and educational resources of the United States Government and other agencies were focused on the unwed mother, with little interest or concern for the supportive needs of the father. He was primarily sought out to give financial aid and support for the child, with little concern shown for his personal, educational and vocational future. As a matter of fact it is common knowledge among professionals that a large number of high-school dropouts are young men who father out-of-wedlock children. They feel they have to support the child by dropping out of school and taking a low-paying job. Many of these jobs are without any future. The young men unfortunately have no guidance and assistance from school or social agencies to help them sort out their confusion and frustration.

The young father is still, in the main, the forgotten man. His need to build up his own confidence in viewing himself as a worthwhile human being is great. His need for sex education and family planning, including an understanding of parental responsibilities as they relate to the many challenges and problems involved in child-rearing, is a necessity. However, the young unwed father is often unavailable for help because he fears punitive measures will be taken against him.

How can we help him build up confidence in our willingness to help him?

A first requirement is that we reassure him of the confidentiality of our relationship with him. We can suggest that his ability to trust us will take time, but that we will try through our actions to establish trust. We can suggest that we are willing to help, and that while we don't know all the answers, we will share with him our thoughts about possible solutions. He needs to know that we respect and accept him as a human being worthy of help and support.

The Webster School Experiment

The Webster School in the District of Columbia was the first public school in the United States established for pregnant girls. It was funded in 1963 as a demonstration school by the Children's Bureau of the Department of Health, Education and Welfare for the three-year period, 1963 to 1966. It was supervised by the Board of Education of the District of Columbia in cooperation with the District Department of Health and Department of Welfare. Since 1966, the school has been operated through the regular District of Columbia Board of Education budget. Since the school's establishment, over 160 cities nationwide have set up interagency efforts to provide comprehensive services to school-age girls who live at home during pregnancy and most often keep their babies. The agencies involved may be the city and county health or welfare department and community action groups which are Federally or locally governed.

Because Webster School was the first, and in many instances the model, for providing sex education, personal and family counseling, continuing education, medical and nursing care, and nutrition education, its programs of sex education and sex counseling merit examination.

Those girls who, upon entry or during the course of enrollment, seemed to have emotional and social problems were counseled individually. At the time the girls were admitted, written permission to administer psychological tests was required from their legal guardians. The pre-test given to each girl, coded so that she did not have to reveal her identity, was compared with a similar post-test given after the 18-week period. The test dealt with Social-Sex Attitudes. The inventory covered statements dealing with dating, marriage, child-rearing, sex attitudes and practices, and love and its different meanings.

The girls participated in weekly group sessions. The object of the sessions was to assist the students in gaining a better understanding of acceptable social attitudes toward family relationships, child care, and sexual behavior, and to build up personal understanding and self-esteem.

For the most part, the attitudes of the girls toward marriage and child-rearing reflected socially acceptable attitudes. However, they were unclear about the role of the family and the father. The girls also expressed uncertainty about how a mother should feel and act toward a child when he misbehaves. Many girls had preconceived and limited notions about the degree of success and acceptability it would be possible for them to attain in social, family and community situations. In addition, the girls often seemed uncertain of the importance of love and companionship in childbearing and child-rearing.

Specific sex information was provided by the nurse and the physician assigned to the project. However, the school's main means of altering the students' sexual behavior was through group counseling. It should be noted that it was the school's official policy to refer girls to their own doctors, clinics, or hospitals if they asked for birth-control information. In addition, many girls received their prenatal care from a maternity clinic closely associated with the school. There they had an opportunity to talk with the project physician about birth control and to enroll in a birth control clinic.*

Three objectives of the school which related to the programs involving sex education and counseling were:

1. By avoiding interruption of schooling, to increase the likelihood of the girls returning to regular schools and continuing in school after childbirth.

2. To provide consistent, coordinated health care that would reduce the incidence of poor pregnancy outcomes.

3. To serve the girls in this program in such a way that they would be less likely to have further out-of-wedlock pregnancies or, if they were married, to postpone later pregnancies until after their graduation from school.

The 487 girls who attended during the three-year period of 1963–66 were junior and senior high-school students (seventh through twelfth grade). In addition to the regular secondary-school curriculum, and health and social services, each girl was involved in 18 weeks of group counseling, for one hour a week in a group of approximately fifteen girls who were all in the same class and approximate age range.

Such techniques of group interaction as role-playing, presentation of case profiles, student leadership of discussions of attitudes expressed on the Social-Sex Attitude Inventory, and written statements of problems were employed along with films, charts, and other visual aids. The students wrote evaluations of these sessions at the end of each 18-week series which were used as guides for future discussions.

In the second year new areas of discussion were added based on problems the girls brought to the group. These included the problems of combining the responsibilities of motherhood with going to school, the question of continued relations with the putative father, and ways of dealing with possible conflicts between the emotional needs of infants and those of very young mothers.

* Complete record of the project from 1963–66 has been published by the Children's Bureau, Research Report No. 2, 1968. For sale by Supt. of Documents, U.S. Printing Office, Washington, D.C. 20402.

Within the group-counseling situation it was also possible to discuss attitudes toward birth control, adoption, foster-care, and abortion in relationship to the quality of life for families. Specific methods of birth control could not be discussed at the school because of a Board of Education ruling in existence at the time. However, at the present time this is permitted.

The Social-Sex Attitude Inventory was a valuable clinical tool. The girls were interested in discussing certain of the statements. They also were interested in role-playing some of the issues involved. Irrespective of the medium used to start the group sessions, a group-centered approach was used whereby the peer group raised questions with each other, felt free to confront each other with differences. The girls were informed during the introductory sessions that no answer or statement was "right" or "wrong" but that they would have to weigh each situation, and look for the negative and positive points, and try to come up with a solution that satisfied all the parties involved. They understood that the counselor would be a "resource" person but that they were in charge of the group.

When the group worked together with single statements from the Inventory, each girl had an opportunity to select the statement she wished to discuss. She was given the advantage of playing the role of counselor. She could ask for volunteers from the group to discuss their response to the statement and then share her impressions. After that the discussion was open.

An interesting by-product of this form of group counseling was the confidence and pleasure it gave the girls when they performed the role of counselor. This was a first time for many to assume a leadership role in the peer group. Although there were slight modifications in language and some additional statements added as time went by, the core of the Inventory was quite constant during the three-year period.

The following chart shows the results based on the group sessions and other services which related to attitude changes.

PERCENTAGE OF GIRLS WITH SOCIALLY ACCEPTABLE ATTITUDES
BEFORE AND AFTER ATTENDING PROJECT SCHOOL

	Pre-test %	Post-test %	Change %	
Dating	52	73	21	(plus)
Marriages	88	98	10	(plus)
Child Rearing	55	84	29	(plus)
Social Sex Attitudes	69	80	11	(plus)

Analysis of the individual clinical profiles made for each girl reveals that the personality trends included evidence of inadequate ego development reflected in such qualities as: *a*) immature behavior in personal, social and family relations, *b*) lack of judgment, and *c*) lack of appreciation of the relationship between academic performance at school and job-placement opportunities. In addition, a majority felt that their relationship with their mothers was unpleasant and that their mothers disapproved of them. Of course it is important to consider the social-economic conditions of poor people which precipitate these situations.

In the main, the eleventh- and twelfth-grade students appeared more concerned with getting married than with preparing for a job after graduation and therefore developing good business and academic skills. They were highly motivated to perform well in the home-making skills. But, on the other hand, motivation toward the academic subjects was poor and academic performance reflected this. This attitude may have been influenced by the 22 married students who appeared to dominate the group and to whom the other students looked for leadership.

Recommendations to Improve Current School Programs

These recommendations based on the study which relate to sex education and counseling and which are relevant to most programs are:

1. Establish a follow-up process to see that girls re-enter school as scheduled or as soon as is appropriate and that during the crucial first year, contact with them is maintained to provide the needed support.

2. Put greater effort into helping school officials, teachers, and counselors to understand the problems and needs of returning school-age mothers. Encouraging school continuance by these girls should be seen as a total school responsibility.

3. Include in the program adequate and accurate birth-control information as a part of health instruction. (This recommendation needs to be included in such a way that it is viewed as a realistic goal for all individuals in their search for quality family life.)

The young men who become fathers need school-sponsored programs which are carried on with a view toward helping either the individual males or the couples achieve maturity and thus become more able to cope with the problems of parenthood. Where schools are not ready to carry on the work, community programs will be needed to fill the gap.

Also, during the three years of the project, group-counseling and education sessions were developed for the parents and guardians of the girls. Some of these sessions were held during the lunch hour, while others were conducted during evening hours. The subjects discussed included:

1. Social-sexual needs of adolescents.
2. Opening up communication between adolescents and parents.
3. Building a sense of maleness and femaleness in children and youth.
4. Teaching about human sexuality to children before they reach puberty.
5. The fact that parents are sex educators from the time children are born, and communicate attitudes and values in verbal and nonverbal ways.
6. What community social and health resources are available to adolescent parents and their families?
7. Moral issues involved in family planning and birth control.
8. Nutritional needs of adolescent pregnant girls.
9. Infant care and development.

At the present time, community health centers, maternal and infant care centers, family-planning centers and planned parenthood organizations are deeply involved in educating and counseling the adolescent parent. However, there is a lack of jobs, manpower training, continuing education programs, and decent child-care centers which will care for infants under one year of age. These deficiencies are seriously hampering the ability of the young people to make the fullest use of their opportunities.

On the positive side, as more competent educators and counselors work with these young people in a supportive way, they are helped to develop values toward themselves and toward each other that will hold out the promise of a cohesive family life filled with loving and caring people.

Abortion Counseling in Adolescent Pregnancy

In spite of the legalization of abortion in all of our states and the emergence of medically effective abortion clinics, abortion for both counselor and counselee—and for sex educators as well—remains a difficult and, in the words of David R. Mace, "agonizing decision." Sex educators and counselors need to comprehend the social, legal, religious and personal attitudes, values, laws, and conflicts involved in the subject of problem pregnancies and abortion.

The client seeking counseling help is unable to reach a firm decision on her own. She is looking for clarification, interpretation, more facts, and a warm, accepting person who can help her reach a decision that will help her and her partner, and that will give her comfort. The sex educator and counselor, in addition to being a knowledgeable and patient listener, should be prepared to help the client move toward exercising the most realistic option available in making a prudent decision. The necessary knowledge for the client would include:

1. Abortion as a medical operation.
2. Attitudes of the family, close friends, and the community.
3. Moral issues.
4. Practical personal concerns.

Sex counselors should specifically provide patients an opportunity to freely discuss the various emotions that torture them. A major one is the fear of being rejected and their anxiety which this sense of injustice creates. The counselor also needs to be prepared to deal with the patient's anger, withdrawal, and fear.

David R. Mace in his book *Abortion—The Agonizing Decision* lists the following five requirements which need to be explained to the patient before she is ready for an abortion:

1. She understands what abortion means and is sure that this is what she wants.

2. Her own judgment is not being unduly subverted either for or against abortion by coercion from her husband, her parents, or friends.

3. In making her decision she has considered how it will be likely to affect her conscience and her value system.

4. She has thought through the possibility of accepting the pregnancy as an alternative to abortion.

5. She is knowledgeable about effective methods of contraception and their availability.

The process of problem-pregnancy counseling is a difficult aspect of sex counseling. The preparation and scope of experience of the counselor which is involved in the various other types of sex counseling applies equally to the process of pregnancy counseling.

Sex Education and Counseling of the Handicapped

Unfortunately, our children, youth, and adults who are categorized as "handicapped" have all too frequently been deprived of the generally available sex education offered to normal young people in the same school district, county, social or health agency.

Many teachers and counselors have reported that the handicapped children under their care resort to masturbation and other auto-erotic activities as a source of release of tension. They also report there is a great need among the children to cling to and touch each other and adults for emotional security, perhaps more so than children who are not handicapped.

Mrs. Medora S. Bass, a sex educator and counselor, deserves much credit for researching and pulling together the bits and pieces of research and curriculum materials which are currently available. She notes that parents of retarded children are "extremely afraid of any kind of sexual expression on the part of their adolescent children. There seemed to be an underlying fear that their children will become involved sexually, or that they will take advantage of someone else. There also exists the fear that more retarded children will be born as a result of the sexual encounters of their children."

These fears have a basis in fact, but keeping both child and parent ignorant about human sexuality only aggravates the problem. Sex education for handicapped children which accepts the fact that they are sexual human beings with sexual needs will help promote realistic programs geared to the limitations imposed by the form of the handicap, and so help the children and their parents to cope effectively with sexual pressures and urges.

Because of the limitations on the right to marry imposed by some states on people considered severely retarded, the sex educator and counselor should check into the laws concerning the right to marriage in the state where sex education takes place in order to plan and develop a realistic curriculum with realistic objectives. It is important to note that the wisdom of such laws has been questioned by some specialists. Many of these experts feel that severely retarded couples should be sterilized and then permitted to marry. In this way they could partake in the satisfactions of married life without the great responsibilities involved in child-rearing. However, the National Association for Retarded Children considers marriage for those with I.Q.'s between 25 and 50 to be inadvisable.

Most experts in sex education believe that courses for the retarded ought to include decision-making problems around the issue "Should retarded adults have children?" This would be constructive in the following ways:

1. Help the retarded form a realistic self-concept.

2. Help the retarded accept their limitations as they relate to the responsibilities of parenthood.

3. Help the retarded to understand the process of reproduction.

Special-education teachers recommend social-drama techniques with puppets, painted paper bags, pictures and simple drawings as visual aids in teaching the retarded about boy and girl social-sexual attitudes and behavior. The special-education teachers feel that formal sex education for the handicapped should begin at the preschool level as with normal children. The physical sexual development of the retarded children follows the same pattern as with normal children, and the need for sex education appears to be just as great or even greater than with normal children.

An important study was conducted by Dr. Jean L. Bloom in 1968 in connection with a sex-education program for homebound high-school adolescents who suffered from severe emotional or physical problems. The study was concerned with the adolescent's development and understanding of himself as a sexual being and with his knowledge of human growth and human reproduction. The course was conducted on a coeducational level, and included: a) biological facts of human growth and reproduction, b) feelings and attitudes about sex, and c) family relations, learning a sex role, learning to behave responsibly as adolescents, concerns of parents when children date.

Parental permission was obtained. The lecture discussion method was used. Films were used as lead-ins to discussions when appropriate. Pamphlets written in simple language and with good illustrations were used for discussions on venereal disease. The combination of lecture, films, review of pamphlets, and group-centered discussions based on the preliminary presentation seemed to motivate and aid the learning situation for these handicapped adolescents in a positive way. After a 12-week course in sex education was introduced, a statistically significant increase in sex knowledge took place. This optimistic note should inspire more educators and counselors to accept the challenge of working with the handicapped in this critical area.

Mrs. Medora Bass, consultant on mental retardation to the Association for Voluntary Sterilization, recently surveyed the literature as it relates to sex education for the handicapped and listed, among others, the following twelve conclusions:

1. There is little in the literature concerning family or sex education for the handicapped.

2. The letters and interviews reveal that many specialists working with the handicapped believe the handicapped are in need of sex education and information on genetics as much—or more—than the non-handicapped.

3. There are some programs, recently developed, which have not been reported, and there is duplication of effort because of this lack of communication.

4. Providing the handicapped with proper learning experience does not necessarily require formal, specialized courses. Small discussion groups and individual counseling are sometimes used successfully.

5. Some retarded couples are aware of their inability to rear children and want to prevent conception.

6. There are little data reported on the attitudes of the handicapped and their parents toward voluntary sterilization.

7. There is a need of more studies to develop and evaluate methods of helping the handicapped relate their disabilities to their responsibilities as parents and as members of their community.

8. There is need for research in the child-rearing practices of the retarded.

9. Groups of parents of the retarded have recently become aware of the sexual problems of their children to the extent of discussing them in small meetings.

10. There seems to be a tendency for the retarded to be more hesitant about asking questions pertaining to sex than the non-retarded.

11. Some junior high schools in privileged communities have no sex-education programs of any kind.

12. There is need for books for the retarded written at their interest level but at an easier reading level.

Handicapped children are more in need of sound sex education than the normal child since their parents are less often able to inform them. Also, their curiosity may be greater because of their limitations. For the well-being of the handicapped child and his partner a childless marriage may often be advisable. Therefore, the handicapped should be given instruction on contraception.

Our rapidly growing experience has made it clear that adolescent pregnancies, abortion counseling, and problems of the handicapped call for special training skills and knowledge. The teacher or counselor can carry her fair share of the responsibility when she is particularly aware of the unique educational methods suitable for teaching and counseling the handicapped. When the counselor is sensitive to the many delicate dilemmas which confront the man and woman involved in a problem pregnancy she can move with patience and rational thought in a manner which is suitable to the patient's needs and readiness. Counseling in these areas is a science *and* an art, and the former can be learned to the point where it can elevate the creative sense in the learner.

5

Developing Communication Skills

Before the sex educator and counselor can ask where those who need help stand today on sex education and counseling, he needs to know where he stands. On this issue the public is as varied and confused as is the professional. The people are coming in droves—from schools, social-service agencies, family-planning centers, planned-parenthood affiliates, university health centers—seeking guidance, seeking a climate where they can explore the various options open to them to learn about their sexuality and how to cope with their problems.

The previous generation, because of the "head-in-the-sand" attitude of so many of its members, is in real danger of losing touch with—to say nothing of control over—the behavior, attitudes and value systems of the young. A new society is emerging but too many of us are still talking and thinking in terms of the old. Suddenly, to our shock and dismay, we discover that we are not being heard by the young. They are off somewhere in another age, following paths we have never known—communal living, partnership without marriage, group sex—and our calls to them do not seem to reach their ears.

It is ironic that we can clearly and effectively communicate with a space capsule circling the moon thousands of miles away, but we cannot seem to communicate with the teenagers in our own household on matters very close to our hearts.

Coming to Terms With One's Own Sexuality

It seems apparent that during the essential communication process—whether between youth and educator or educator and administrator, or counselor to counselor—our self-awareness as a sexual individual male or female is of major significance.

Our awareness ought to embrace our feelings about ourselves as male or female, our family position—including the attitudes of our parents toward us—our attitudes toward our *male* and *female* colleagues, our attitudes toward our white and black colleagues and clients and students, and the feelings they arouse in us.

Our attitudes toward nudity, adolescent pregnancy, masturbation, abortion, homosexuality, contraception, divorce, group sex, and extramarital sex relations are of major significance in the effectiveness of the sex-education and counseling process. These are the realities of human sexuality.

In the past it was a relatively easy matter for professionals to discuss problems with clients and students, and feel that if they, the professionals, were effective from the *neck up*—that is, knew the facts, and understood the problem through analysis and rapport with the client— they could write the *correct prescription*. No longer is that sufficient. Much in human sexuality is communicated through verbal and nonverbal signals. Sexual gender, clothes, language, age are all part of the communication process.

It is a first priority that we develop to the best of our capacity and bring into focus our sexual self-image. If this is difficult, we must call on the resources of workshops which include sensitivity training in human sexuality and training in verbal and nonverbal skills. The American Association of Sex Educators and Counselors at its national and regional sex workshops and institutes includes sensitivity sessions of sixteen hours, ten hours and eight hours geared toward awareness in human sexuality. Films, attitude inventory tests, role-playing, case presentations, psycho-drama—all are among the methods which may be used to develop sexual awareness.

Use of the Social-Sex Attitude Inventory already referred to in Chapter 4 can help shake up the layers of unconscious conditioning that inhibit us from understanding and accepting new ways in human sexuality. Educators and counselors can use this Inventory in group discussion as a means to explore their preconceived attitudes toward sexual behavior, compare these attitudes with their peers, discuss their thoughts and feelings openly, and hopefully appreciate the scope of the irrational cobwebs they have harbored for so long. It is good to know that this process of self-confrontation has helped many people to reformulate their attitudes and so become better prepared to deal with their own sexuality and that of their students and counselors.

Of course it is always possible for the teacher to develop his own

inventory as he comes across statements and questions that are controversial or based on myths, or that he feels would handicap his students
and therefore need further discussion and exploration.

The Sex Knowledge and Attitude Test (SKAT) by Harold I. Lief and
David M. Reed of the University of Pennsylvania is widely used in medical schools. It can also be of value to undergraduates and nonmedical
students training for allied health and sex-education work. SKAT is an
omnibus research tool developed as a means for gathering information
about sexual attitudes, sex knowledge, degree of experience in sexual
encounters, and a diversity of biographical information. The test has
been under development since 1965, and its more recent revisions have
been standardized and cross-validated on approximately 4,000 U.S.
medical students. A manual of references concerning the effectual data
is available. Four standardized attitude scale scores and two knowledge
scores are obtainable from the SKAT. The attitude scales are as follows:
Heterosexual Relations, Sexual Myths, Abortion and Masturbation.

A sample of the test statements follows, with either T (true) or F
(false) to be circled after each statement.

The spread of sexual education is causing a rise in premarital inter-
course.   T   F
Parents should stop their children from masturbating.   T   F
Impotence is almost always a psychogenic disorder.   T   F
Most people believe premarital intercourse is socially acceptable.
                                                    T   F

Learning the Language

Before we can communicate with skill, we need to learn the language
of human sexuality and the feelings this evokes within ourselves and
within the people we are trying to reach. This aspect of the matter has
already been explored in Chapter 2. As stated there, communication becomes clearer when both the receiver and the sender perceive the message
in the same light. When a black child tells me "Black is beautiful," I feel
him saying, "I am black, and I like myself and take pride in my blackness." And when I respond, "Yes, I agree, black is beautiful," I hope he
senses my feeling that black and white are equally beautiful and that I
am glad he takes pride in his blackness.

Therefore learning the language and its variations in feeling tone will
help us, whether we are at the sending or receiving end of the wire.

Before we can communicate with skill, we need to learn the language
of human sexuality and the feelings it evokes within ourselves and

within the people we are trying to reach. At one level at least, the feeling tone behind the words is more important than the words themselves. When the teacher grasps the feeling tone behind the words, she can react in a supportive way. The fact remains, however, that there is a core vocabulary in human sexuality.

Our understanding of the meaning of the words listed in the Glossary in the back of this book constitutes a basic core in the vocabulary of sex. However, just learning the dictionary definition is hardly enough. It is necessary to understand the feelings these words evoke within ourselves, the fantasies that blow around in our minds, and the feelings they create in others. Communication at its best involves self-awareness of our feelings about the thoughts we are sending through our words, voice, gestures, body movements and any other nonverbal means of communicating we use. For example, the second-grade student raises his hand, teacher nods, and the child says, "I have to leave the room." Teacher says, "Please wait until I finish this arithmetic problem on the blackboard." Child responds with anxiety, "But I have to go Number One right now." The teacher, realizing the feeling tone of anxiety on the part of the student, without any verbal response, takes the pass and gently beckons him to leave the room. Obviously she totally accepted his usage of the expression, "Number One" for "urinate" and responded to his feeling of anxiety with support and effective reaction.

Learning the language involves learning the language of the neighborhood, the ethnic and religious attitudes and feelings toward sexual expressions and behavior, and colloquialisms commonly used in the clinic or classroom by patients and pupils.

Some sex educators make the mistake of insisting that the children in their classroom drop from their vocabulary words such as "wee-wee," "dick," "ding-dong" in referring to the penis. They insist that the only correct word for penis is "penis." They refuse to understand the vocabulary of the home and neighborhood. The language that parents and children are comfortable with, and which is socially acceptable to their friends and neighbors, ought to be acceptable to the teacher. She can then introduce the universal language of sexuality and explain to her students (and parents) that knowing both levels of language will help them to communicate with people wherever they may be.

As was pointed out earlier (cf. Chapter 2) in a somewhat different context, many elementary-school children go through a period of using slang and "dirty" words such as "shit," "fuck," "bastard," and "bitch," often as shockers without even understanding the meaning of the words expressed. A teacher or counselor needs to stop and consider the context in which the words are used and the situation which provoked the usage before responding. The teacher may wonder *a*) if the youngster is trying to show off and attract attention, *b*) has he been unfairly put down by a teacher or classmate and is he responding with anger, *c*) is he using words which he hears at home and uses out of habit, or *d*) is he so upset about school, or some other situation, that he is hardly aware of his choice of language in expressing his deep anxiety?

When the teacher grasps the feeling tone behind the words she can react to the feelings in a supportive way. When the student has calmed down, she can tell him that she knows the meaning of the words he used, but that maybe he doesn't; then she explains them matter-of-factly. He should be told that these are words he shouldn't use in class. Besides, these are slang words, and there are many more appropriate words in which to express his feelings.

Learning to Listen With the Third Ear

The expression "listening with the third ear" (listening for the feeling behind words) is the phrase of Dr. Theodor Reik, a lay psychoanalyst, whose book *Listening With the Third Ear* many have found to be most helpful. The teacher or counselor who learns the art and science of listening with the third ear will be able to understand the fears, the joys, the anger, the love, the jealousy, the compassion, the suspicion, the trust, and the many other emotional feelings that are expressed through words which often are used to cover up the true feelings behind them. The trained person, who catches the feeling, can respond to the caught feeling in the communication and offer responsive support. This helps the sender to ventilate, open up, and behave in a more trusting and healthy way because he feels the receiver of the message understands and accepts him.

Obviously this training in listening takes time to master. It is, however, both teachable and learnable, and that is what really matters. The *reflective* statement or question which reflects the feelings expressed by the sender helps to convey understanding and encourages amplification of the problem.

Let's look in on a counseling situation where the client has difficulty expressing his conflict as to whether to break off with his girl or continue his relationship with her. He expects to enter college in another city, and this has him worried. The counselor uses the technique of listening for feeling and asking reflective questions:

Mr. A.: But we're in love and we were planning to marry some day. It's hard to think about that now . . . and I just don't know what she and I should do. . . . I'll be away and we'll be apart. I've been thinking, especially when you're planning to get . . . you know, not to be together.

COUNSELOR: You have been wondering whether, when you are away, the relationship will work out? [*This question indicates that the counselor is trying to understand his feeling. If the client feels the counselor understands him, he will continue to tell him more.*]

MR. A.: Yes, it is a problem and it worries me. I never realized that something might happen while we are apart. But I guess it won't happen, she will still love me.

COUNSELOR: What particularly concerns you about that? [*Counselor asks for clarification and tries to help the client become more specific in identifying his fears. This helps the client work with both his feelings and his reasonings in sorting out the situation.*]

MR. A.: Well, what bothers me—a lot of my friends are separated and . . . and something happens between the two. . . . It's just not the same as before. They get involved sexually with other people.

COUNSELOR: You feel that being separated and apart for a long time will hurt your relationship too? [*The question conveys understanding.*]

MR. A.: Yes, that's it. If I didn't have to go away, things would work out. It's going away that bothers me. She doesn't know I'm anxious.

COUNSELOR: You haven't discussed it with her?

MR. A.: No. Because she believes that anything we plan together will work out, even our having sexual relations.

COUNSELOR: So you are wondering whether to continue having sexual intercourse?

MR. A.: Yes.

In this situation the reflective questions and statements helped the client to open up and to express some of his fears. Reflective questions also help to increase rapport. The counselor, in pursuing this line, would try to help the client talk things out with his girl friend about his fears.

Dean Johnson, in *Marriage Counseling, Theory and Practice*, notes:

At times reflective comments may be used by the counselor to help the client express what he is feeling and thinking. Moreover, reflective comments enable the client to examine and evaluate what he is saying. Frequently a client will express thoughts and feelings without recognizing exactly what they mean to him. When these verbalizations are reflected to him, he may be rather surprised that these thoughts and feelings are really his own.

In the classroom, whether the group is small or large, the sex educator can use reflective questions or statements to help students examine and understand their feelings and judgments about a variety of sexual conflicts and fears.

Recently in a junior-high-school class where dating and sex play was being discussed, one of the students engaged in the following dialogue with the teacher:

GIRL STUDENT: Boys are out for what they can get. They'll try any kind of sweet talk to get you to lay down for them.

TEACHER: You feel that all boys are selfish when it comes to sex, and there isn't a single nice one around.

GIRL STUDENT: Oh! I didn't mean that. I meant it's hard to meet a nice fellow who really cares about girls and their feelings.

TEACHER: Let's wonder a minute about what you and your friends feel a boy looks for in a girl he would like to introduce to his best friend as his girl. [*By reflecting with students the teacher can help them work through their tendency to stereotype in their broad generalizations and begin to express feelings and thoughts about themselves and the opposite sex so that they can formulate values and norms that will help them form heterosexual friendships with some confidence in each other.*]

Reflective statements and questions can accelerate rapport in both individual and group counseling and in the classroom.

Exercises in Sensitivity

During the past fifteen years the author has developed a "reflective" exercise to use in training adolescents and professionals to listen for and reflect the feeling level in various communications. It involves listening and observing both verbal and nonverbal clues that the sender wishes to convey. In her "Affective Learning" workshops, the exercise has become a standard part of the core curriculum because of its popularity with the various groups.

It is advisable that this exercise be used after the group has been together and worked together for at least four hours in intensive interaction. When practiced by an ongoing group, such as a class which meets over a period of weeks or an ongoing counseling group, the exercise can be repeated at different intervals for reinforcement. Of course, the decision to present a particular technique is arbitrary and will depend upon the emerging needs of the group.

REFLECTIVE EXERCISE

Seat a group of eight to twelve people with the leader in a circle. Each person should have a pencil and a blank sheet of paper. Explain the exercise in the following way:

This is an exercise to help us tune in on emotional feelings that words alone do not communicate. To help us along, each of us will write about a true incident which had an emotional impact upon him. In relating the incident, use the first person, and refrain from using any emotional terms to describe your feelings—that is, your actions, reactions, thoughts and feelings. Use approximately one side of the blank paper. If you need more space, by all means use both sides. Try to do your story in ten minutes. It may seem hard at first, but you will get into the swing of it. If you find you have a tendency to use emotional words, just scratch them out.

After the group has finished writing, call for a volunteer to read his story. Members of the group will individually attempt to reflect the reader's feelings at the time of the incident which is described. You can use introductory phrases such as: "You felt . . . when this happened," or "You may have felt several emotions . . . ," or "I wonder if you felt like . . ."

After several members of the group reflect with the reader, he then shares with the group his emotional feelings at the time, and receives additional spontaneous supportive feedback. Continue with other volunteers who wish to read their story.

Sometimes a group will ask for an example. In which case the leader may help the process along by sharing with the group a short story such as the following:

I was twenty-two years old at the time. My fiancé was to meet me at 2 P.M. on the corner of 57th Street and 5th Avenue in New York City. We were planning to select an engagement ring that Saturday afternoon. I arrived at the appointed time and waited for him until 2:45 P.M. He didn't show up, so I phoned his apartment. His friend Tom, who shared the apartment, answered the phone and when I inquired about my fiancé, he told me he had gone off on a weekend trip with Mary, a close friend of mine.

This exercise is satisfying to most members of the group. It has been used with school trustees, principals and headmasters, therapists, doctors and others in the helping profession, and with classroom teachers, as well as with secondary school students.

The satisfaction of being able to listen and become aware of hidden feelings is very pleasurable to the ego. It is satisfying, too, because it is an intimate situation usually not shared in public and one that brings the individual and the group closer together. Also, it is satisfying to the storyteller to find that many in the group understand and are able to empathize with his feelings in a supportive way. It is helpful in developing one of the most critical needs in affective education and communication.

It is interesting to note that most people relate stories that are sad and frustrating and which call for great strength and fortitude to cope with them. Few participants bring up joyous emotions associated with happy and satisfying situations. Some groups have pondered this at sessions following the exercise and have supplied a variety of reasons. Perhaps other groups can raise this issue too, and explore reactions.

FINGER DANCING

Sensory awareness of one's rhythm, creativity, and cooperativeness can be heightened both for the teacher and for the students by using this exercise done in dyad form. If the group is heterosexual, it is best that the dyads be formed by counting off 1, 2 . . . 1, 2, etc. In some instances partners will be mixed sexually, in other dyads persons of the same sex will share the experience. The teacher introduces it by the following or similar words:

I will play different musical rhythms for you, and without verbal communication you can share a dancing experience. Who will lead or follow is up to you. This is your experience. You may use the finger dancing as an introduction and become involved in other dancing or rhythm movements with your body according to your feelings. This is your creative moment, and you can take it from there.

Note: The rhythms are played on a record player or tape cassette for 15 minutes. During this time three distinct rhythms are introduced. The first is folk music, the second is a polka, and the third is a Benny Goodman jazz rhythm or some Beatle music. Both have a strong "beat." Other rhythms can be used, depending upon the age and interests of the group. Music that the group likes and is familiar with should be used.

The dyads then form a group of five dyads each, or ten people, for the feedback with a leader. The initial reaction for the mixed dyads is one of pleasure, whereas the all-male dyads reflect tension and uneasiness because of culturally imposed fears. They worry about being teased or observed by the others. This often leads to a discussion of cultural influences in male and female touching and dancing patterns—those which are socially acceptable and those upon which strong censorship is placed.

The groups usually are ready to talk about common feelings of both the facility and frustration in communicating their preferences, negative feelings and pleasures. The following questions may be used by the group leader in facilitating communication during the feedback session:

1. How did you decide who would lead? Did you exchange roles of

leader and follower? How did you feel in each role? How did you guide each other? Did you feel any dissatisfaction or frustration? If so, how did you handle it? When you found your partner responsive, did you express in some way your pleasure and satisfaction?

2. How far in body movements did you carry the rhythms?

3. Would you have preferred other rhythms? Why?

Note: The sharing and communication skills in nonverbal rhythm-sharing can be used with children from kindergarten through college years, and of course with adults as well.

TRUST WALK

This exercise is also known as the "blind man's walk" and is helpful in developing sensory awareness, trust, and nonverbal communication skills. It can be used with both children and adults. The exercise is done in pairs and the feedback is centered in circles of ten or twelve people, composed of couples who participated in the trust walk and a leader.

This exercise can be performed indoors or outdoors. Except for the cold winter months, the outdoor experience can be more interesting because of the many alive and growing natural plants and trees.

Where young children are involved, the instructions need to include a statement concerning the responsibility of the leader or guide for the safety of the blind man.

After pairing off: *Instructions*: One is to close his eyes and the other will be the guide. The guide is to provide a variety of sensory experiences in touching, feeling, smelling, tasting, body motion, and so on. He is to be as creative as he can in selecting these experiences. *Two examples*: "It's fun to run while you are blind and being led," and "It's interesting to encounter another person while blind, especially if the other is blind too." Try not to identify or categorize while you are blind. "Just experience what is happening and how you feel about it." After about ten minutes the partners switch roles. The leader or guide becomes blind, and the blind person becomes the guide.

The participants are usually amazed at the degree to which they could trust each other. They are fascinated by their ability to tune in to new sensations about their surroundings which before they had taken for granted.

The intimacy that developed between the two people in the dyad was mentioned frequently. Especially when people agreed that the one experience helped them to learn more about each other than months of working and lunching together.

This exercise can be used in group-counseling sessions involving sex partners and couples encountering difficulties because they don't trust each other. In schools for example, the dyad for the trust walk may pair a headmaster and a student, a trustee and teacher, and any number of status-mixing combinations which can lead to a new recognition of each other as human beings eager for understanding and acceptance.

ME AS A KID

This exercise was used during the White House Conference for Children in 1970 with the delegates who were assigned to the "Identity" Forum. It has since proven useful in communication work with primary-school children, adolescents, teachers, school and college counselors and administrators, and sex educators and counselors.

The group consists of eight to twelve people seated in a circle with their leader. Each is given a large drawing sheet, approximately 24 x 12 inches and a small crayon or drawing pencil.

Instructions for junior and senior high-school students: "Let us each draw a picture as we saw ourselves in the primary grades." For college students the instruction can state, ". . . draw a picture as each of us saw ourselves as a child. Each of us can select any age that stands out in his mind and feelings." For teachers, counselors, staff, or parent groups, the instructions would relate to the age of children whom they are teaching or counseling, or the age of the children in a given family.

The instructions should also include the following statement: "Before you start drawing yourself at a particular age, think about your appearance at that time, the activities you participated in, and the people you related with. You might want to include the important people or activities in your life, whether they made you happy or unhappy. Please take about ten minutes. This is a rough sketch, an impressionist drawing. We are not artists who expect to have our work exhibited or compared on its artistic merits."

When the group have finished drawing their pictures, a request for volunteers is made by the leader. As each person volunteers, he or she first holds up the drawing, shares his impression of himself and describes some of the particular settings or people he drew and their relationship to him. Often the individuals in the group will share some of the following feelings. These have come out spontaneously or are initiated by the leader at appropriate times during the discussion:

1. Occasions that one enjoyed or disliked (school, sports, church, Christmas, birthdays, visits to relatives, vacation).

2. Feelings about pets, bicycles, books or special equipment or furnishings.

3. Friends or peer group relations. Agreeable or disagreeable situations.

4. Nature and outdoor growing things like trees, grass, flowers, streams, sunlight, pebbles, and hard surfaces.

THREE-PART EXERCISE IN COMMUNICATION

The group is paired off and each dyad shares the exercises. Then five dyads form a group of ten for feedback concerning the experience. The dyads are instructed to sit back to back and, without turning their heads, attempt to carry on a conversation. After about five minutes ask them to stop and express their feelings.

The group members usually express feelings that talking without nonverbal cues is a very exasperating and frustrating experience. They become sensitive and appreciate the advantage of being able to observe another person and use the many nonverbal cues that can be picked up in face-to-face encounters.

The second communication exercise in the series of three instructs the pairs to turn their chairs around and face each other. Without talking, they are asked to communicate by using only their eyes. They are also told to become aware of how they feel as they do the exercise; if they want to look away that is permissible, but to be consciously aware of whether the "eye-to-eye" experience makes them feel embarrassed, silly, or intrigued—whatever feelings they experience.

After a few moments they are to sit back, close their eyes and "See whether you have some ideas about your partner." The five dyads form their group and share their experiences.

The third part of the three-way communication exercise involves closing eyes and having the partners in the dyad communicate only by touching hands and in any other way they mutually desire.

George I. Brown, in *Human Teaching for Human Learning*, expresses the thought that this exercise helps the participants discover the significance of less conventional ways of communicating. They are able to feel confident in being able to make contact with another human being in unorthodox ways. The progression of the exercise is designed to move participants from very little risk to more risk. Almost everyone talks, but few would risk touching except for shaking hands or back slapping.

It is interesting even in our Western culture to see the spontaneous display of affection and sympathy shown by men for each other in full view of the public eye on the basketball court or football field, where winners hug each other in joy, weep when they find a friend has fallen in pain, pat each other's buttocks in appreciation of scoring or playing well, and end by lifting the hero high above the crowd. Yet, in the world of work and the world of academic and social relations, the straight jacket of propriety is snugly set about the body by these same men, and is only to be set free by alcohol or other artificial means.

In all the exercises discussed here, it is important to remember that the experience heightens awareness of self, but the sharing of the experience in the group creates the kind of communication of feeling which reaches to deeper levels of sharing with others. The protection here for participants is the general level of trust and openness that is shared, and the supportive help which the leader brings to the group. When teachers or counselors are not trained to lead groups, a person who is capable should either train the teachers and counselors or work along with them.

At the American Association of Sex Educators and Counselors (AASEC) and American Association of Marriage and Family Counselors (AAMFC) workshops for training teachers and counselors, the first day of a five-day intensive experience is devoted to communication and self-awareness exercises and group experiences. The evaluations of participants after completing the workshops speak very positively of the value to themselves in building warm relationships, in learning to listen, in developing awareness of nonverbal cues in conversation, and of being able to apply many of the exercises later in their own job experiences with children, youth and adults.

The teacher's or counselor's decision to use a particular technique or exercise must depend upon the readiness of the group and her perception of their readiness. It is wise to start from the least risk-taking exercise and go on to those that involve more risk. Building on satisfying responses gives the individual the reinforcement that precipitates trust and openness.

Ideally, a teacher or leader should have an extensive repertoire of techniques and approaches and should be able to create new techniques the moment the need arises. For example, puppet shows, newspaper clippings, art, architecture, sculpture, movies, or even film strips, can be used. Also, many games involving nonverbal means such as charades, which act out a range of emotions, can be of value. Techniques involving touch, smell, hearing, tasting and movement can be included by planning and participating in experiences that seemed worthwhile to carry back to work.

Often teachers and counselors raise the questions: Will my students lose respect for me if I become one of them? Don't they need to look up to the teacher or counselor in order to learn?

The answer seems to be that the students see the teacher or counselor as a human being, and whether they respect him or not depends upon their perception of him. Being a "brain" doesn't necessarily compel respect if the teacher or counselor is a bully or a snob to boot. Students can relate and share, and feel the freedom to explore and to grow, when they are guided by a humanistic teacher or counselor. Worthwhile group experiences develop these kinds of feelings between teachers and students.

Sensitive Areas in Teaching and Counseling

Although some thoughts and ideas have been expressed earlier in this book on prevailing attitudes and feelings toward sensitive subjects, for example: *a*) sexual intercourse outside the marital state, *b*) homosexuality, *c*) masturbation, *d*) nudity, *e*) "dirty" words, *f*) abortion, and *g*) birth control, it may be prudent at this point to explore some of the effective approaches for training and teaching.

THE LIFE LINE

Within recent years the author has devised a life-line approach for training in these areas. This technique came into being when it was discovered that on many occasions individual teachers would take several contradictory positions on masturbation depending upon the age of the masturbator. This also happened frequently in discussions on nudity and out-of-wedlock coitus. For example, an individual teacher expressed the feeling that it was normal for a child of four months to play with and enjoy his penis. The same teacher was upset to find a second-grade girl in her class playing with her vagina while sitting at her desk during the arithmetic session. In other words many teachers and counselors were confused and often took both sound and irrational positions on the same subject. Age seemed to be a critical factor in shaping their attitudes. To bring this out for discussion, it may be helpful to draw a life line on the blackboard and hand each member of the group a copy of it on an 8 x 11 inch sheet of paper. The life line looks something like this.

Instead of opening the discussion in the group with a broad question such as "How do you feel about masturbation?" the question asked was "Would you feel differently about a child masturbating at four months than you would if he were four years?" Any of the various ages listed could be used depending on the responses and the discussions provoked. This helps to surface underlying and unexpressed feelings which many of our professionals hold. But once having been confronted with specific situations, we find that group members tend to sort out and assess their feelings in a reflective fashion. Specificity through specific situations has been a helpful approach.

In using the life-line approach for discussions on homosexuality, the group appear to gain valuable insights into their ability to distinguish between homosexual behavior practiced by heterosexuals and behavior by people who identify themselves as homosexuals. Many situations evolve around small children who like to dress up in clothes of the opposite sex, who tend to strongly identify with the parent of the opposite sex, or whose life-style or appearance is that of the stereotyped "sissy," "queer," or "tomboy." Specific situations brought up for discussion help the group to understand the influence of the absence of a parent from the home, the social and cultural practices in the home or community, and the developmental play and tasks that children need to experience to reach security in their sexual identity. The life line helps to negate the clichés and stereotyping associated with this sensitive area.

Nudity discussions that seem to rock the boat and create much con-

AREAS FOR EXPLORATION

1. Masturbation

2. Homosexuality

3. Nudity

4. Premarital sex behavior

5. Pregnancy

6. Birth control

7. Abortion

Life Line

4 months	4 years	14 years	24 years	44 years	64 years

fusion relate to public and private appearances and age of the person. Discussions concerning appropriateness of nude bathing, nude sun-bathing, bathing two children of different sexes in the same tub, seemed to clarify foggy notions held by many of the group participants.

Discussions on abortion lent themselves to sharp differences in the group as they viewed religion of the patient, marital situation and age. The life line helps to bring this into the discussion because age involves the family situation especially in the case of minors.

Language discussions, especially around the range of four-letter words which are commonly used, such as "shit," "fuck," etc. often appear to be acceptable or unacceptable based on age of the speaker and the place or circumstances under which they were uttered. It is not uncommon to hear an adult in the group say "It's O.K. for me to say 'Oh, shit' because I can use it with discrimination and I also have alternate appropriate words at my command. For the six-year-old, he should have his mouth washed when he uses a 'dirty' word, in order to make sure he doesn't develop bad habits."

Our discussants will weigh the equities involved in their attitudes and pick away at many of the inconsistencies they have clung to for a long time. The cathartic benefits are manifold. Teachers and other group members hear their colleagues utter the "unspoken and forbidden words" without falling apart, and gain confidence in the feeling that "words are not dirty" but rather the mental and emotional feelings we have about them may be "dirty." They become more comfortable in speaking and hearing others express long-forbidden words. Then the group can move along to discuss appropriate language.

Often I will suggest to a group that many people feel "nail" is a clean word, whereas "screw" is a dirty word. The reaction is one of laughter. They appreciate how ludicrous we sometimes are.

GRAFFITI BOARD

The Graffiti Board is another icebreaker for opening up verbal discussions on particular "dirty" words. On the blackboard or on three large posters hung before the group or placed on a rack are written three terms:

sexual intercourse   *penis*   *vagina*

The leader calls for volunteers to write on the Graffiti Board synonyms for each of the three. Soon the blackboard is filled. In a recent workshop session over 150 words were placed on the blackboard. Age, culture, community, and ethnic groups all contributed to the richness and variety of expressions. After this exercise the group discussed language used within the intimacy of the home, among friends, and language used in casual conversation with acquaintances or professional colleagues. Distinctions were made between the verbal and written word. The most significant aspect of the Graffiti Board is its application in the classroom and in sex education with parent and community groups.

These sessions have many benefits:

1. They take the sting and fear out of sex language.

2. They help the listener reach out to grasp the feeling tone of the speaker and enable the listener to understand the context in which the word was said.

3. They help teach children, youth and adults the meaning of words and social distinctions in their daily usage.

4. They help to eliminate moral judgments about people who use sexual language freely.

FAMILY PLANNING

Family-planning and birth-control education has become less sensitive and less fraught with fear during the last few years. The mass media's concern with the problems of human ecology, population crisis, and the quality of family living has heightened our awareness of the efficacy of teaching and talking about family planning and contraception. In addition the Women's Liberation movement has helped women to assert their human rights for decision-making concerning when and how many children they will bear.

No longer do we talk about whether or not we should make family planning a part of the sex-education curriculum. Rather, our focus is on how can we best integrate it into the program.

In our training group we introduced the film *Roots of Happiness*. This film shows two families—one family in which children are loved, spaced and wanted. The other family has children living in a crowded situation in a home permeated by anger, fear, and anxiety. The following discussion explored the many facets of effective family planning vs. no family planning and the effect upon the human condition.

The group approached the area of teaching youth about family planning in the following way. The need for teaching family planning in schools stems from many factors. The more salient and forceful reasons include:

1. Healthy and happy children are usually those who are wanted and cared for as members of a family group.

2. The health and emotional well-being of parents is closely related to their ability financially to maintain an adequate standard of living for the number of children in the family. In group discussions with adolescents, a review was made of the average cost of living for a family of two, three, or four persons with the budget including the cost of raising a child until the age of eighteen. Taking a hard look at the financial facts of life was a first for many of the young people. After each discussion, several usually expressed the opinion that "I didn't realize it costs about $20,000 to raise a child. I guess I'll wait to have one until I can afford it."

3. Family planning has a potent impact on the world's concern for the population explosion.

4. Many families today have more children than they want or can adequately care for because of ignorance about family planning.

5. Many young people, of junior and senior high-school age, are not prevented by social or moral strictures from having sexual intercourse, yet they rarely use birth-control contraceptives. This is due mainly to ignorance.

6. The body of knowledge related to family planning is of sufficient importance to the health and welfare of all individuals as to make depriving young people of this information contrary to sound principles and practices in education.

The social and personal need for family-planning knowledge is essential. Such knowledge can decrease illegitimacy and venereal disease and help young people and children to avoid miserable lives. Early marriages can often be postponed. Early divorce, broken homes, and homes fraught with emotional tension can frequently be avoided.

If it is agreed that family planning is an essential part of family-life and sex education, then who should teach it and in what manner should the subject matter and attitudes be taught?

In the first place, a teacher who is sensitive and comfortable with the subject ought to be chosen. He or she can be a health educator, nurse, counselor, psychologist, or any competent professional who has a solid interdisciplinary background, is familiar with the subject matter, and is sensitive to the feelings, understandings, and social, religious, and cultural background of those whom he teaches. It is important to avoid a judgmental authoritarian approach. Explaining and clarifying in a supportive, comfortable way the questions of students is most helpful in the process of family-planning education.

A student-centered approach in which the group can explore and survey differences of opinion and the basis for decision-making can lend reinforcement and strength to the program. Case studies, role-playing, and class panels help the students to explore attitudes and feelings.

Programs in family planning, where possible, should include the parents of the young people. The classes should be held separately, but both classes might include core materials. This parallel approach is helpful for improving communication between parents and their children. Many successful family-planning programs have included resource people from the community—from medicine, nursing, law, and religion.

Family planning is a growing part of the health-education curriculum, and the need for training personnel is a challenge to educators. Through training laboratory procedures, educators and counselors can appraise their old behavior patterns and attitudes and look at new ones. By participating in affective interaction with others, these educators and counselors are afforded the opportunity to grow in self-awareness and in the nonverbal and verbal skills so necessary in the sex-education and sex-counseling process. Communication skills are learned through participation in sensitivity groups, encounter groups, marathon groups and the laboratory movement. All of these share the common goal of helping each participant to recognize and face in himself and in others many levels of functioning. These include emotions, attitudes and values. They assist the learner to evaluate his behavior in light of the response it elicits from himself and others. He then can learn to integrate these experiences into a more effective and perceptive self. Communication skills can be learned by preschool children on up through the aged. Of course the experiences that best accelerate the growth process are those which are reasonably suitable to the task readiness of the learner.

6

Techniques for Teaching

It is important for sex counselors and sex educators to remember that the prime sex education and counseling takes place in the home. From age zero until the child goes to school, parents and family are sex models, sex communicators, sex teachers and counselors, so that the growing child's sense of his identity, his image of masculinity and femininity, his values and his behavior are overwhelmingly influenced by his parents and other members of his family. Even when he goes to school, teachers merely supplement the basic attitudes and values taught in the home. Thus, when the counselor is involved either individually or in a group with his patients or clients, he needs to be aware of the relevance of their home-inculcated learning to what they say or do.

In the realm of human sexuality, whether in counseling or education, the goal should be the preparation of people to cope with their internal sex pressures and with their own self-image, and to deal with the social and environmental impact of sexuality that impinges upon them day after day. At the heart of meeting the needs of human growth and self-actualization in a democratic society is the need to learn problem-solving at its best. But before they can become competent problem-solvers, people as individuals, students as individuals, and counselors as individuals need to feel free and responsible.

Man is a social animal. Especially during adolescence, the peer group appears to be the most significant model for checking out, reinforcing or discarding values, attitudes and behavior. The peer group is more valuable in the educational or counseling setting than the one-to-one teaching or counseling situation.

Group-Centered Approach

In the group-centered approach we can help the student become freer and more responsible by increasing his sense of his own power to take responsibility for his behavior, by providing experiences that make available ways to become free, and by making possible the actual experience of increasing freedom.

Especially in the group where collective freedom exists, each member of the group has the right to question, to check his perception of others, to check how others feel about him. The group, with its freedom, can set limitations on behavior, goals, and judgmental statements. The group, or individuals, can exercise responsibility by confronting and encountering others in the group, or the group as a whole.

In this atmosphere of freedom and responsibility, human growth and human judgment expands and is enhanced through problem-solving. It is important for each member of the group to be able to say with confidence, "I feel free, I feel responsible."

When a group-centered approach is used for teaching human sexuality or in counseling, the group should be limited ideally to fifteen people as a maximum. However some aspects of the approach can be used in large classrooms of up to forty pupils.

Actually, the group-centered approach to learning is not so different from what good teachers and sensitive counselors have done ever since sex teaching and sex counseling began. They know the need for the student to feel free to question, to contradict, to be anxious and worried. They are aware of their own limitations, their own fears, hostilities. They understand their motives for teaching and have mixed feelings about themselves. All of this creates the humility that good teachers feel, along with an awareness of themselves as non-judgmental humans.

The theory and techniques of the group-centered approach in sex education and sex counseling have been developed over a period of fifteen years in the training of teachers, counselors, psychologists in human relationships, and in teaching children and youth. The experimental aspects of the method have been used in teaching preschool children, elementary school children from kindergarten through the eighth grade, and secondary school youth. Parent groups have also been involved during the experimental period. Validation of the concept is still continuing.

During the past seven years the group-centered approach has been evaluated by behavioral scientists as part of two Government grants. The first involved over 400 girls at the Webster School (1963–67) for pregnant school-aged girls. This was funded by the Children's Bureau, of the Department of Health, Education and Welfare. The girls were pretested with psychological instruments; namely, a social sex attitude test and a sentence completion test. It was found that in the main the girls had *a*) a poor self-image of themselves as women, *b*) inadequate ego strengths to cope with daily problems, *c*) inadequate sex education, and *d*) immature understanding of their own sexuality and that of their male partners.

As a result of the group-centered approach helping them develop self-awareness and self-acceptance of their sexuality, plus understanding of problem-solving techniques through "reality testing," definite changes in the girls' attitudes occurred.

The girls in the project felt that they had a more realistic image of themselves, their situation, love, their partner's feelings, and an understanding of their relationship. They felt that they had developed more realistic judgments concerning whom they would choose as sex partners. The girls actually selected more appropriate marital partners than the control groups. Ninety per cent returned to regular school.

The second project (Title III, ESEA Project) was developed to train counselors, teachers, psychologists and others in the group-centered approach to be used in a school setting in counseling pupils, staff and parents in the area of sex, personal and family living. The project was conducted in the District of Columbia and involved training staff to counsel and teach in inner city schools. An independent research group hired to evaluate this project found that after one year of training and on-the-job supervised training: 70 per cent of the trainees *a*) changed their attitudes toward their own feelings concerning sensitive areas in sexuality, and *b*) were able to develop programs for children and youths which their students, colleagues, and parents of students found helpful.

How does this relate to teaching sex education in other situations?

1. We need to be aware of how we are coming across. We can no longer stand up as the "expert" without concern as to how we are coming across to our students. Are they afraid to ask a question for fear they will appear stupid, or can they risk asking the expert any question?

2. We need to be aware that the student wants to know how we feel about him as an individiual or group member, rather than as a performer.

3. The students want to know whether we like them, whether we feel they can make it, whether they look good to us. We need to perceive these feelings.

What matters for us also matters for them. Yes, they want the facts. They want us to wipe away the cobwebs of ignorance. But they also want us to be aware of them (as they are aware of us) as human beings involved in a relationship.

The group-centered approach involves more than dialogue. It involves many of the counseling concepts and techniques which effective people use a good deal of the time. From this perspective, sex education is viewed essentially as a *growth experience*. In this context sex education serves our human understanding of our sexuality, our relation to each other as woman and man, boy and girl.

But it is precisely our relation to our sexuality, our relation to one another that we have somehow lost and which the group-centered approach hopes to put together. Our touch, our feelings, and our sense of our sexual reality have been dulled and have lost the dignity and meaning they had for us as children. Hopefully we can reach out with trust and openness through satisfying group experiments.

Our relationship to our sexuality and our relationship to one another which we want and need is implicit in the group-centered approach to sex education and counseling. It is also implicit in training youth and adults in human relationships both in and out of the classroom.

THE GROUP RELATION WITH THE TEACHER

It has long been recognized by professionals that such human qualities as warmth, understanding, permissiveness and acceptance are relevant in promoting freedom to think, to feel, to err in judgment, and to try again. This is further enhanced in a group where the teacher or counselor is understanding and well disposed toward individual members and to the group as a whole. This creates the beginning of an educational or counseling climate that is conducive to trust and openness on the part of all the participants.

When the behavior of the teacher communicates to the group the confidence that all the group says is accepted without criticism, the group feels that in this relationship the teacher or counselor is cooperating in helping the group to experience a non-moralizing approach to understanding the sexual social behavior of human beings.

The relationship in the group (which becomes an important factor for each member in the sex education process) is similar to the therapeutic relationship. The sufficient conditions which Dr. Carl R. Rogers, the eminent psychologist and pioneer in nondirective counseling, defines as three qualities of the therapeutic relationship in his book (*Counseling and Psychotherapy*) are likewise a necessary and sufficient condition for establishing meaningful relationships in sex education or counseling whether these occur in the classroom, clinic, adult-education center, at informal gatherings or in the parlor of the hospital ward. They belong in every classroom where the teaching of any subject takes place.

1. *Genuineness*. Within the teaching or counseling situation the teacher is freely and deeply himself and his actual experience is accurately represented by his awareness of himself.

2. *Unconditional Positive Regard* (nonpossessive warmth). A warm acceptance of each aspect of the students', parents', and counselors' experience as being part of the individual in the group.

3. *Accurate Empathy*. Understanding the individual's awareness of his own experience.

For the group experience to be effective, it is necessary for the people in the group to perceive the teacher's genuineness, warmth and empathy. Where the group feels the teacher's genuineness, warmth, and empathy, this feeling may serve as a catalytic agent in developing trust, openness and movement toward challenging and enriching experiences.

The responsibilities of the leader in setting up a problem-solving situation as part of the group-centered approach to sex education and counseling are manifold, but irrespective of the setting or age of the group, the steps described below can and should be followed:

1. Center the learning experience in a small group.

2. Present the group with a problem which is of common interest to group members.

3. Build confidence in the group to work together with the problem.

4. Offer the group the opportunity to explore the problem and determine their readiness to work with it.

5. Help the group to see several sides to the problem and determine what, if any, additional information or expertise is necessary.

6. Emphasize the importance of sharing and trusting in problem-solving.

7. Reflect within the group the difficulties involved in problem-solving.

8. Encourage openness and diversity of opinions as a means of exercising options.

9. Make the group aware that the process is often as healthy as the solution.

10. The group should learn that peer-group sharing is cathartic and supportive.

11. Build ego strength in decision-making through peer-group awareness of common sharing of similar problems.

12. The group should learn to view the leader as a resource person instead of an authoritarian figure.

13. Develop closeness and empathy through the group experience.

14. Develop a willingness to test out new experiences, attitudes and feelings elicited from the group experience.

The teacher understands that all members of the class are capable of assuming responsibility for their sexuality according to their age and social development and that within the limits of this development they will, in the group, attempt to make the best choice for themselves.

The teacher helps the students perceive her in her supportive role in the following ways:

1. She encourages group participation.
2. She accepts silence and other nonverbal forms of communication.
3. She intervenes in a manner that motivates a desire on the part of the group to explore the various options open for decision-making.
4. She avoids projecting a "right" or "wrong" approach to a problem.
5. She reflects with the group their feelings of frustration, anxiety, disappointment and also joy and satisfaction.
6. She doesn't push the group along at her pace, but accepts the rhythm and mood of the group, so that she is able to help them see it through.
7. She projects a feeling of maturity and support without being opinionated or judgmental.
8. She uses praise and sets limitations that are reasonable and conducive to the group's experience and self-awareness.

REACTIONS OF STUDENT GROUPS

Student reactions to the group process in general were good. They felt the group was very important to them. Some of them insisted that they wanted to know how each one felt about, for example, premarital sex before they voiced an opinion. Many individuals in the group said they were learning from one another. It mattered much that someone else felt the same way they did. Some rejoiced when they learned that what had caused deep feelings of guilt within themselves was an acceptable form of sexual behavior for many. In work with parents, some mothers expressed a feeling that they felt freer in talking about their sexuality with their children and with their husbands. They felt that the group work was responsible for this change.

Within the peer group, especially where the group is heterogeneous, the self-actualizing process of each member as male and female is enhanced. In a warm accepting atmosphere, the group takes on a responsive role along with the sense of freedom felt by group members.

We felt that we were on the right track, but had not gone far enough. Would the group-centered approach work for other groups? The interdisciplinary group-centered approach was then used with pregnant school-age girls. Each girl was a group member for eighteen weekly sessions. The group chose the topics from a melange which they developed with the assistance of the leader. They were interested in serious problems such as adoption, whether to marry the putative father, what is love really about. They discussed the positive and negative aspects of each situation, and during the process they gave one another support and humor. They gained depth in their relationship with each other. They came to the group looking and feeling miserable and alienated, but soon found friends in the group with whom they could share common problems.

The negative power of the group was very impressive too. Several girls who planned to give their babies up for adoption became ambivalent because of group pressure. The group was against adoption. It was hard for one or two girls to face up to the group, especially when their status at school depended so much on group acceptance, yet it was important to bring up this delicate situation. It was presented to the group as a situation that happened in another city, and the question was posed: What was the group going to do about it, as problem solvers? This called for the teacher to reflect with the group, to give them the freedom to express hostility, to permit the girls to make judgmental statements, to allow them to verbalize judgmental sanctions and rejecting attitudes. They gave expressions to many stereotypes—"She is selfish," or "She doesn't love children." Some said a girl who would give her baby up is a heartless mother. It was suggested that the group reflect upon the girl's needs as a growing woman, on her potential as a wife or mother, as a wage earner, on her right to an education; and to weigh all of this with the baby's needs for attention, a home, and loving care.

What was best for each of them? They thought this problem through. They expressed anger and frustration. They argued back and forth, and after three sessions were more flexible and less emotional. Some were supportive and on good terms with the girl who wanted to give her baby up. They were involved and learning to check out their feelings and help their peers check out theirs. Many developed a desire to understand more and to help the others understand. They were becoming aware of themselves and the others as feeling people.

In the second project parents of young children shared in the group-centered approach and shared problems concerning parent-child relationship. They discussed prepuberty sex, "dirty" words, and disciplining children. The relationships in the group were open and became more trusting as communication was facilitated. Each adult helped her colleague discuss her concerns by sharing and relating with warmth and concern. They found they could share a common problem. The group helped in problem-solving.

And so it went—upper income, lower income, students, teachers, preschool, college level. It was possible to change attitudes and behavior. It was possible to help others feel freer, more comfortable in their relationships, and with a greater willingness to verbalize and examine their feelings and compare them with others. This was also working for counselors, psychologists, and administrators. The concept was more than dialogue. It involved accepting one another's feelings, with problem-solving involving an exploration of options and group involvement.

The group's reaction to each individual member is an important component of the theory. It is important to understand how the individual member perceives the group reactions and his ability to check out misunderstandings. The group can be both supportive and rejecting of one of its peers. The problem of working this out is best accomplished under the guidance of a qualified leader. She is the catalyst responsible for creating the cohesion in the group while accepting the individuality of each member. She is also responsible for perceiving how the group reacts to her leadership.

CASE DISCUSSION FOR FACULTY AND STAFF

The catalytic experience can be varied depending upon the needs of the group. In working with teachers and counselors in the clinic, it is frequently helpful to introduce a particularly sticky case which needs many heads and hearts to take that sober second look at the problem. Or if a teacher or counselor has a knotty professional sexual problem, she may bring it to the group. In most clinics or schools an interdisciplinary team usually makes up the group. This is of great advantage to participants because each can see and feel the problem from a variety of windows and see the options open for decision-making.

The case discussion is also a great equalizer of personality types. The doctor is at the same level as the classroom teacher, and the nurse, psychologist, and social worker can make no claims to having all the answers to the problems. In many instances the parent-aide—often considered around school buildings as low woman on the totem pole—comes up with the most practical reasonable insights and solutions to the case and the personalities involved.

Young people, especially adolescents, enjoy coping together on cases, and where the leader can help them feel free and responsible, they will attack the problem with both sensitivity and zest. They informally are constantly acting as counselor to one another and need very little coaxing in order to become involved.

Case Study—"Put Yourself in His Place"

John is seventeen years old. His girl friend Sally is sixteen years old and pregnant. Before her pregnancy they were both planning to go to college and had tentatively decided that when they completed their four years of college education, they would find jobs and then marry.

John, a senior in high school, now wants to get a job and marry Sally so that she can leave school to have the baby and stay at home to mother his child. Sally herself is confused. She is twelve weeks pregnant and isn't sure she wants the baby. She would like to stay in school and continue on to college. She feels John should do the same.

1. What would you do if you were John?
2. What would you do if you were Sally?
3. How would you go about helping them understand each other's point of view?
4. Would you involve the parents in decision-making here, or anyone else?

Additional case histories can be constructed from composite situations at school by asking students to submit them in writing without signing their name, and from newspaper clippings.

Other Resources

FILMS

There are many informative films for use with adolescents, such as:

Phoebe: A Story of Premarital Pregnancy, McGraw-Hill Book Co., (1965), 29 minutes. A prize-winning film that captures the mental and emotional reactions of an unwed girl on the day she realizes that she is pregnant.

(The group can discuss what they would do if they were Phoebe, her mother, or her boy friend.)

Quarter of a Million Teenagers. Available from the health department. 24 minutes. Film deals with adolescents and the problem of gonorrhea and syphilis.

(If you were a parent how would you help? What do you feel your responsibility would be in dealing with this problem if you were the sex educator in the school that these boys and girls attended?)

The Merry-Go-Round. McGraw-Hill Book Co., 23 minutes. About a relationship between a boy and girl who are faced with decisions about sexual involvement. Three authorities comment.

(Ask each student to be an authority and share his comments with group.)

TAPES

"What is Love?" "Youth Speaks Out," "Parents Discuss Problems With Their Adolescents," "Teenager's Problem of Whether to Keep Her Baby or Give It Up for Adoption," are typical discussions by groups using the group-centered approach.

The tape "What is Love?" is a video-taped discussion by eighth-grade parochial-school boys and girls who discuss the differences between puppy love, physical attraction, infatuation, and the love that exists between people who wish to live together in marriage. The discussion was precipitated by a student's question. He was concerned because "so many people say different things about what love is." He asked for the counselor's opinion of what love really is. Instead of answering the question the counselor asked him what he thought it was. It was suggested to him that the counselor wasn't avoiding answering him, but that she would have a better notion about his question after he had described his feelings. He said they were confused. He wanted to be in the girl's company, he enjoyed holding her hand and dancing with her, but he found it difficult to talk to her about his feelings. He was feeling differently about himself. He didn't know how she felt about him.

It was suggested that maybe the entire group would be interested in exploring the question. He agreed and the discussion started. Several teachers in the school were interested in having their students join the discussion. It was felt, however, that the group of twelve had worked together and that changing its size and introducing new personalities would tend to set the group back. Instead, the teachers were asked whether they would like to use the video-tape discussion as a means of starting their own groups. They could first view it, and begin from there.

Video-tapes and plain sound tapes are valuable techniques in sparking group-centered discussions. They can be used in a variety of ways:

VIDEO TAPES

1. The group can view themselves and see anew both the verbal and nonverbal ways in which they communicate. It is both fascinating and frightening to see oneself for the first time interacting with others in a group situation. The self which others see, but to which we are blind, is shown to us through a realistic medium.

2. The tape can be used with other groups at workshops and school or clinic sessions to spark discussion on both content and process of the group experience which was viewed.

3. Where a parent discussion is viewed by children, it helps them to discuss and experience the problems and concerns of parents and vice versa.

4. The video tape of a group discussion is a good medium for those viewing the tape to analyze the communication techniques used, the level of participation, the role of the leader and other factors which are helpful in understanding the group-centered approach.

SOUND TAPES

When it is made a common practice during a project to tape all discussions, it will frequently be discovered that many students, parents, and teachers will want to listen to a replay privately. Many leaders use tapes of lectures, group discussions and expert panels that are heard at professional conferences and share them with their colleagues for discussion and implementation. Tapes of discussion on homosexuality, abortion, family planning, nudity and premarital sex by adolescents have been popular subjects for listening and group discussions.

Role-Playing

Role-playing is a valuable medium in which to act out one's feelings and attitudes while interacting with others in a social situation. Parent-child relationships, teacher-student relations, and peer-group relations may all be explored. Through role-playing, attitudes can be changed and new insights into one's feelings can be discovered. It can also bring into focus faulty approaches to problem-solving.

Role-playing is often called socio-drama because it applies to any kind of dramatic educational or therapeutic method in which the participants portray their own feelings, behavior, and attitudes or those of others.

Usually the situation is one that involves a normal type of interpersonal conflict that has been experienced or anticipated by the group members. The problem or situation chosen for role-playing is usually of concern to all or most of the group members. Role-playing is primarily concerned with education in communication and self-awareness, and re-education or modification of attitudes and behavior when indicated, or as a reinforcement of one's current attitudes and behavior when they appear to be satisfactory and successful in problem-solving. The benefits of role-playing may involve therapeutic assistance, but role-playing for classroom and clinic use in sex education and sex counseling would seem to be primarily for healthy people whose problems and concerns are within normal range. It should not be intended as therapy.

How does one begin in setting up a role-playing situation, and once having set it in motion, how can maximum benefits be reaped from the experience?

The problem or conflict may be introduced by the teacher or counselor as one she feels the group is ready to tackle. It may be a problem that was discussed by the group, without satisfaction, and she feels that by acting it out they can gain more insight and understand it more clearly. It may be a conflict which the group suggests, or which an individual or pair desire to act out in order to experience it and get into the situation at a deeper level.

The problem is eventually introduced to the group in a well understood and defined manner. Where it arises spontaneously the leader needs to get some feedback from the entire group to make certain that they understand the problem.

When the role-playing program is prepared ahead of time by the leader or teacher, each player's role should be written down on a 3 by 5 inch card and handed to him to read. After he understands it, he in turn reads it to the group. They are then free to ask for clarification concerning a profile of the character and his attitude and behavior.

Instructions such as the following may be helpful both to players and to group members:

"You are about to see members of our group [give names] playing a role and interacting with each other. From our experiences in the group, we feel that listening, understanding and helping each other become more perceptive when put together in a situation which helps us solve our mutual conflict.

"Even though there are only _____ actors on stage we are all participant observers. We will be listening, feeling, identifying and feeling at times both with them and out of it, depending on what goes on. We will also be sharing their concern with finding options and arriving at a reasonable solution, mutually agreed upon. Let us see how well we can work together."

When the group has been through the experience together, this lengthy introduction is superfluous and need not be used. However, for people new to role-playing, the leader should be explicit and state the goals and the roles of all group members.

Where a leader observes a good deal of passivity in a group, she should try to check it out with the group. Frequently it will be discovered that the situation being role-played is not relevant, or that insufficient structuring took place and the observers were not clear concerning the need actively to listen and experience the situation.

After a conflict has been dramatized and a solution worked out, each player is asked a) how he felt playing his role, b) did he feel the other players understood his feelings and his attempts to solve the problem; was he aware of their feelings and their attempts to work it out? The group is then asked to discuss the roles and its appraisal of the communication that took place during the interaction and the quality of the problem-solving involved.

When the group has explored the various aspects with the players and with each other, others may volunteer to play the roles, or the players may desire to reverse roles in order to take the opposite position as a starting point.

The method involves three types of dramatic experiences according to Ronald B. Levy in *Psychodrama and Sociodrama in American Education*. The types are 1) personal, 2) interpersonal, and 3) societal. The personal experience affects and permeates the individual in a way peculiar to him. The interpersonal experience is social and helps to remove interpersonal blocks between participants. It is the experience shared when two or more group members dramatize common problems together. The societal experience results when the group members play roles that demonstrate some societal disorder.

The actors are usually volunteers. Forcing or assigning a group member to take a role is a sure way to inhibit spontaneity and freedom to interact with the other actors. The teacher or group leader must be willing to permit the actors and group to explore the problem as they see it, and to express their thoughts and feelings freely and with candor. Otherwise it will have little effect in surfacing feelings and thoughts that have remained hidden.

Free expression is essential to stimulate the group to recall and identify their own related experiences. Where the leader attempts to control and manipulate the discussion, the quality of the group's observations of the role-playing and their reactions will suffer and become negligible.

It is wise for the teacher to tell the group openly that some situations are not appropriate and suggest another. She should not permit the group to go ahead and then attempt to direct, control or suppress expressions of true feelings.

For example, a group recently wanted to role-play a situation where two homosexuals were in conflict over anal-genital sexual intercourse. One partner preferred such intercourse whereas the other favored oral-genital intercourse. Because this was a public-high-school group, it was felt for many reasons that this was inappropriate and not relevant to the main discussion, which involved differences in attitudes toward homosexuals by psychiatrists and members of the Mattachine Society.

In instances where role playing is used with elementary children, there should be close cooperation and communication between teachers and parents. Parents have been known to complain to the principal that certain teachers were getting children to spill private family problems in front of the whole class. What had really happened, of course, was that a particular child had spontaneously acted out her role in the family as she perceived it.

When a teacher anticipates some misunderstanding, she would be wise to discuss the entire role-playing procedures with the parents, have them go through a role-playing experience of their own choosing, and explain to them its value in sex education and counseling. This method of orientation usually brings forth great enthusiasm and support from parents.

Role-playing as a method of beginning a group-centered discussion is sufficiently flexible to be used from preschool through adulthood. By watching children in the preschool and kindergarten play house a novice will gain confidence in the children's ability to act out parent roles or sibling roles, to the point of dressing up from heels to hat in whatever they feel is appropriate gear for the situation. Watchful and sensitive teachers have often used snatches of the spontaneous role-playing as a point of departure for a more structured situation which the children act out for the entire group.

WHO SHALL ROLE-PLAY?

The importance of having participants volunteer was discussed earlier. At times the teacher or leader finds that no one wants to volunteer. She may patiently suggest to a participant whom she feels is ready but reticent, "Would you like to help us out by taking a role?" Usually the ice is broken with the first volunteer and others soon follow. If, however, no one volunteers, it is best to drop the idea. It would seem that general resistance by the group reflects a lack of readiness on their part to risk acting out the role. On some occasions the group may ask the leader to take a role. When it is felt this will accelerate the process and help the group, the leader may appropriately join in and play the role.

The observers may function in a variety of approaches other than as individuals who are listening, observing the interaction, and analyzing the problem-solving approaches attempted by the actors.

The group may split into two or three segments, depending upon the number of actors participating, and each segment identifies and closely follows a particular actor. This procedure is sometimes referred to as the split-group identification.

For example, where the role-playing concerned a fifth-grade student who in anger yelled "Fuck you!" at a teacher who threatened him with suspension because he had "a dirty mouth and wasn't fit to associate with decent children," half the group was assigned to identify with the student, whereas the other half identified with the teacher.

ROLE-PLAYING SITUATIONS

Situations involving role-playing which effectively involve the interest of groups include:

1. Interference by parents in selection of friends, setting curfew hours, selection of clothes, and other situations where adolescents feel their desire to be independent is threatened.

2. Primary-school children's concern about parental preferences for siblings who are of a particular sexual gender, stereotyping their roles and play activities in the family, and parental reluctance to discuss sexual questions with them.

3. "How far do you go on a date?" is still a provocative role-playing situation fraught with conflicts. It involves the length of the relationship, depth of intimacy between them, and judgment concerning the expectations and outcome of the boy and girl. The range of acting-out includes their attitudes toward sexuality, peer-group attitudes, the outcome as it affects their present and future relationship, and the risks involved. Pregnancy and drop-out situations are also relevant.

4. Students in grades from the seventh through the ninth (early adolescence) are concerned with how to get together. They feel awkward and embarrassed at starting a conversation, sensitive to their physical appearance, not sure how they come across on the dance floor, and wonder what others' likes and dislikes are. They often feel as though they are on another planet when at their first dance, party or school affair.

Role-playing concerned with social procedures and manners of socializing when flexible and reasonable can help a young man or woman over this difficult period. Typical situations used are:

1. Making a date on the telephone.

2. Saying good night after the school dance.

3. Deciding with friends what to wear to a Halloween party.

4. Giving a record- or tape-playing party.

5. The question of whether house parties should be chaperoned frequently comes up in class discussions.

With the college-age group, problems are more adult and run along these lines:

1. Decisions on choice of method of birth control to use.
2. Whether to continue a pregnancy or have an abortion.
3. Early marriage and possible difficulties.
4. College drop-outs.
5. Extramarital sex relations.
6. Conflicts arising out of bisexual roles.
7. Homosexuality and social and legal sanctions.
8. Parental interference in mate selection and mode of life-style.

Role-playing situations which have been improvised with adults include:

1. Difference in attitudes between men and women toward sexual intercourse.
2. Variations in sex play.
3. Attitudes toward masturbation.
4. Problems of dating of divorced or widowed adults whose children resent the "stranger in the house."
5. Family conflict arising from adolescent pregnancy and parenthood.
6. Conflicts between partners which are aggravated when one wishes to obtain professional help from a sex counselor and the other resists.
7. Marital problems involving sexual dysfunctioning, i.e., frigidity, premature ejaculation, etc.

Since about 90 per cent of the people in the United States marry, group-centered discussions around role-playing need to include the selection of marital partners, setting realistic goals, problems common to all marriages, family life and social-psychological needs of children and family members. Also the different types of family life-style can be explored through role-playing. The teacher can use role-playing to present model sexual developmental tasks from early childhood through adulthood.

A trained sex educator can help students explore the sexual behavior appropriate in dating along with the pros and cons of adolescent mate selection. Here is a role-playing situation performed by members of an eleventh-grade class in a ghetto school:

The class has been discussing whether a girl should ask a boy into the house after a first date. The scene is set at the door of the girl's apartment where she lives with her family. The boy, seventeen years old, asks if he can come in. The girl, also seventeen, says she is tired and wants to say good night. The boy looks disappointed and then in an angry and awkward way says that the least she can do is to invite him in for ten minutes because he has taken her to the movies and for hamburgers too and that cost him five dollars. He does not think he is getting his money's worth. The girl replies that she thought the good time they had, and the progress they made in becoming friends, was more important than paying by kissing or deep petting.

After the scene was played, the class talked over the issues and concluded that a real man respects his girl friend's wishes. They also discussed the fact that the sexual urges of boys and girls are different in nature and degree during the high-school years, and that girls should know their behavior can often be distressingly provocative to boys. Boys are easily stimulated by a girl's figure, the way she wears her clothes and her flirtatious remarks. Girls are stimulated by romantic feelings of love, music and soft lights, and an atmosphere of tenderness. The role situation apparently sparked a good deal of interaction and discussion between the two sexes in the class. They were able to ventilate their anger and frustration over some of the students' rigid remarks. For many the session meant greater trust and understanding.

Other Teaching Aids

It is apparent that sex educators ought to become familiar with the best in contemporary literature and with the approach to art forms which emphasizes the human aspects of sexuality. The humanities have been sadly disregarded by sex educators and counselors as resource teaching tools. Yet with the importance of a humanistic approach to human sexuality, it would seem highly appropriate to tap the rich lode of imaginative literature after our students leave their early childhood behind them. Primary, secondary, and higher education can become more vital for students when we engage them in the sensibility and sensitivity of literary works. Literature has much to give. It provides insights into motivation of sexual behavior, into interrelationships, it deals with diversity for both individuals and their cultural milieu. An outstanding advocate of this approach is Dr. Rose Somerville. Many of her ideas concerning the use of literature have been incorporated in what follows.

LITERATURE

Everyone loves to hear or read a story involving love, hate, jealousy and compassion. Whether the story is true or fiction, it can nevertheless keep us enrapt with interest. Have you watched the faces of little children sitting on the floor during storybook hour in the library? Can you recall the number of times you wept in the darkness of a movie house, and later wondered why it had such an impact on you? Do you have a small dog-eared volume of poems tucked away on your shelf, which you turn to through the years just to catch a moment of a precious feeling?

Haven't most of us felt that the reason Shakespeare and other great writers have been praised and read through the centuries is because of their gift of understanding the universal passions, weaknesses, strengths and towering nobility which lies within each of us? Literature is probably one of the richest sources for teaching and counseling human sexuality within the context of human relations.

The short story has many advantages. The theme, style of writing, development of characters, and relationships are put in a compact form which allows an overview in a short span of time.

In story selection, the teacher can select themes to help her students develop awareness of stereotypes, cross-cultural differences, and various family designs which affect sexual attitudes and behavior. Psychological and social insights are revealed in good writing, and a good short story can have greater value to the reader than 600 pages of didactic material with which he cannot identify and which is written in a dull and dry fashion.

The Short Story Index is recommended as a helpful source. Almost a hundred of its subject headings are sex and family related. They run the gamut from adolescence, adoption and adultery to woman and youth.

The short story, when used in the group-centered approach, will enable the group to probe into the major concerns and problems of the leading character and others, his self-image, the motivating factors which relate to his behavior, the quality of his interacting situations, the options available to him, and the outcome.

Obviously, a checklist approach would be self-defeating in the group's discussion. It can stultify and negate the essence of effective interrelations. However, once the group is trained in using group-centered techniques, they will have the mental set for delving into the various segments of the relationships.

Dr. Rose Somerville, a well-known family-life teacher of teachers, has written a fine booklet concerned with the use of the short story in teaching family and human relationships. In the course of her discussion she says:

Adolescence is a favorite subject of short-story writers. In many instances they are recalling their own difficulties of growing up and coping with role discontinuities that are characteristic of American society.

Characters in their teens and early twenties are therefore frequently key figures in stories about mate selection, parent-child and sibling relations, sexual standards, family disorganization, aging and bereavement.*

Dr. Somerville delineates other relevant themes such as "Dating and Mate Selection," "Sex Standards," "The Unmarried Adult," for short-story selection.

Plays ranging from *Romeo and Juliet* to *A Raisin in the Sun* can be potent catalysts for adolescent groups to explore the range of identity and family relationships.

A Raisin in the Sun by the late Lorraine Hansberry is the story of a Negro family living on the South Side of Chicago. It revolves around the decision of the family to use a sizable sum of insurance money for improving their status. The conflict occurs when three of the family members assert their ideas on how the money should be spent. These conflicts allow for insights into each family member's personality, including his sexuality.

According to Dr. Somerville, "Groups who have used this play were able to deal with conflicts concerning *a*) a family matriarchal pattern as is typical of many Negro families, *b*) Walter's inner struggle to become a "man," *c*) Mamma Younger's realization of Walter's need to become the head of the house, *d*) Beneatha's preoccupation with nonassimilation, and *e*) speculation as to how the Younger family fared in the all-white neighborhood."

The universal appeal of reading and composing poems is a delightful experience for both elementary and junior-high school students (grades five through nine). During the elementary-school years, magazines such as *Children's Digest* and *Jack and Jill* are interesting resources.

ART AND MUSIC

Art as reflected in paintings, sculpture and photography is a meaty means for stimulating discussion. The works are often known by hearsay to many of the students and are highly respected. A view of art works by way of slides, or a field trip to museums offers an experience which can be a refreshing change of pace in the curriculum. It will also offer many learners the opportunity to familiarize themselves with art works that they have heard about but never seen. Michelangelo's "David," Rodin's

* From "Family Insights Through the Short Story" by Rose M. Somerville in the Human Relations and the Family series, edited by Paul Vahanian (New York: Bureau of Publications, Teachers College, Columbia University, 1964).

"The Kiss," Degas' "Women Bathing," for example. In addition Stei-chen's "Family of Man," a remarkable study of cross-cultural life from infancy to old age, can bring new insights and feelings to young and old alike about love, courtship, marriage, birth, nudity, adolescence, and family life.

Through modern music and its lyrics our young people express their sexuality and feelings in explicit ways. Their dance forms and rhythms, accompanied by rock 'n' roll music rhythms are capable of expressing their sexual feelings and fantasies. Using their music and their lyrics as a source of developing awareness of the message that is being sent to them may help to precipitate discussions concerning attitudes toward love, de-sire, friendship, and other aspects of their relationships.

A study conducted for the President's Commission on Pornography and Obscenity was concerned with erotic influences of the mass media on adolescent girls. It arose out of a group discussion as to where the girls had experienced their first sexual intercourse. The girls in the group were pregnant adolescents who had been talking together for about two months on a weekly basis and were open to this type of group discussion. It seemed that most of the girls had their first sexual experience either in their own home or in the partner's home during the day when their par-ents were out of the house, or when they were there in the basement playroom or in a room where the TV or record player was kept. Together the couple had either watched TV, played records, looked at comic books or read together true-story romances. The girls felt that the lyrics from the records, and the TV scenes, reflected their feelings and those of their partners. For many, this influenced their behavior at the moment when they were feeling close to the other.

Discussing lyrics and listening to music in a group in class or clinic might help young people talk about their sexual emotions and the reac-tions these forms of the mass media precipitate. It might be helpful to them in making realistic decisions concerning their sexual behavior and the responsibilities involved.

Team Teaching

Team teaching is not new in educational circles. It has been used to great advantage in developing interdisciplinary approaches in the social and behavioral sciences. School systems have used team approaches both for remedial and developmental tasks. However, this approach to sex education has been utilized in the main at the college and postgraduate level or inservice. Its use needs to become more comprehensive and include all grade levels. Where team teaching has been incorporated into the curriculum in an organized fashion, the results have been more than satisfactory.

Team teaching involves the services of an interdisciplinary team who truly implement an interdisciplinary curriculum. The rationale for using the team approach is:

1. An individual teacher does not have as rich a background and the specialized knowledge and skill in the various disciplines necessary to develop and teach human sexuality, as do a group of individuals who are competent specialists in their respective fields.

2. Students relate to different people according to their particular background and experiences and learn better from some teachers than others. Therefore in the team-teaching experience they have an opportunity to have a variety of learning experiences and hopefully will find some of the teachers compatible with their particular needs.

3. Team teaching breaks up the monotony of students having to share experiences, no matter how rewarding, with the same teacher day in and day out. The variety of style of different teaching personalities can add spice to the school room situation.

4. Team teachers give the teaching team greater manpower, more resources, more creative thinking, and cooperation in getting the job well planned and performed. The team can also rotate as discussion leaders and become involved from time to time as resource teachers in other educational areas outside the team course.

The team can function under a coordinator or become its own coordinating committee. For optimum results, the team should be involved in the planning, organization and teaching portions of the program. Ideally the teachers should also be compatible as colleagues and comfortable in working together. During the planning period the following objectives might be reviewed:

1. Specify the goals the program wishes to achieve.

2. Each team member interpret to the other members her concept of her role as a team member. Where overlapping occurs, the team decides who is best qualified to do the job.

3. Work out channels of communication among team members, so that a basic structure is established for progress reporting, evaluating, modifying, and working together regularly on reaching the goals of the program.

4. Team members should be allowed to volunteer for the programs.

Core Teaching Teams at various age levels might well include:

1. Preschool: teacher, nurse, social worker and/or psychologist, pediatrician and parent.

2. Elementary level: teacher, nurse, pediatrician, counselor, family-life and sex educator.

3. Secondary level: school counselor or psychologist, English teacher, nurse, sex educator, and sociologist.

4. College level: sex educator, college physician, counseling psychologist, sociologist, marriage and sex counselor, and gynecologist.

Many school and agency teams have also included lawyers, psychiatrists, ministers, anthropologists, and others, depending on their availability and the scope of the program.

The family-life and sex education team at the Webster School, for instance, consists of a physician (ob/gyn), nurse, social worker, clinical psychologist, nutritionist, counselor, and home economics teacher. With patience the team was able to blend after six months of hard confrontations and a realistic appraisal as to who would do what job best. The role of the principal as coordinator helped to give each team member a real sense of her important role on the team with the clear understanding that no member was more valuable than another as far as the overall effectiveness of the program went. There may be a tendency for those with higher professional degrees to work under an illusion that as team members they have greater authority and power to make team decisions. Once the point is established concerning equal opportunity for all in decision-making, then the idea of a hierarchy of authority among team members can be eradicated.

LECTURE AND DISCUSSION GROUPS

In lecture and discussion groups the team can frequently function as a panel, each presenting a different perspective of the same subject, followed by questioning one another, and then allowing the small discussion groups to follow up with the issues raised by the team.

For example, in a fifth-grade class the subject under discussion is "The Meaning of Adolescence." A team consisting of the teacher, a nurse, psychologist and/or counselor present the following material, possibly over three one-hour sessions:

Nurse
1. Physical growth during adolescence.
2. Differences in growth rates between girls and boys.
3. Influence of endocrine glands on growth.
4. How human life begins—male and female reproductive systems —fertilization and conception.
5. Physiology of menstruation and personal hygiene.

Psychologist or Counselor
1. Social and emotional growth goes hand in hand with physical growth during adolescence.
2. Psychology of male and female toward their sexuality during adolescence.
3. Adolescence as preparation for adulthood
    a. Freedom and responsibility in sexual behavior and interpersonal relationships.
    b. Friendship and dating.
4. Normalcy of sexual urges and feelings, and behavior.

Teacher
1. Prepares library shelf of books in class for sessions.
2. Coordinates the topics with the two specialists.
3. Answers questions by students in follow-up sessions.
4. Refers students with special problems which she cannot assist them with to appropriate resources both within the school and the community.
5. Assigns further readings and relevant experiences for students.

Using the Expert

When news gets around that the expert is coming, it creates a stir in an often apathetic atmosphere. It may precipitate informal discussions among both students and faculty as to what this expert is going to say and "tell them." Often staff feel defensive because an expert is brought in. The attitude seems to be: "Why can't I do the job? Do they think I don't have the ability? Why do they spend the money on an expert? It could be put to better use on books, film strips, slides and other teaching materials."

ADVANTAGES

The considered advantages can be categorized by saying that the expert
—brings fresh approach to the subject,
—brings the prestige of recognition and authority to a subject which engenders fear and suspicion,
—offers an in-depth approach full of substance to areas which are often superficially discussed,
—develops motivation and continued interest in the subject.

DISADVANTAGES

The disadvantages are often pitfalls that occur because of faulty preparation both in orienting the school and the expert to the situation. They can be categorized somewhat roughly as follows:

1. The faculty must be told of the proposal for an expert and discuss the feasibility of his presence. During the discussion, hidden anxieties will need to be discussed openly. The expert is then seen as a supportive asset lending strength to the program rather than posing a threat.

2. The expert must be told about the goals of the program and his role in the total picture. Otherwise he will fail to grasp the contribution he is expected to make.

3. If the expert is merely assigned a topic, he may use the same speech or lecture he has given to other groups. This can be highly inappropriate to the program in your school. It is much better if he receives an outline of the entire program, along with specifics concerning your expectations from him. Also, try to schedule a face-to-face meeting with him before he makes his presentation.

FOLLOW-UP PROCESS

When the expert appears to have fulfilled the expectations of those responsible for the program, utilizing him for further recommendations based on his observations and the feedback from students and faculty can do much to strengthen a new program. The expert may encourage the school personnel to write or call for further assistance. This assistance may deal with parent education, bibliography, in-service training programs, referral resources, or use of other specialists.

Teaching Decision-Making

The teacher's preparation and confidence in her role as group leader is essential for the success of the program. Many teachers are highly skilled in techniques, but feel that when they change to the new role of catalyst they will lose the respect of their students and counselors. Of course this is contrary to the evidence. The evidence is accumulating that where empathy, respect and genuineness exist in a relationship that is open and trusting, then behavior change and learning take place. With confidence, the teacher becomes the catalyst for freeing the individual rather than controlling him.

The teacher's best preparation is training in the nature of good human relationships. Specifically this necessitates a knowledge of group dynamics, personality development and defense mechanisms, an understanding of the concepts of the group-centered approach accompanied by training in human sexuality, sociology of the family, family planning and contraception, along with an awareness of her limitation and prejudices in particular areas of human sexuality. Sensitivity training may be helpful to those teachers who need to become more sensitive to their feelings and more aware of how other people react to them.

TEACHER'S SPECIFIC PREPARATIONS

The teacher's understanding of the problem-solving approach should be in harmony with the accepted guidelines for group-centered approaches and should contain the following specifics:

1. The physical situation should be considered. The classroom or counseling room must be cheerful and informal. Movable chairs or cushions should be arranged in a circle, with seating arrangements for all on the same level. Teachers should avoid sitting behind their desks.

2. Whether the introductory medium is a film, case study, role-playing situation, news item, or question or problem posed by the group, the teacher should review and check the item as to its relevancy, motivating factors, interest for the group, and that it is of sufficient substance to create a satisfactory problem-solving situation.

3. The problem should provoke conflicting feelings and attitudes in the group. If all of the group members are more or less in agreement, obviously it would be better to select another problem.

4. The teacher can find a wealth of material for problem-solving by collecting questions that students ask, and by drawing on problems that are common to the students. Caution must be exercised in the selection process so as to avoid any identification by the group as being the problem of a group member or another classmate. Changing names, locale, and dates can help mask the true identity of the people involved, and thus create a comfortable feeling among the group members.

ESTABLISHING THE RELATIONSHIP

It's hard enough to establish rapport with one person. How to do it with a group of people in a reasonable length of time so that they can get started on the problem? This is a not uncommon question asked not only by the neophyte but also by the experienced teacher. In connection with this, patience and an awareness of the difficulties involved in establishing trust, interest and openness in a group situation are the first prerequisites in helping to get started.

The following introduction has frequently proven to be helpful:

"I'm Mr. ————, and I'm very pleased that I have been given the opportunity to share a group experience with you. I find it as difficult as do most people to find easy answers to problems. I see my role here as helping you as a group member, perhaps as a resource person, or to help in any way the group wants me to serve. Each of us can help by concentrating on the group work, respecting one another's right to differ, and to be as honest and candid as possible in expressing our feelings. I will respect your right of privacy, and your desire not to speak when you don't wish to, as I know you will respect mine.

"May I suggest, however, that the more involved we become in the group process, the greater impact we will exercise on strengthening the group. We all can benefit in developing a closer relationship with the group. It helps when we experience our feelings rather than expressing thoughts about situations that occur in the group. By experiencing a feeling, I mean reflecting with the group: 'I feel anxious now, I also feel ready to start. I don't know how it's going to end, but I feel it's going to be a good experience to share it with you.' "

By thus putting her role and feelings about her relationship with the group in clear perspective, the teacher affords her students the opportunity to accept or reject that role or to ask for further clarification. She then encourages them to feel free to differ, encounter, and express their feelings toward the group work and each other as the work progresses.

SETTING UP THE PROBLEM

As indicated earlier in this chapter, the problem should evolve easily from prior discussion of activities which are relevant and which the group wishes to tackle. In setting up the problem, the facts should be clear and known to all members. It is wise for the teacher to check with the group to make certain that they have all the facts. They should be clear as to their role as group people. If a film is being used, they may need some structure as to what they should look for, or what question needs to be explored. In role-playing, they need to know the types of observations they are to make. In a discussion of a particular case history, they need to know the reports and findings of "experts" or "professionals" associated with the case. They may ask for additional facts. If this is necessary, then the group can change into an investigative committee and collect the necessary data.

After the presentation, the group will prepare to work and look at the pros and cons in the situation. It may be germane at this point for the teacher to caution the group that the goal is to solve the problem and in so doing to attempt to find several options. In this way the group can look at the strengths and weaknesses of the possible solutions, mull them over, and then decide which seem most reasonable.

Listening to one another helps, especially when it is felt that differences are occurring. We can help each other see our differences, if we listen to both the words and the feelings behind the words.

During the course of a problem-solving session with eleventh-grade girls, one of the girls asked the group how they would advise a pregnant girl who planned to give her child up for adoption. Several girls responded with open hostility to the question and answered that they would advise against it. The group felt this was a subject they wanted to pursue. So the problem was scheduled to be clarified and presented the following day:

An eleventh-grade girl named Mary, aged seventeen and pregnant, wishes to complete high school and go on to college, and feels she would accomplish this best by giving her baby up for adoption. The boy whom she dated and by whom she conceived is no longer interested in her or her pregnancy. He feels their relationship was a mistake and that it is best that they break off. He has made no plans to help her financially and she does not wish to take the matter to court. She lives with her grandmother and two aunts. Her mother lives in another city, having deserted her when she was four years old. Her mother's mother has taken care of her since that time. She feels that the baby would be better cared for in an adoptive home by foster parents who want the baby. She feels her grandmother would be taxed healthwise with this extra burden. She knows her grandmother would never refuse to take the baby, but she feels the baby will be better off with adoptive parents who want and are able to take care of a baby.

The majority of the fifteen girls in the group were against adoption. Some were more adamant and hostile than others. The teacher sensed their feelings and reflected with the group. "You appear to be opposed to adoption. I feel you believe Mary should keep her baby." Their nonverbal and verbal responses indicated that indeed they did and that they agreed with what the teacher caught as their feelings about the situation. It was important for the teacher to sense their need to express their negative feelings.

The therapist was aware of the impact of focusing on Mary rather than the problem of adoption. And, in presenting the situation, she said it was a problem that arose in another city. By changing the location, she hoped to make the student who had raised the question more comfortable in the group, and the hostile members in the group more open to her.

After presenting the facts to the girls the teacher asked their advice.

Would they be counselors? She told them that as counselors they were free to explore all the angles and to express whatever feelings or judgments they felt were real to them.

WORKING THROUGH CONFLICTS

The discussion started. The group experienced and shared their hostility and expressed it vocally. "She is selfish. She doesn't love children! A girl who would give her baby up is a heartless mother." "You seem to feel upset about adoption. You feel she is doing the wrong thing, and that bothers you," said the leader. "Yes, yes," came the response from the group. When the anger became a bit diffused through some individuals reflecting on the group's part concerning their feelings, it was suggested that they might want to consider the girl's needs as a young woman growing toward maturity and wonder about her potential as a wife, mother, wage earner, and her right to complete her education. After the group thought about that it was suggested they should consider the baby's need for affection, care, decent housing and nutrition.

The group appreciated the big job ahead and they were willing to tackle the issues one at a time. They wanted to hear from each girl as to how she felt about these conflicting needs and what she felt was a reasonably good solution. Over and over these questions went round: "What is best for the mother? What is best for the child? Can a solution be found that will be satisfactory for both baby and mother?" After three 1½-hour sessions some members seemed to become more flexible and less emotional, while others appeared supportive and in sympathy with the pregnant girl's dilemma. They were really experiencing in many ways the conflicts that are common to pregnant teenage girls who need to work through the serious problems of adolescent pregnancy. They were learning to check out and reflect on their own feelings and were recognizing the emotional feelings of others in the group. They could say to each other: "Cool it! Take it easy. You sound better when you don't scream!" Or helping one another to develop their thoughts by such comments as, "That's a good idea. Let's hear more!" or "You're sharp, and really cooking with brain food!"

The group reached a decision after the sixth session that the pregnant girl would have a better chance to make a life for herself by continuing school, and that the baby would be better off with foster parents who loved and wanted it, and that the baby should be put up for adoption through a reliable social agency.

A group-centered approach which emphasizes respect for the uniqueness of each learner and is concerned with the individual's attitude and feelings appears to be an excellent method for both teaching and counseling in the area of human sexuality. Among the techniques which help learners and counselees concentrate on their feelings and attitudes are case discussions, films, tapes, role-playing, literature, art, music, and the dance.

Team teaching reflects a truly interdisciplinary approach to human sexuality, especially where the team works as an integral whole through intensive planning and in sharing the teaching responsibilities. The expert can then function as an auxiliary member rather than as the central figure in the teaching program. It is important to remember that all sex education and counseling which has relevance and meaning in the day-to-day experience of the learner needs to be decision-making oriented. These techniques are at the heart of the group-centered approach. Well-learned decision-making techniques can help the learner grow in independence and in his ability to cope with his sexuality.

Settings Where Teaching and Counseling Take Place

Home

It is important for the sex counselor and sex educator to always remember that the prime sex education and counseling take place in the home. From age zero until the child goes to school, parents and family are sex models, sex communicators, sex teachers and counselors, so that the growing child's sense of his identity, his image of masculinity and femininity, his values and his behavior are overwhelmingly influenced by parents and members of the family where he lives. Even when he goes to school, teachers merely supplement the basic attitudes and values accepted in the home.

When the counselor is involved either individually or in a group with his patients or clients, he needs to be aware of the impact of home life. When children return home from school they are again interacting with the intimate and significant people in their lives. Therefore, it seems incumbent upon those in teaching and counseling to give great consideration to the cultural, social, and interpersonal relationships in the home. Ways must be found to develop educational programs which will parallel and supplement family sex counseling, so that parents and children can work together on new information and attitudes and values. During the day, meetings can effectively be scheduled to which parents may come for "coffee and conversation," luncheon meetings where they can bring box lunches, or afternoon meetings. In order to work with fathers, evening meetings are most feasible.

Remembering that the home is the central place where sex education is an ongoing business for better or worse, those on the professional end of the guiding rod will need to take into account the educational process that takes place there.

Church

The churches of the three leading religious groups in the United States —Protestant, Catholic and Jewish—have formed an Interfaith Council for sex education and have published a remarkable statement which agrees that sex education needs to be taught and that the school, church, and home should work together in developing sex education programs.

The National Council of Churches through the Reverend William Genné, its Coordinator of Family Ministries, has exercised a tremendous influence in having family-life and sex education programs introduced in religious school classes, youth groups, week-end retreats, sermons, week-end workshops, parent education seminars and teen-age sessions. In addition the organization has published many pamphlets available to ministers, teachers and family members.

Through the American Association of Pastoral Counselors, Marriage Council of Philadelphia, Menninger Foundation, American Association of Sex Educators and Counselors and other groups, many ministers are receiving training in sex counseling.

The Catholic Church has developed curriculum and training opportunities both for parochial-school teachers and counselors, and for priests. The boards of education of a number of dioceses in the United States have supported family-life and sex education programs. Father James McHugh is National Director of the Family Life Education Division of the U.S. Conference of Catholic Churches. The division has published many pamphlets, has a fine newsletter called *The Leader*, has summer workshops at Catholic University, and has a strong regional network of Family Life Direction and programs.

The Rochester Diocese has one of the best curriculums for school-age children and parents for Catholics in the United States. Dr. Gerald Guerinot has directed this program. He is also on the Training and Standards Committee of the American Association of Sex Educators and Counselors.

The Unitarian Church recently embarked on an intensive week-end program for parents and adolescents which involves several forms of media—books, slides, movies, lectures and small-group discussion. The work was spearheaded by Dr. Deryck Calderwood. The theme is entitled "About Your Sexuality." It has incorporated many of the approaches recommended here in training educators and counselors, and in teaching youth and parent groups—the theme of developing awareness through films and slides depicting physical intimacy and sexual intercourse, the problem-solving approach to education through small-group discussion, the breaking down of language barriers through open communication on sexual terminology, and reading material concerned with sensitive areas in human sexuality.

The Reform and Conservative arms of the Jewish faith, have, through their national organizations, published material on family-life and sex education for distribution to member synagogues and temples. Seminars and courses are offered for adult members on Marriage, Adolescent Growth and Development, Communication in Family Relations.

In all three of these religious groups, specialists are brought in for evening lectures and group discussions.

Peer Group

Probably next to the influence of the home during early childhood and pre-adolescence, the peer group during adolescence and thereafter is the strongest influence in the sex education of youth and adults. This strong statement is supported by the recent national survey involving thousands of young people undertaken by the President's Commission on Obscenity and Pornography. This same Commission also conducted a survey in which it asked members of the American Association of Sex Educators and Counselors whom they thought were most influential in the sex education of youth, and the majority of responses selected the peer group as having the greatest influence. One need not look very far to ascertain the peer group influence in pre-marital sex relations, group counseling led by peer leaders, campus "hot line" services operated by peers.

Mass Media

Considering comic strips, commercials on TV cartoons, full-length movies, plays and musicals, records, magazines, and books, we can state with some sense of reliability that we are surrounded by sex from day to day.

It seems that the mass media specialize in sex and violence, and that the producers, writers, composers and others who find the right combination are certain of financial success, even though the work may lack artistic or literary merit. *Playboy* and *True Story* Magazines and explicit pornographic works are best-sellers. The recordings which our youth buy and listen to over and over again have as their major theme love and sex. In many instances both the rhythms and lyrics are explicit in their sexual messages.

Recently sex educator Dr. Sol Gordon capitalized on the interest of youth in comic books, and used subjects such as masturbation, contraception, and homosexuality which he presented by drawing crude sexual characters, who mouthed sensible sexual attitudes concerning these sensitive areas. It remains to be seen whether this approach will work by aiding in the communication of sexual information and attitudes to young people.

Schools, K–12

Private schools, parochial schools, public schools and Head Start and preschool programs now generally support family-life and sex education. The National Education Association, with a membership of over one million teachers, the American Association of School Administrators, representing school superintendents and other school administrators, and many N.E.A. member organizations support sex education and family-life education. In public schools, a specific curriculum for sex or family-life education is set up and taught by a particular department, especially in the secondary schools. The elementary schools usually use team teaching or generalists assisted by the school counselor, nurse and doctor.

The Head Start and preschool programs closely tie the subject of family life into the general health curriculum and encourage active participation of parents for the teaching of the vocabulary of sex, explaining the coming of the new baby, and building confidence in being girls and in being boys. Much of the education involves games, group activities and field trips.

The private or independent schools are utilizing sex education as a part of human-relations training. As consultant to the National Association of Independent Schools, the author has traveled across this country, conducting teacher and staff training workshops. The thrust is on developing a frame of reference which involves flexibility and nonjudgmental attitudes in teaching human sexuality. The setting for teaching is the teachable moment as part of a history, English, science or social-studies class curriculum or as an elective for students in secondary grades. Where possible, parent education is included.

In certain states restrictions are placed on the scope of the curriculum and the selection of readings and audiovisual material. Some systems prohibit discussion on birth control, abortion, masturbation and homosexuality. Some school systems prohibit use of SIECUS guides. Those who are working in or with school systems should review, with school boards, both state and school-district regulations and laws concerning the teaching of family-life and sex education.

Clinics

Clinics associated with medical schools, hospitals, or community and mental health services are generally confronted with adolescent sex problems, marriage problems, and parent-child relation problems involving poor people. The workers in adolescent and pediatric outpatient clinics deal with problems of unwanted pregnancies, venereal disease, early marriages and separations, incest, contraception and family planning. Many of our psychosomatic illnesses are caused by sexual problems between family members. Anxiety and other symptoms of emotional problems are frequently caused by deep feelings of guilt concerning alleged sexual wrongdoing.

When these clinics have pamphlets, films, and other handouts available to patients in public rooms, these audiovisual materials are gobbled up and often motivate patients to raise questions. They are given reassurance from the material that it is healthy to discuss sexual problems and family-life concerns, and that these matters are shared by many people. They are helped to realize that they are not alone in their perplexity.

Having a professional or paraprofessional trained in family-life and sex education as part of the clinic staff serves several helpful purposes:

1. She can be a resource person in clarifying the problem and helping the patient receive early attention.

2. She can be a resource person for the clinic staff through maintaining a library of materials dealing with family-life and sexual materials.

3. She can conduct classes in family-life and sex education as part of the educational experience of all patients who visit the clinic.

4. She can check out patients who need special help and encourage them to use the family-life and sex education resources of the clinic.

5. She can make herself available to other community agencies for guidance and assistance in their programs for children, youth and adults.

Social Service Agencies

Social workers and volunteers working in social agencies are confronted increasingly with problems concerning adoption, marriage, unmarried teen-age parenthood, unwanted pregnancy, school dropouts, birth control, abortion, separations, divorce, extramarital relations, runaway youth, suicide, and homosexuality.

During the course of preliminary interviewing, the social workers find that many of the problems involve human sexuality. These include lack of knowledge of the reproductive system, serious problems of sexual identity, depression following an abortion, conflicts between youths over sexual activities, and many other major and minor considerations.

Today, a few schools of social work are training graduate students in marriage and family counseling. Also social agencies in some of the larger cities are offering in-service courses and seminars. Staff members are also being encouraged to join the American Association of Sex Educators and Counselors and other groups.

Family-Planning Centers

Over 500 major family-planning centers and hundreds of satellite groups in the United States are funded by the Office of The National Family Planning Center, Department of Health, Education and Welfare of the U. S. Government. The purpose of these family-planning centers is to offer free medical, educational and social services when voluntarily requested by citizens to do so. When minors request family-planning services, each center is guided by the applicable laws in its community.

In addition to physicians, who examine, prescribe and fit contraceptive devices, the nurses assist and also hold individual sessions on method instruction. Community workers and social workers handle social problems concerned with the family. They make referrals to other agencies, assist in developing a social sexual history for each patient. Referrals for sickle cell and pregnancy tests are made. Also, referrals are made to fertility, genetic, and psychiatric clinics. Food needs and housing facilities are checked.

The health educator and counselor is responsible for the family-life and sex education services at Howard University's Family Planning Center. The services include slide talks on social-sexual development from infancy through adulthood, social sexual changes and behavior patterns during adolescence, reproduction, genetics, parent-child sex education, counseling on specific marital and sex problems, group work with adolescent girls and boys, and group discussions on the obstetric and gynecology wards dealing with family-life and sex education.

Also, the Family Planning Center serves the University Health Center, and these comprehensive services are included in the family-planning package. Each student sees the sex educator and counselor for an initial screening to share basic knowledge and attitudes with her.

Many coeds at college have never discussed sexual matters with anybody, even with their boy friends. Yet many are coming for birth-control information and devices and saying, "May I have some pills," fully expecting someone to hand them a package of pills and that will be all there is to it.

Some are fearful of the first pelvic examination which is part of the routine. Other examinations relate to the pap smear, urine analysis, and sickle cell blood test. It takes patience and understanding to relieve these young women of their anxiety in dealing with these procedures and to help them understand the personal and professional concern of the staff for their health and welfare. On many occasions students ask for a woman doctor because of shyness. And for this reason many centers have a woman doctor in addition to the males.

The problems presented at the Family Planning Center are varied. The chances are these problems are presented in most places where marriage and sex counseling takes place. Patient problems most frequently discussed include:

Abortion counseling. Counseling on the decision, and post-abortion counseling on depression, changed relationships, and health problems.

Sterilization counseling. (Vasectomy proceedings are being discussed and when these become operative, counseling male partners will be included.)

Frigidity.

Conflicts concerned with an inability to have an orgasm.

Mixed attitudes toward self concerning femininity and masculinity.

Premature ejaculation. Negative attitude of female patient and the anxiety created in the male because of his inability to please her.

The demasculinizing female. She rejects her role as helper in improving sexual potency of her partner, and subjects him to humiliating interactions where she holds him responsible for her failure to enjoy sexual intercourse and reinforces his guilt by comparing him with men who have previously satisfied her.

Being overcritical of family-planning devices to the point where apathy exists and none is used.

Resistance to the use of recommended birth-control device because mate or member of family is against its use.

Superstitions and myths about birth control and family planning which prevent effective use of birth control.

First out-of-wedlock birth, abortion of teenagers, thirteen to eighteen years of age where they are invited to join a group with peers for education and counseling.

Second-out-of-wedlock pregnancies for all age groups. Patients are invited to join a group with their peers to discuss similar problems.

Marital conflicts centered on sexual matters:

　　Extramarital relations.

　　Family separations. One of the parents comes and goes creating instability in the home with accusations of sexual promiscuity.

Requests for assistance and models in discussing sexual development with their children and youth.

Premarital counseling involving sexual informatinon and discussion of areas of adjustment in interpersonal relationships.

Requests for pamphlets on sex and family-life education.

Menopause. Need for reassurance of femininity and patient's capacity for continued sexual pleasure, including factors involving the male's perceptions.

Parent-child conflicts centered on sex play of child (masturbation and mutual play with peers), dissatisfaction with sexual attitudes of child's friends and dating partners.

Infertility problems. Feeling of inadequacy as a female due to inability to have children.

Universities and Colleges

In many universities and colleges, counseling usually takes place at the University Health Center, Dean of Student Affairs offices, Counseling and Guidance Centers, dormitory counselors who reside in the dormitories and counsel there, and "hot line" and group counseling sponsored and operated by student groups. Interested faculty and administrators are often available to the students who seek their help.

It is not surprising that the sex education may be funneled during a lecture by a staff member during orientation week, and cozied in between "drug abuse" and "how to study."

The Student Government office may sponsor a "Sex Series" or a one-shot performance where a packed auditorium listens to the "expert," a few ask questions, and the next day most students return to their usual routine without the benefit of any feasible follow-up plans for realistic education.

In addition, courses in human sexuality are offered by various college departments: Science, Sociology, Biology, Psychology, Anthropology, Education (especially Health Education). In some of the more conservative institutions, the courses are labeled Family Living or Family Life Education.

Many of the colleges and universities pour thousands of dollars into these programs with little feedback concerning their success and without an over-all evaluation related to their content and objectives.

As a former Director of Guidance and Counseling at a large university and as one currently engaged as a consultant at a University Health Service and working with many college officials, it is the author's impression that integration is one of the pressing needs in the current scene. All too often the respective programs are fragmented and each piece is initiated by an interested person without much thought to the over-all goals of the services and courses. The University Health Center, which is usually directed by a physician, is frequently different in its philosophy and approach to counseling from services offered by the Guidance and

Counseling Centers, the latter being directed by a psychologist. The same might hold true for the other segments which offer counseling help.

These differences in point of view may be confusing to the students who need help and a sound base for support. The need for a coordinating and cooperating mechanism is essential to prevent overlapping of services, further the easy routing of student referrals, and aid the mutual growth and expansion through central administration and communication channels.

Many students are discouraged by the ostrich approach that some colleges give to unwanted pregnancy, illegal abortions, dormitory living arrangement, and referrals to community resources, and have initiated their own counseling services. Some of these are handled in a professional manner, under supervision and in consultation with the college administration. Others are autonomous or seek guidance from sources outside the university. Professional personnel, in turn, are concerned about the adequacy of unsupervised counseling, the legal responsibility to parents for services administered by students in university facilities, and the lack of communication when something goes wrong, such as an attempted suicide, hemorrhaging from a poorly performed abortion, a hasty marriage induced by a pregnancy, or a school dropout.

The Mattachine Society for male homosexuals and gay liberation groups for females are present on many campuses. In addition to serving as social supports for their student members, they also offer counseling. Here, again, there should be concern for the approach used in counseling the uninitiated male or female adolescent who, because of a single homosexual contact, worries about their identity and in seeking help through counseling may be pushed into a homosexual frame by an overzealous student counselor.

It cannot be urged too strongly that colleges and universities must insist on training in the counseling process for those persons acting as sex counselors.

Graduate Schools

It is at the graduate school level that the greatest gap exists in graduating trained professionals to do the job. In some ways those who are responsible for curriculum development in preparing professionals to cope with and plan for the horrendous problems in the world around them are like the proverbial ostrich who hides from reality by burying his head in the sand. At present most medical schools offer some material in human sexuality. The Center for the Study of Sex Education in Medicine is the major catalyst in arousing medical educators to develop human-sexuality and sex-counseling programs. Dr. Harold I. Lief directs this program from the Center at the University of Pennsylvania. Too frequently, doctors, who have the greatest demands put upon them by patients, are often the least trained. The medical schools that do offer courses have doctors, lecture services, postgraduate lectures, clinical training during OB/GYN and psychiatry clerkships during their third year. The research programs and texts authored by Masters and Johnson have had a strong effect in opening the minds of physicians to the needs of their patients.

Nursing schools have done practically nothing to introduce training in sex education and counseling. Individual instructors focus on the subject in studying the adolescent or in early childhood nursing needs. It is approached here from the crisis and remedial intervention angle. Many schools, however, hold one day or weekend institutes which they sponsor together with other local professional groups or schools.

University departments of education have been involved in a realistic fashion in molding programs that make sense. The health education programs at both New York University and the University of Maryland offer majors in sex education. The home economics departments at several large state universities, through land-grant funds, have developed programs which include family relations and early childhood development. Such programs may provide supervised training for practitioners.

The ministry, through its theological and graduate schools, and especially those of the Protestant faith, includes family-life and human-sexuality courses in training men and women for the ministry or as religious educators. Some of the training schools for ministers offer their students internships at pastoral counseling centers. The Menninger Foundation in Topeka, Kansas, and the Marriage Council of Philadelphia have worked cooperatively with the church groups as training centers.

At present many of the graduate schools offer Master and Ph.D. degrees in family-life and sex education. But, at the present time, it is ironic that no graduate school in the United States offers any graduate degree in either sex or marriage counseling.

Schools of social work appear to be introducing some aspects of human sexuality into their family practice courses and supervised agency training. A recent text by Dr. Harvey Gochros, a professor of social work, which deals with sex education for social workers hopefully will stimulate further interest. The number of social workers concerned with the plight of the unwed mother is helping to develop individual awareness of poor preparation to do the job effectively.

Health Departments

In recent years both state and municipal departments of health have offered maternal and infant care services, prenatal and well-baby clinics in addition to other health services. The maternal and infant care departments, in addition to medical care, now offer sex education, family-planning services and social-psychological services to teen-age mothers and to adults. A majority of the patients with low incomes who are entitled to these services are young mothers in their teens, some still attending school, others being dropouts.

The well-baby clinics offer ample opportunity for staff to discuss social-psychological and sexual developments during early childhood with the young parents when they report on routine visits for nutrition, immunization and other health needs.

The Department of Health, Education and Welfare has funded programs associated with both the Head Start program and health departments for young children under the age of three years. These health and early-childhood development programs include family-life and sex education for parents. Staff personnel working in this area are usually doctors, nurses and social workers. The team approach is frequently used. Many of these professional people have had the benefit of special training in human sexuality and counseling.

The emerging need for massive sex education and counseling has served as an impetus for the development of programs in various settings. No longer is the public-school classroom the dominant medium for dispensing sex education on the current scene. Clinics, churches, mental-health centers, family-planning clinics, hospitals, social agencies, independent and parochial schools, adult-education centers and planned-parenthood groups are emerging settings for sex-education programs and are attempting to meet the demands for effective sex education and sex counseling. The need for training professionals, paraprofessionals and volunteers who are motivated to work in these settings is a necesasry and exciting challenge.

8

Model Training Programs, I

During the past twenty years, a number of training programs have been conducted in a variety of settings. They run the gamut for training personnel to work in settings from preschool to twelfth grade, college, graduate schools, family-planning centers, religious centers, parent groups, and community health centers.

The effective training programs have much in common. The ineffective ones were second-rate and poorly conceived imitations of those that worked. The effective programs shared these features: .

1. The administrative head of the organization supported the training program and was involved in the program from beginning to end as head of the advisory group.

2. The training objectives were in harmony with the needs of the group with whom the trainees were eventually to teach or counsel. This involved identifying the problems and objectives as the first order of planning.

3. The training programs were interdisciplinary.

4. The training programs dealt with both content and skills and techniques involved in humanistic teaching and counseling.

5. The trainees were supported and supervised in their practice experiences.

6. The programs took into consideration the learning experiences and methods that were most meaningful to the trainees.

7. All the consultants and teachers of the trainees received an overview of the program and conferred either individually or in groups with the head of the training program before active participation.

8. The training programs were designed so as to provide for an evaluation of their effectiveness through valid instruments such as question-

naires, personal interviews for pre- and post-testing, and observable behavioral changes.

9. An interdisciplinary advisory group which represented the consumer interests (those whom the trainees were preparing to teach or
counsel) met from time to time with the training staff to assist through
advice and counsel.

10. Training in small-group dynamics, especially as it affects the
teaching and counseling of human sexuality, was a part of the core curriculum of all the successful models.

11. All program participants had a core bibliography for reading materials and audiovisual aids. Also a small reference library was available
at a convenient place for use by the trainees.

Preschool Training Program

The goals and content areas of a model preschool training program,
developed through extensive experience, can be outlined as follows:
1. Goals
   a. Training program with staff (teachers, counselors, nurses, ad-
      ministrators, etc.).
   b. Training staff to use the group-centered approach in their work
      with both parents and preschool children.
2. Content Areas
   a. Developing self-awareness as a girl or a boy along with pride
      in self. Through various forms of play, storytelling and discus-
      sion, trainee reinforces self-awareness and pride in self as a girl
      or a boy. These healthy attitudes develop ego strength, coping
      powers and relationships between peers and others which are
      satisfying and successful.
   b. Develop pride and satisfying relationships within the family
      through respect, affection, reasonable forms of discipline, and
      understanding one's feelings and behavior. The family's mem-
      bers whom trainees taught and counseled were suffering from
      many social ailments: broken homes, poverty, affection depriva-
      tion, inadequate supervision, unreasonable discipline and isola-
      tion. It was necessary to start somewhere in building family
      awareness, family roles and family relationships which could be
      satisfying and enhance family closeness and pride.

Our concepts and training program grew from the notion that staff
need to *understand* and *accept* each family as they find them, and that
with respect and loving concern, we can help parents and children to
develop an identity within the family that will be conducive to building

healthy attitudes and behavior as individuals and family members. With these two major conceptions, it was necessary to develop a training situation that would be realistic and meet the needs of the population involved.

An important instrument, developed for use in preparation for the training program, was the following questionnaire designed to discover the background, training interests, and needs of those who were to participate in the program. A similar questionnaire has been used, with slight modifications, for Head Start programs, elementary, secondary, college and professional schools:

TO: Trainees in the Sex Education and Counseling program.
SUBJECT: Survey for Planning Training Program.
    Since (date) _____, (name) _____, Director of the Planning Project, has been meeting with some of you to plan together a training program in individual and group counseling and education, and curriculum development in the area of sex education and counseling.

We are using a survey form to obtain your views concerning your needs and recommendations for effective planning. Your interest and involvement during the planning stage is essential for developing a successful program.

We will be in touch further through meetings, workshops, conferences and training sessions, so that you will be assisting us during all the planning phases.

    Kindly complete the following items as best you can: ·

PLANNING PROJECT
SURVEY OF STAFF NEEDS AND RECOMMENDATIONS

Name: _____

Title: _____

School: _____

Educational Background:
Undergraduate Degree_____, Date_____, Major_____, Minor_____
Graduate degree(s) & Date_____, _____, _____,
                                          Areas of Study_____
(I.) Check the *areas* of study in which you have taken courses in both the graduate and undergraduate levels.
Personality_____   Marriage and Family Law_____
Counseling Principles_____   Family Relations and
Group Counseling_____   Sociology_____
Sex Education_____   Testing_____

Parent Education_____   Learning Theories_____
Nutrition and Health_____   Leadership Training_____
Dating, Courtship and Marriage_____   Communication Problems_____
Family Finances_____

Please scale your preference concerning the following methods for training. Number 1 will indicate your first preference, whereas number 6 will indicate your last preference.

Lecture and Discussion_____   Small Group Seminars_____
Demonstrations_____   Case Conference_____
Supervised Practice and Observa-   Tape Recordings and Super-
tion_____   vision_____

Please indicate other preferred methods of training, if any:

_____

_____

_____

Kindly list the types of problems presented to you or your colleagues involving sex, personal and family living by both students and parents which reflect the concerns of many:

1. _____

2. _____

3. _____

4. _____

5. _____

6. _____

7. _____

8. _____

9. _____

10. _____

AREAS OF CONCERN

The format of the training sessions was geared to the preferences of the trainees. Following is a list of the types of problems presented to the trainees by parents of preschool children involving sex, personal and family living, which reflect their concerns at home and in school:

—communication problems between parent and child, teacher and child, parent and teacher,

—interpersonal conflict and rivalries,

—overcrowded conditions at home,

—family framework of one-parent home, mother working, dependent children,

—lack of vocabulary for body names and functions,

—sex language and exhibitionism,

—poor hygiene and nutrition,

—child's identity problems,

—poor economic conditions,

—autoerotic and heterosexual body play,

—lack of intellectual stimulation at home,

—alcohol and marijuana,

—teacher's ability to discuss sex,

—attitudes of unwanted pregnancy at home.

TOPICS

The first semester of the school year was devoted to weekly two-hour training sessions. These training sessions were conducted by staff and guest consultants. However, in line with the group-centered approach, many of the trainees assumed leadership roles in the group. A well-rounded outline of very specific content was followed, as can be seen from a summary of the topics included:

Orientation: Group-Centered Approach and Concepts in Family Life and Sex Education. *Discussion and distribution of kits.*

Parent-Teacher Relationships: Working Together in Family-Life Education. Organizing and Maintaining a Parent Group. *Demonstration and discussion.*

Pregnant School-Age Girls: Reactions of Family Members and Preschool Children. *Discussion and readings.*

Curriculum Aids and Activities Developed in Sex and Family-Living Education at Preschool Level. *Discussion. Bibliography compiled and distributed.*

Female Identity in Black Women. (Studies used to illustrate the problems: *Black Rage* by William H. Grier and Price M. Cobbs. *Poverty's Children, Telling It Like It Is*, compilation by Luther Jackson of several Hylan Lewis studies.) *Group discussion on case analysis.*

Effects of Racism on Black People in America and Ways to Remedy It in Home and Classroom.

Techniques of Group Counseling: Use in Classroom and Counseling. *Role-playing and discussion.*

Areas of Parent Concerns in Family-Life and Sex Education. *Techniques for initiating group discussion.*

On-the-Job Projects: A Team Approach to Preschool Small Group. *Discussions on leaderless group involvement.*

Erik Erikson's Theory of Child Development Relative to Play as a Social and Psychological Development in Sexual Patterns in Children. *Aggressive behavior discussed also.*

Art Education for Young Children in Building Self-Awareness. *Slides, curriculum, materials. Discussion and demonstration.*

Parent Education: Range of Human Sexuality. *The challenge of developing awareness by children of maleness and femaleness and how it pervades all aspects of their lives.*

Preschool Language and Behavior in Family-Life and Sex Education. *Materials and methods that can be used to develop creative play activity in sex and family life.*

The Use of the Reflective Technique in Group and Individual Counseling. *Demonstration and practice session.*

Records and Other Teaching Materials Used in Helping Children Understand and Self-Direct Aggressive Feeling. *Demonstration and discussion.*

Organizing and Leading Parent Group in Preschool. *Demonstration and discussion.*

PRACTICUM PROJECTS

The trainees were advised to begin planning for their on-the-job projects midway through the course. Some guidelines were offered:

1. Focus on the needs of preschool children and their parents in family-life education and sex education in your schools.

2. Utilize the benefits gained from the training sessions.

3. Wherever possible, a school team approach should be used.

4. Children, parents and other staff members should participate.

5. Utilize the group-centered approach.

Project proposals were submitted, received by the staff and readied for application. All necessary revisions were reviewed with the trainees before each proceeded to implement her proposal. The projects reflected innovations in curriculum in sex and family-living education both at the preschool level and at the parental level. They focused on realistic concerns in self-awareness, sexual identity and family life. Many teachers worked with both children and parents.

One project concentrated on a central theme that involved all the preschool children in the school. It focused on the theme, *Who Am I?* The purposes were as follows:

—to help the children learn and develop awareness, that each one has worth and dignity,

—to develop self-knowledge and to build positive self-concepts,

—to emphasize the uniqueness of each child through sexual and racial pride and family composition,

—to emphasize the contributions that each child can make to his family and school.

With this basic theme in mind, each teacher developed her own materials and methods.

Several types of projects and activities developed were described as being particularly stimulating and exciting. A representative assortment is described below:

1. One teacher had the children lie down on the floor and she drew an exact outline of their bodies. Then each child could cut, shape, and paint his face and clothing as he saw himself and then stand next to his paper image for a photograph.

2. Individual books were made for and by each child containing self-portraits, family portraits, pictures of home and school, along with a page of the child's weight and height.

3. The class developed and made a TV out of a cardboard carton that was cut out in front for a screen. Two attached rollers and a scroll would show and tell through drawings about each individual child. The illustrations were their self-portraits, photographs brought from home, descriptions of height and weight, and drawings of each child's family and home. The children could play with the TV during the day in their doll corner. There were also circle discussions, songs and finger plays used with the children around the theme of self and family relations.

4. A parochial preschool class conceived the idea of a VIP (Very Important Person) Day for each child. On his day the parents of the child came to school with photographs, movies or mementoes of their child and told the class why their child meant so much to them. The response was overwhelming. Many fathers took time off from work to speak to the class. Mothers brought photograph albums and movies. The principal of the school, who had not participated in the project directly, tried to attend as many of the VIP sessions as she could. Each VIP had a crown to wear and was able to introduce his parents to the rest of the class. The parents were invited to spend the rest of the day at school.

Both parents and children thoroughly enjoyed this teacher's project. Where parents were not available, guardians or a surrogate parent came. Most of the preschool groups involved both parents and children in their project.

5. One preschool group focused on the aggressive child and on ways in which this aggression could be directed constructively. The teachers in the project decided to involve all the teachers in their school. Each kept a list of cases of aggressive behavior noted in her classroom and the ways in which they were able effectively to rechannel aggressive behavior. One of the best devices was the kicking of a pillow with the face of a monster drawn on the front. When kicking or hitting was noted, the teacher would ask the child to visit the monster, who could be kicked and hit as much as the child wanted. Clay dough, musical devices, and physical chores were also found helpful in lowering aggressive tendencies. Parents were then invited to visit the school for meetings. Art workshops were cleverly used as a drawing technique and the parents were delighted with their own art abilities. After these initial workshops, parents came weekly for sewing and discussion groups where the discussion was focused on problems in the home and the ways in which parents could handle them. The teachers suggested some of the ways they had found helpful in dealing with the children in school and the parents shared ways in which they handled them at home. The parents could see that their problems were not unique and many helpful suggestions arose from these weekly meetings.

6. One project involved weekly trips to various places in the community. This was done with the idea of introducing to the children various male and female roles in homes and in society and to show when these tend to be separate or when they tend to blend. The teacher hoped to build a sense of male and female pride among her children. The trips included a visit to the home of one of the children, where the mother proceeded to demonstrate her duties as a housewife and mother. Another trip was to a barber shop owned by the father of one of the children, where he demonstrated his skills. These trips were continued weekly for a period of two months with the permission of the parents. Photographs were taken of the children and placed in a scrapbook along with pictures drawn by the children after each trip.

SUPERVISION AND TRAINING

During the on-the-job training, each teacher was visited three times. This enabled observation and informal discussion concerning the activity and goal of each project. Teachers felt comfortable during these visits, free to discuss their successes and problems. Frequently, one of the staff was called in to help with a parent discussion meeting or to watch a special session with the children. Three- to five-year-old children have a short attention span and the teachers successfully arranged project activities and time spacing to meet these needs.

Materials such as tape recorders, bibliographies and books were loaned to teachers when requested. The project paid for and equipped each participating school with a number of books and pamphlets on sex education and counseling.

Throughout the training sessions, time was spent during each period in self-awareness training. The training focused on "sensitive" areas confronting participants both in counseling and in the classroom. The use of a "life-line" diagram was presented to each.

Following are some of the conclusions reached and processes used by the trainees. Their information may serve as a guide to other trainers undertaking a program to prepare professionals and aides for teaching and counseling.

1. Professionals and other school staff need to search and share their attitudes with parents. Ideally they should organize a small task force and expand after conflicts and concerns have been established.

2. Parent discussion groups are mainly concerned with:
   —personal and social health (prevention and care),
   —personal and family roles,
   —peer-group activities,
   —discipline—(methods and concepts),
   —helping children develop a satisfying self-image as male or female,
   —setting limits for children which they can accept.

3. Demonstrations with teachers reversing role and playing parent figures and parents or playing teacher roles in one-to-one interviews and in group discussions concerning personal and family-life problems.

4. Parallel education of parents at one level and their children at another held during the same semester is more effective than teaching children without parent education.

5. In the black community little boys are being dominated by women in their daily life patterns and need to be separated from women adult figures at appropriate intervals. They need male teachers and others with whom they can identify. The experience in school should be realistic and supportive so that the child can learn to cope more adequately with his real-life situations. The teacher can also help the mother to understand the need to respect the males in her family. It is important to help children and parents to see through the stereotypes concerning black males

and black females such as "women are matriarchal and aggressive," and "men are lazy and no good."

6. Ideas from the trainees on activities calculated to develop a concept of family:

Puppet plays	Photos of family
Songs	Finger play
Parent day—role reversal	Parent–teacher conference
Parent observations	Flannel board activity
Play house	Papier-mâché and wooden
Drawings of family members	figures for family

7. Play is an important social and psychological experience. Through play the child learns trust, autonomy, initiative and industry. The preschool child can grow in imaginative play by practising and sorting out roles. He can play out his anxieties. It is healthy to act out these feelings during this period.

8. Teachers cited these examples of channeling aggressive behavior in the classroom:

Making a punching bag of old clothing	Playing musical instruments— real or imaginary
Workbench	Clay
Free-style painting	Imaginary activities for children in confined spaces
Singing in groups	
Relay races	Free-running in the gym and outdoors

9. Art is an excellent outlet for fears and emotions, and can help the preschool child to better understand himself and his surroundings. He can project through art his feelings about his family and his relationships with family members. Children go through various stages in art growth from scribbling to preschematic, to schematic and to realism.

Of particular interest are the main conclusions reached by the training group as the result of their intensive experience together:

1. Today we see emerging in our culture and neighborhoods various forms of family life—commune, one-parent families, foster-parent families, unwed-parent families, three-generation families, with mostly similar strengths and weaknesses. The child's orientation toward his family needs to be positive.

2. Language usage concerning physical sexuality is colorful and at times difficult for teachers and others. The group arrived at accepting language as being meaningful to children and that they can learn different expressions but to help them understand that some words are clearer and more meaningful than others. Some words are better understood by more people than others.

3. Teachers also felt that preschoolers using the bathroom together was good educationally and helpful in showing the naturalness of the body and its functions.

4. Parents can be motivated to attend parent sessions by setting sessions at convenient times:

—in the morning before work,

—after lunch when bringing the children to school,

—evenings.

Having children perform in the classroom or assembly will draw parents to school and the parent discussion sessions can follow.

5. Songs or records are effective ways of having children learn about their feelings and sense of family and the new baby.

6. Often projects involving parents are a good beginning for starting discussions in family life. Sewing, making and giving Christmas presents, costume-making, and set-building can be effective methods of sharing.

7. Role-playing should be reinforced through talk, play or other activities. Mealtime is good for socializing and talk in addition to feeding.

EVALUATION BY THE PARTICIPANTS

At the time the on-the-job projects were being completed, an unsigned written form of evaluation of both the training and project experience was distributed to all the trainees.

The trainees rated the areas in which they felt their knowledge had increased in the following order:

New techniques for group counseling	67%
Concrete ideas and suggestions for use in the school	56%
New insights and awareness about problems of family living	35%
Factual information in the area of sexual behavior	33%
Increased self-understanding and self-confidence	25%

Other gains attributed to the program were a desire to broaden personal concepts and to pass on new ideas, the opportunity to exchange ideas with others, and the use of the bibliography.

The application of both theory and method to the trainees' own work was rated as follows:

Training relevant to work responsibilities	95%
Opportunity to implement training	94%
Dissemination of information and theory about sexual behavior	57%

Change in their own attitudes and behaviors in work
    situations   50%

Use of new techniques in handling of children or parents   33%

On the question of possible changes in future training methods, the trainees voted as follows:

No different from its current form   57%

More frequent meetings if time permits   25%

Fewer meetings (Only one out of the 68 responded affirmatively)

As for specific training methods, the majority stated preferences for more general lectures, case conferences, free discussions in smaller groups, demonstrations of group counseling with children and parents, and audiovisual techniques. Twelve trainees requested more outside reading, while nine preferred less. Only one third of the group felt the need for more individual consultation with staff members. The group also felt that more informal meetings during the second semester and more demonstration groups would be helpful in future training sessions.

Some of the comments found on the evaluation forms give a more comprehensive picture of the participants' feelings:

"I have become more aware of problems encountered by children living in overcrowded homes and have learned new techniques for parent discussion groups."

"I feel the program has been very conducive to my understanding of sex education and family living in lives of inner-city children. I formed a very close relationship with parents of our center through points I learned from the program—very valuable."

"I have become aware of the need to discuss with the parents the sexuality of their children. One way is by letting the parent tell about the child's behavior and how he handles it and then letting other parents tell how they handle the same problem."

"I learned the importance of purposeful listening and reflective questions. I have learned about books and other materials and methods which help teachers in improving the self-concepts of the children. The program has helped me feel more confident in dealing with parents."

"Particularly useful to me was the time we spent learning how to bring about participation through 'therapeutic' questions and responses."

"My misconceptions and errors were that my understanding of our sexual natures and sexual behavior was narrow. I thought of sexuality in terms of factual knowledge. I believed that childhood conditions affect maturity, but somehow didn't tie it all in with our sexual nature's development."

"I developed new ways of communicating with young children and ideas for more active participation in programs. The program has helped me in expressing to the children the individuality of each child and importance of each child."

"The majority of the techniques used were directed toward helping pupils establish a positive image toward themselves and others. With the parents, through conversation and newsletter, I have tried to establish good relationships so that channels of communication are always open."

"It provided the opportunity to meet with others of similar work conditions to exchange ideas."

The philosophy of the group-centered approach in training brought out the responsibility of the trainees to make it their program. They each felt they had a stake in its success and their individual progress. This accelerated their interest and accounts for the success of the program.

Training Program for Elementary and Secondary Schools

The kindergarten to twelfth-grade training program received the Pacesetter's Award from the President's National Advisory Council on Supplementary Centers and Services. The Council recognized the program as outstandingly experimental, creative and innovative, and on July 1, 1970 awarded the citation to the author of this volume, who created the program and served as its director.

The training program took place from 1967 to 1970 and included the training of over 1,000 teachers, counselors, psychologists, social workers, nurses, school administrators, and parent and student aides. Approximately 150 of the 1,000 received intensive training and on-the-job supervision for one year during the three-year demonstration period.

This Federal-funded pilot project was concerned with both counseling and education training. All teachers were called upon to counsel from time to time, and all counselors, irrespective of their professional discipline, were involved in the educational process and concerned with learning theory and techniques. The program was therefore planned to include both counseling and teaching, theory, skills and practical experience. Also, by mixing counselors and teachers together in the same learning experiences, they were able to share many divergent points of view and approaches to the process of learning and counseling.

The project began on July 1, 1967 and ended July 1, 1970, involving trainees who either were employed by or worked directly in the District of Columbia public, parochial, and independent schools. Since the program was founded on a demonstration research grant, it was necessary to set up several hypotheses which could be subjected to evaluation. An independent group was retained to evaluate the program at the end of each year.

The hypotheses set forth were: *1*) counselors, teachers, psychologists, nurses and other professionals can be trained within one year to develop skills and competency to teach and counsel children and youth in sex, personal and family-living problems, *2*) by developing these competencies the trainees can provide other school professional personnel in their school buildings the opportunity to benefit from the project, *3*) the ongoing curriculum, whether formal or informal, in both group counseling and family-life education would be enriched, and *4*) laboratory schools would be established for practicum purposes at elementary, junior and senior high-school levels.

The need for such a project was obvious in many areas. One out of every four problems presented is a personal or family problem. These run the gamut from conflicts in parent-child relations, early teen-age marriages, teen-age female dropouts due to pregnancy and male dropouts due to putative fatherhood and its accompanying financial problems, dating and courtship questions, problems caused by lack of adequate supervision, and personal and social dilemmas surrounding the school-age mother who returns to school after the birth of her child. These problems affect the academic performance of the student. Pupil personnel staff have strongly expressed a need for training in group theory and counseling with youth and group work with parents both to prevent and to solve the growing number of problems. The professionals felt a need for knowledge and training in an interdisciplinary approach.

Within the school setting the focus would be centered on identifying problems, understanding the interdisciplinary dimensions and learning skills required in short-term group counseling and for teaching. In addition, the trainees would be encouraged to refer problems beyond their competency to specialists and community services.

Specific ideas structured the program. One was that the trainees should be strongly supported and supervised in their work. A second was that they should be given a broad interdisciplinary point of view. A third was that the program should combine theory and practice, taking into consideration the learning experiences and methods that were most meaningful for them.

During the first year 45 trainees were involved in the one-year intensive training course. They included principals, teachers, public-health nurses, school and clinical psychologists, psychiatric social workers, school counselors, attendance officers, and pupil personnel workers. Of this group

26 held master's degrees, two held graduate degrees in divinity, and 17 held bachelor's degrees. During the third year of the program the trainees included high-school seniors and parent aides who had not earned a high-school diploma.

The emphasis was on education, interdisciplinary intervention and group counseling. The significant body of information concerning human sexuality and significant male and female roles from childhood through adulthood was explored. In addition, practicum experience was provided within a familiar school setting.

The conferences held with staff members, students and parents highlighted the need for total personnel involvement in each school. Traditionally the principal, by reason of her authority, is the key person. She determines the time and utilization of personnel in her building. She bears the major responsibility for the educational programs in her school programs. An interested principal can mobilize the strength of her staff and the support of the community to initiate a multidisciplinary program at all grade levels in her school. The school which had the most successful program—as measured by staff, parent and children involvement—was led by a principal who believed in the program and was actively involved at all stages of planning and implementation in her school.

Trainees were asked to rate methods by which they felt they could best learn the theories and techniques to be covered. Most of the professionals ranked Lecture and Discussion as their preferred choice, with Demonstrations second, Small Groups Seminar third, Supervised Practice and Observation fourth, Case Conference fifth, and Tape Recordings and Supervision sixth.

Conferences held with pupil personnel professionals, administrators, parents and youths indicated that the dominant problems which concerned the greatest number of schools were:

Sex Education
Family Planning
Parental Guidance
Parental Discord
Economic Problems
Teen-age Pregnancies
Neglect
Alcoholism and Narcotics
Teacher-Parent-Child Problems
Lack of Motivation
Nutrition and Health
Communication Problems

Early Dating in the Elementary Schools
Sex Promiscuity
Inadequate Male Image
Lack of Privacy
Overprotective Parents
Boys and Girls in Family Sleeping in the Same Bed after Puberty
Sexual Assaults and Incest
One-Parent Family Problems
Exposure to Adult Sex Activities
Homosexuality

The ones that were stressed as the concerns of many in home and school where the professionals worked included 88 special areas of concern. These presenting problems reflect the scope and severity of concerns confronting school personnel whether they were teachers or counselors.

Obviously, during the training period it would have been impossible to cover the underlying factors involved in the various types of conflicts, problems and confusion inherent in the presenting problems. The emphasis, of necessity, would have to be on the relationships between parent-child, sibling relationships, student-teacher relationships, parent-school relationships, and staff relationships, so that sufficient empathy and understanding could be developed for helpful insights and effective problem-solving.

During the first semester of this first year of training the group of 45 met weekly from 8:30 A.M. until 10:00 A.M. at centrally located parochial schools. Adequate space was provided for a round-table discussion, taping of sessions, and demonstration. Since the structure was fluid, the trainees were asked to put in writing some of their expectations. They were informed that these comments would influence the direction that the training would take.

A sample of their comments which were helpful to the staff follow:

The following list contains many of the areas in which this in-service can be most helpful: awareness, listening, background knowledge in personal and family living problems, group dynamics and leadership, team work, how to plan *with*, not *for*.

I would hope that the practicum content would help me to identify the key causal or conditioning factors in specific cases: What are the key factors, relationship, attitudes, etc., which we must assess to really analyze in a comprehensive way, the child's or family's difficulties? I am particularly interested in how to reach and involve parents in school and community problems.

During this program, I hope to *1*) develop better understanding of the problems of teen-agers and children and of their parents, *2*) increase knowledge and improve techniques toward helping these children and parents cope with their problems, and *3*) cooperate with other personnel in developing a program through which groups of children and groups of parents can share their problems and explore solutions.

I expect to gain help in providing effective consultative help to teachers, counselors, parents, principals and students in my role as school psychologist on the part of the student's life which involves the family and interpersonal relationships. With older students that will involve problems about dating, family supervision or lack of it. I hope to gain better understanding and insights into family interrelationships and conflicts and their effect on the student and how to help the student and family to make an effort toward alleviating and diminishing their problems. I wish to learn how to give them aid in using community resources.

A school nurse listed the following:

... *a*) to help me gain better understanding not only of other people's problems but problems which concern me, *b*) to have more confidence in counseling other individuals with their problems, *c*) to feel that by my contacts with other qualified personnel I shall learn to handle many phases of a problem, not only the "health aspect."

A parochial-school teacher wrote as follows:

At this time my knowledge of student counseling and guidance is very limited. This is my first course as such. I expect to learn procedures and techniques for helping children and their parents. My contact with elementary children has been in the capacity of classroom teacher only.

I am looking forward to mastering techniques in counseling that I know I lack, and learning about areas of family and personal living to which I have had little exposure.

In my work I have perhaps been more lax than I realized. This is involving the parents more in the child-school relationship so they can feel a part of the entire problem rather than just a parent-child disciplinary agent in the home. Also I hope to learn new and better techniques in talking and working with the children and parents and in understanding their attitudes and values. I am looking forward to new, practical approaches to my work.

I would hope that this course would make me more aware of the needs of pupils and parents in my community. Increased expertness in group counseling is another need. A knowledge of the agencies which can provide help beyond my ability. More specific knowledge of the other disciplines represented.

A health-education teacher wrote:

Through this training program I hope to gain more insight on how I can communicate with pupils and their parents on health matters. Usually in the school, the counselor, principal, and the health and physical education teacher are involved more intimately with children than are other teachers. Therefore, this program would be beneficial to me in every respect.

CONTENT, TRAINING AND EVALUATION—FIRST YEAR

Taking into consideration the goals and needs of the trainees, a number of outstanding consultants who were familiar with school personnel and

problems were invited to participate as teachers in the training sessions.*
Some of the topics covered in the sessions included:

Human Sexuality and Role Identification
Building Awareness in Family Communication
Illegitimacy and the Social-Psychological Factors Involved in Teenage
    Pregnancy and Guide Lines for Counseling
Counseling Parents of School-Age Children in Family-Life Problems
Group-Counseling Techniques
Goals in Counseling and Therapy
Techniques in Organizing and Maintaining Parent Groups in a School
    Setting
Preparation and Organization of the Case Conference on Unwed Mother
Sex and Family Law
Mental Health in Family Relationships and Sex Education
Health
Social-Psychological Implication of Venereal Disease
Group Discussion on Sexual Behavior of Elementary School Children at
    an Inner-City School
Adolescent Obstetrics
Health, Social and Psychological Needs of the Pregnant School-Age Girl
    and Her Family
Sensitivity Training with the Trainees
Areas of Sensitivity
Masturbation
Homosexuality
Obscenity
Premarital Sex Relations
Family Planning and Birth Control—Its Use and Abuse in Teaching
    Situations in a School Setting
Use of Consultant in Developing Consultation Service
Use of Film as a Teaching Tool in Sex, Personal and Family Living.

Every training session was tape-recorded. One demonstration session
conducted with eighth graders from a parochial school was video-taped.
The tapes served many purposes. A number of the trainees requested
them for use in staff conferences at their respective schools. Others
wanted the tapes for personal replaying in order to reinforce some of

* Patrick Accardi, Mary Calderone, John F. Clark, Paul B. Cornely, Elizabeth
Herzog, Lorenzo Jacobs, Warren Johnson, E. James Lieberman, Gordon Lippitt,
Eleanore Luckey, Esther Schulz, Marjorie Schumacher, Clark Vincent, Gerhard
Neubeck, James A. Peterson.

the concepts and ideas that seemed important to them. The director used the tapes in consultation sessions with school personnel who were not trainees, but who had heard about the sessions and wanted to hear the tapes. The tapes are being transcribed for the purpose of including the material in a school guide for use by the trainees and others. The video tape proved to be an extremely useful tool in sparking group discussion in separate sessions held with trainees, parents, and students.

The practicum experiences were diverse both in quantity and quality. Some lasted the full term of the second semester and involved as much as ten to fifteen hours per week for some of the trainees. In many instances two to six professionals who were not trainees were involved in the project, whereas in some situations the trainees went it alone. However, in all instances the practicum appeared to meet a real problem which faced the participant in her respective school setting and a realistic attempt to work through that problem. In addition to clearing the practicum experience with the director, all of these projects were cleared with the principal in each school.

Practicum experiences were based on the explicit assumption that there is no one right way to conduct a group discussion, consult with staff members, counsel individuals, refer a student to a community agency, but that each person develop his own style which is right for him because it is an integral part of his own personality. The instructors, including the consultants, were people with a variety of backgrounds. Among them were sociologists, psychologists, marriage counselors, sex educators, doctors and lawyers. In spite of their different initial orientation all shared in the belief that a) training and practice should be along interdisciplinary lines and that the best results are obtained when b) teaching and counseling is client oriented and is tailored to their needs as expressed by their verbal and nonverbal feelings.

Inherent in the nature of a pilot program is the need to test and evaluate innovative procedures in order to have a basis for effective change. The objectives were clearly set forth in the accepted proposal and form the basis for the evaluation. The director was sensitive to informal suggestions by trainees and others, verbal reactions to procedures during group discussions, and formal (inventories, interviews, observations, practicum experiences) methods of evaluation. This included feedback from the trainees, supervisors, parents, and school children.

An adequate measure of evaluation of the various group sessions could be reasonably made by having the teacher note before the session three central ideas, attitudes, or facts that she would like the trainees to learn from the session. The trainees would then note three central ideas, attitudes, or facts which they learned from the session. The teacher-trainee perception of the session would then be compared for effectiveness of communication. This procedure took place during every training session. In general, at least two thirds of those attending each session accurately perceived what the teacher perceived as central to the learning situation. The laboratory schools in actuality became the schools where the trainees were employed. They knew the children, parents and staff, and their work dovetailed with the principal's needs as the latter saw them.

As in the Preschool Training Program discussed earlier, a questionnaire was submitted to the trainees which required no signature. One question asked the trainee to specify the areas of knowledge in which he felt most improvement due to the training. The resulting rank order was as follows: new techniques for group counseling (67%), concrete ideas and suggestions for use in the school (50%), factual information in the areas of sexual behavior (25%), new insights and awareness about problems of family living (25%).

The following rank order of responses was obtained regarding the use made by the participants as a result of the training: dissemination of factual information (50%), use of new techniques in handling of children or parent (50%), changed their own attitudes and behavior in their work situation (70%).

Regarding the specific method of instruction, there was a general desire for additional lectures, case conferences, and individual consultations, with not more than six participants desiring fewer presentations of these types. All respondents, however, expressed desire for more demonstrations of group counseling and education and more presentations of audiovisual techniques. The only method of instruction not favored was outside readings.

Half of those responding to the questionnaire offered their personal reaction to the program as a whole. Among these about half found the program to be "excellent" and "useful." Several expressed specific requests for more individual training and more emphasis on techniques.

Many of the trainees' comments on gains in group counseling dealt with the ability "to reflect" with the group on sexual matters and "keep the group discussion going." In working with other members of their staff the following comment by a trainee represents many of the trainees' feelings. "I've been better able to understand some reactions of teachers to apparent sexual behavior of the children in their classes—and to work closer with them irrespective of our different points of view." In discussing changes in their own attitude, a common response was "attempts to understand the other person's point of view have been most relevant for me."

The major concrete idea which could be implemented was "more group counseling and group dynamic approaches. I have improved sensitivity and eagerness to listen."

An unsigned questionnaire dealing with the practicum experience was submitted to the trainees toward the end of the year. A sample of typical answers of the effects on practicum participants follows. Children: interest aroused, motivation to meet more, learn to verbalize feelings, express fear and anger, behavior modification (a few). Parents: interest and desire for more meeting, learn to express problems, to communicate with child and school, improve understanding of child—awareness, expressed desire for school to help in sex education, cooperative. Staff: increased their interest, were "impressed," and more helpful, referred more cases and want more counseling groups set up, staff relationship within schools improved.

Among all the parochial schools involved, there were no unfavorable comments. All had initiated sex-education programs with children, staff and parent groups, using the interdisciplinary approach for the first time. The fact that schools which were not included asked to share and participate is another favorable sign. The professionals who contacted the director for assistance, heard about the program from the trainees. Whenever the director visited schools and demonstrated group-counseling techniques with parents, comments made to the director and staff were very encouraging.

Because the elementary-school personnel are generalists first and specialists second, the most effective cooperation and leadership was reflected in enthusiasm, effort and outcome. The setting is small, leadership and control comes easier and a closer relationship exists with staff and parent group. The parents are also available at this level for school meetings and conferences during the day. The team approach generally worked well and is becoming a pattern in the trainees' school at the elementary level.

In addition to the extensive training, five city-wide one-day workshops were held for those teachers and counselors who could attend. These took the form of lecture and small-group discussion.

CONTENT AND TRAINING—SECOND AND THIRD YEARS

During the second year, the trainees were professionals primarily involved in teaching and counseling at the elementary-school level. Sixty-two participants were from public and parochial schools. The emphasis during the third year concentrated on a three-level approach:

1. Training for other staff members in consultation skills and group work.
2. Training in group work with students in the elementary schools.
3. Training in group work with parents.

The schedule established during the first year was followed: weekly sessions held at local schools for one semester, and on-the-job training held during the second semester.

Emphasis was placed during the training sessions on *a*) team teaching and discussion on an interdisciplinary basis, *b*) developing consultation skills and services involving family and personal relations, *c*) training in group-centered approaches with children and adults.

In addition the program also was aimed at helping the trainees to understand their own sexuality so that they could help children understand theirs, their femaleness, their maleness, and their role in the family and society. These are not goals that can be accomplished in a one-shot film showing and discussion. They are best achieved as part of the usual classroom curriculum. Ideally they require a teacher who has both the factual physiological information needed and a grasp of the broader concept of sex and sexuality. The training course aims at producing that ideal.

During the second year the methods in order of preference which the trainers preferred were 1) demonstrations, 2) lectures by consultants from various disciplines, 3) audio visual techniques, 4) lectures and discussion and role-playing.

Over 400 school personnel attended three one-day workshops. The themes were: 1) Family Life and Sex Education in Human Relations Education, 2) The Group Approach—Techniques and Methods in Sex and Family Problems, 3) Language Barriers and Communication in Human Sexuality.

The trainees were asked on the same evaluation form to describe what purpose the content of the workshop served for them. For a third of them the workshops had been a first introduction to sex education, and more than half had found that the workshops provided new insights into particular problems which arose in their work.

As for teaching methods demonstrated in the workshops, 61 per cent of the trainees responding said that the workshops had increased their interest in learning more about techniques; about 50 per cent said that the workshop helped make them feel more confident of their ability to lead a discussion group, increased their understanding of the role of the discussion leader, and alerted them to the special problem of language in sex education. For the other 33 per cent the workshop had been an introduction to group-discussion techniques and had increased their understanding of the dynamics of group discussion.

Questions concerning the use of the all-day-workshop method elicited the following answers:

The workshop introduced me to group discussion techniques (29%)

Increased my understanding of the role of the discussion leader (48%)

Increased my understanding of the dynamics of group discussion (32%)

Alerted me to the special problem of language in sex education (48%)

Made me feel more confident of my ability to lead a discussion group (51%)

Made me feel less confident of my ability to lead a discussion group (0%)

Increased my interest in learning more about techniques (61%)

As the trainees progressed through their basic classroom training they were advised to begin planning their project, and some guidelines were offered:

1. It should serve to fulfill an actual need on the part of children and parents in family-life education.

2. It should utilize more or less the benefits gained from the instruction.

3. It should be planned as a group project in which all members would function as a team whenever possible.

4. It should serve children, parents and other staff members.

All participants completed their assignments. The projects were then reviewed from the point of view of *a*) being realistic in terms of time and staff availability, *b*) training and skills of the team, and *c*) relationship to other projects in the same building.

In two schools where the principals were actively involved in the training process, the projects included assembly programs in which all the school children were present, and all the trainees were involved as one team in the planning. In addition a minimum of four trainees shared in the teaching and group discussions of other projects undertaken in the schools. These included programs of parent discussion groups involving four to six sessions on:

1. Discipline, building family cohesiveness.

2. Building pride and confidence in self.

3. Answering children's questions on body changes and human growth and development.

In several instances kindergarten and primary-school teachers worked closely with the parents in developing programs showing growth in animals, and chickens, and bringing to the children the wonders of being mothers, fathers, and babies in various family roles. They learned care and responsibility and growth by the young through love, respect and cooperation in the family.

The classes in the fourth through sixth grades coordinated into their projects a study of physical changes during puberty, developing greater understanding of the emotional and social aspects of growth and development, and self-awareness.

The counselors and nurses found in their group discussions that the care of children, along with sex and personal problems, were the concern of parents. The parents became involved in the programs in many ways. They attended assembly programs for children on family life and school behavior. They assisted teachers and attended study-group sessions afterwards.

During the second half of the project, the work of supervision and consultation was divided between Dr. Patricia Schiller, Director, and Mrs. Peggy Gorham, family-life education specialist. The former was responsible for the forty-two trainees in the three public schools and the latter took responsibility for the twenty nurses and parochial-school trainees. This seemed a workable plan.

All the trainees were observed at least twice while doing their project, also they called by phone for consultations concerning books, audiovisual aids, consultants, and of course reassurance in what they were doing. Weekly visits were made to the schools and in many instances the trainees visited the office of the director for consultations.

The trainees met in two groups, but both had the same number of sessions and similar experiences. Books, pamphlets and tapes were both given and loaned to them. Each was advised to set up a small library in her building from the materials, books and pamphlets which were distributed. In addition they used additional materials from the office.

The nuns and several nurses wanted to do their projects co-operatively. The following description of their successful joint ventures speaks for itself:

The programs were diverse. Five programs consisted of six to eight classroom sessions with eighth graders; four programs were organized for fifth and sixth graders who exhibited sex or personal problems. One program was a city-wide planning project, and four programs were discussion groups with parents.

Two of the parochial-school principals worked out a joint plan for a one-day workshop in sex education for the eighth-grade children in their schools. They viewed the workshop as an experiment in community relations as well as an educational event. The program took place at a parochial school in the combination auditorium lunchroom where gay "Welcome Assumption" signs were posted. The children were paired off in a between-schools buddy system to assure the making of new friendships. The film "Generation to Generation" was shown to both groups, boys and girls mixed, followed by a short question and answer period. Before seeing the film "Girl to Woman," the girls went to a classroom for a group discussion and question period with two school nurses. Meanwhile, the boys were seeing "Boy to Man" in the auditorium, and they had their chance to discuss and question the school doctor after the film. The children lunched together and then played baseball —Assumption vs. St. Thomas More. The teacher who organized the program was young, vibrant and set a tone which her final report best describes: "We planned a social for the afternoon because we felt it kept the discussion of sex in a real setting—people working together, people learning together. We wanted to dispel the grim, serious-business attitude, and put the knowledge they gained into a wholesome setting . . . open, frank and comfortable." Buoyed by the success of their workshop, both schools plan to have a regular program of sex education next year, climaxed by another all-day workshop and social time.

Another principal of an inner-city parochial school, Immaculate Conception, was also its sixth-grade teacher, instituted an on-going program for fifth- and sixth-grade girls and boys. She divided the teaching between a pupil personnel worker and herself and called upon the physician who donates his time to the neighborhood health clinic and to married couples and parents. They met in groups of eight to talk with the students about discipline, childbirth, and ways to show love and affection. The question period was lively and interesting. Although bearing both a teaching and an administrative burden, not to mention involvement in many of the problems of her students' families, this teacher carried on one of the most thorough classroom-integrated programs that occurred among the parochial-school trainees.

The principal of Annunciation School, whose student body is predominantly white and economically well off was already running a highly developed sex and family-life education and counseling program in her school when she began the training course. She concentrated for her practicum on a special eighth-grade project, an elected committee of children called, "The Life Committee" which was to be responsible for receiving suggestions and complaints about the topics in the "Life" discussions. One of her first efforts was to broaden the children's concepts of roles they could assume as adults. She was also conducting parent sessions, and informal discussions in homes. As the teacher of the eighth grade she was able to incorporate the program into their eighth-grade curriculum.

The exchange of ideas and feelings was often as rewarding for the nurses as it appeared to be for the participants. One nurse, after describing some of the "stimulating" discussions which took place during her six-session program for parents, made the following statement:

I think it was a worthwhile venture for me. I feel I gained new insights into problems faced by many ghetto parents. I also developed a greater respect for their ability to function as well as they do in relation to the multitude of problems which they frequently encounter—the major one being economic.

One nurse, conducting a program for selected parents of children who exhibited special problems in behavior and attitudes toward personal hygiene, encountered what she felt to be an attitude of resentment on the part of the parents because they were identified as parents of problem children. This established a barrier to communication that she was unable to overcome. Her counsel to those who might wish to set up a similar program in future years is that, although those who need most to be reached may not respond, group programs should be voluntary. Some other means—perhaps home visits with a friendly but direct discussion of whatever problem the child exhibits, followed by an invitation to join other parents whose children have problems too, emphasizing the common bond rather than the uniqueness of their problem—might yield far more involvement and success.

EVALUATION

At the end of the school year a similar evaluation form to the one used during the first year was distributed to each trainee for completion.

The trainees rated the areas in which they felt their knowledge had increased in the following order:

New techniques for group counseling	(69%)
Concrete ideas and suggestions for use in the school	(47%)
Factual information in the area of sexual behavior	(38%)
New insights and awareness about problems of family living	(31%)
Increased self-understanding and self-confidence	(25%)

Two trainees felt no particular gain or change from their previous knowledge.

The application of both theory and method to their own work was rated as follows:

Dissemination of information and theory about sexual behavior (66%)

Change in their own attitudes and behavior in work situations (66%)

Use of new techniques in handling of children or parents (56%)

Three had not yet implemented their training in any way, but no one felt it was irrelevant to her work responsibilities.

Half the respondees felt that there was no need for change in the current form of the training program. Two asked for more frequent meetings, in order to have the services of more resource people, more time with those available, and to develop further the techniques explained. Five trainees wanted fewer meetings, with end-of-the-day fatigue and parking problems being the reasons stated. One trainee felt that the program needed complete revision. As for the specific training methods, the majority stated a preference for more demonstrations of group counseling with children and parents, more audiovisual techniques, more case conferences, and more free discussions in small groups. Less than half requested more individual consultations with staff members. Nine trainees preferred more outside reading, but seven preferred less. General lectures were unpopular with the majority. The group also responded in the majority to a preference for informal meetings with the group to exchange ideas and report on progress during the second semester, rather than holding occasional formal scheduled meetings. Five trainees asked for more individual consultation services by staff members because of the different needs of each trainee.

Many of those who responded offered additional, more personal commentary. Two were totally negative and felt that the program produced nothing but fatigue. Another felt that much of the program was not applicable to her needs as a Grade 1 and 2 teacher. Most of the comments were, however, similar in tone and content to the trainee that summarized her feelings as follows:

An understanding of the reactions of others to children's sexual behavior with more tolerance is an outcome, personally, from this course. My contact with pupils was improved, with greater appreciation for open, forthright sexual discussions. I grew as a person along with the pupils.

Three of the trainees made recommendations on behalf of sex education in general, and one is well worth quoting:

There is an urgent need for ventilation on the part of our entire school staff. Many of the problems which I encountered result from misinformation or negative attitudes which exist between home and school. If there were an opportunity for a "retreat" or workshop with the entire staff the participants in this program would have more opportunity for dialogue, leadership and sensitivity.

The third-year training sessions concentrated on training preschool and kindergarten teachers, and counselors. Since preschool was covered in an earlier section of this chapter, we can say in passing that the general format worked well there. For the first time paraprofessionals were included. They added a rich and important dimension to the course discussions, and served as a catalyst for extending the knowledge and understanding of the professionals. Their cogent, practical view of problems showed sharp insights and understanding of children's psychosexual needs.

The evaluation concerning areas of learning of the 68 participants fell into the following percentages:

New techniques for group counseling	67%
Concrete ideas and suggestions for use in the school	56%
New insights and awareness about problems of family living	35%
Factual information in the area of sexual behavior	33%
Increased self-understanding and self-confidence	25%

The application of both theory and methods to their work was rated as follows:

Training relevant to work responsibilities	95%
Opportunity to implement training	94%
Dissemination of information and theory about sexual behavior	57%
Change in their own attitudes and behaviors in work situations	50%
Use of new techniques in handling of children or parents	33%

Some of the comments found on the evaluation forms give a more comprehensive picture of the participants' feelings:

I have become more aware of problems encountered by children living in overcrowded homes and have learned new techniques for parent discussion groups.

I feel the program has been very conducive to my understanding of sex education and family living in lives of inner-city children. I formed a very close relationship with parents of our center through points I learned from the program—very valuable.

I have become aware of the need to discuss with the parent the sexuality of their children. One way is by letting the parent tell about the child's behavior and how he handles it and then letting other parents tell how they handle the same problem.

I learned the importance of purposeful listening and reflective questions. I have learned about books and other materials and methods which help teachers in improving the self-concepts of the children. The program has helped me feel more confident in dealing with parents.

Particularly useful to me was the time we spent learning how to bring about participation through "therapeutic" questions and responses.

My misconceptions and errors were that my understanding of our sexual natures, sexual behavior, was narrow. I thought of sexuality in terms of factual knowledge. I believed that childhood conditions affect maturity, but somehow didn't tie it all in with our sexual nature's development.

I developed new ways of communicating with young children, along with ideas for more active participation in programs. The program has helped me in expressing to the children the individuality of each child and importance of each child.

9

Model Training Programs, II

It should go without saying that all these programs need to be conducted by a sensitive and aware human being knowledgeable in the interdisciplinary aspects of human sexuality, in communication and group knowledge and skills, and accepting of students with problems.

College

The college program should involve:
1. Teaching undergraduate courses.
2. Dormitory counseling and seminars.
3. Counseling in the university counseling center and conducting encounter groups in human sexuality.
4. Counseling and education at the university health service center.
5. A university-wide lecture series open to all students.
6. Pastoral counseling concerned with human sexuality.

Since most college personnel working in this area are either guidance counselors or psychologists, or people with advanced degrees in medicine, nursing and education, the majority receive special training during summer institutes and courses, weekend institutes, or attendance at professional conferences where they exchange and share knowledge and problems with colleagues and pick up significant bits of information which they can follow up with readings and further exchange of ideas.

The American Association of Sex Educators and Counselors (AASEC), the recognized national professional membership organization for sex educators and counselors, found in a recent survey of its membership that they develop their knowledge and understanding through workshops and seminars. However, their graduate studies were in the helping professions such as medicine, law, psychology, social work,

172

education, nursing, home economics, ministry and other allied professions.

The AASEC holds an annual one-week summer workshop for training college personnel. It is an intensive experience in concepts, methods and techniques. Many universities throughout the United States conduct one-, two- and three-week workshops for which they award graduate credit.

In-service training programs are planned from time to time on certain campuses. A model six-week program (conducted during two-hour sessions) developed on the Howard University campus for college personnel training is outlined below:

HOWARD UNIVERSITY

THE UNIVERSITY HEALTH SERVICE
In Cooperation With
THE DEPARTMENT OF OBSTETRICS AND GYNECOLOGY
and
THE CENTER FOR FAMILY PLANNING SERVICES
offers
A WORKSHOP IN HUMAN SEXUALITY AND CONTRACEPTION

This series will be presented in the Conference Room of the University Health Service under the direction of Dr. Samuel B. McCottry, Director of the University Health Service, and Dr. Patricia Schiller, Assistant Professor of Obstetrics and Gynecology, Sex Educator and Marriage Counselor. Subjects of individual sessions are listed below:

Introduction.
    The Language of Human Sexuality.
        Physiological, social and psychological terminology.
Human Sexual Responses.
    a. Differences in physical reactions between male and female.
    b. Issues in erotic stimuli—mass media, drugs.
Contraception: Methods—pros & cons.
    a. Method of discussion of various forms.
    b. Medical research on negative and positive factors.
    c. Leading a group discussion on contraception.
Sexual Problems of College Students.
    a. Communication of sexual preferences and feelings.
    b. Attitudes toward orgasm—female frigidity.
    c. Role of foreplay.
    d. Peer-group pressures.
    e. Communicating sex relations as part of a total male-female relationship.

Individual and Group Counseling Techniques.
  a. Initial interview.
  b. Joint counseling—partners.
  c. Organizing a group.
  d. Group interaction techniques.
Abortion Referrals—Counseling Concerns and Responsibilities.
  a. Decision-making as a patient prerogative.
  b. Abortion—hospital and non-hospital settings.
  c. Parental involvement.
  d. Exploring major relationships with the student.

The elective course offered to Freshmen medical students is described below:

ELECTIVE COURSE OFFERED BY
DEPARTMENT OF OB/GYN

TITLE: Human Sexuality, Marriage and Sex Counseling for Medical Students

INSTRUCTOR: Dr. Patricia Schiller, Asst. Professor, OB/GYN
　　　　　　　Executive Director American Association of Sex Educators and Counselors
　　　　　　　Clinical Psychologist and Marriage Counselor

TIME: Monday, 2:00 to 4:00. Freshmen—second semester

LENGTH: 1 semester—2 hours per week for 13 weeks

Short Description: The course will deal with the psychology of men and women toward their sexuality; adolescent pregnancy and parenthood; sexual problems confronting the physician in his practice with married and single women and men; language barrier in sexual communication; counseling in sensitive areas in human sexuality such as masturbation, homosexuality, abortion, nudity and adolescent pregnancy. Emphasis will be given to attitudes and problems of poor black people. Family planning problems will be included.

Those enrolled will learn counseling and educational methods and techniques in helping patients. Also training in consultation skills in working with inner-city school personnel. Audiovisual aids, role-playing, small-group discussions, and guest consultants will be utilized as well as case studies.

Course Content by Sessions (Thumbnail descriptions)
  1. Social-Psychological Sex Inventory. Pre-test on Human Sexuality Test administered to all students. Overview and philosophy on human sexuality.
  2. Psychology of men and women toward human sexuality, sexism, marital role, family planning and abortion.
  3. Adolescent pregnancy and parenthood in the black community.
  4. Sexual problems in marital relations and techniques of counseling. Psycho-social factors involved in frigidity and premature ejaculation, family-planning breakdowns.

5. Survey of the Masters-Johnson approach to sex counseling and sex education.

6. Physicians as sex educators and counselors in family, pediatric and community medicine.

7. Language barriers in sexual communication.

8. Developing a social sexual history. Practice in using a form instrument in marital and sex counseling.

9. Desensitizing the student in order to discuss sensitive areas, i.e., masturbation, homosexuality, abortion, birth control, premarital sex.

10. Legal and social issues in abortion.

11. Interview and counseling techniques. Individual, conjoint and group. Observations at clinical centers.

12. Patients, school personnel and leaders from the black community will share a panel on "Helping Black People—Young and Old—with Sex Problems."

13. Post-Test. Social Sex Inventory.

Graduate and Professional Schools

Schools of social work, education, psychology and counseling, medicine and nursing are now offering courses. Many still follow the undergraduate pattern of dealing solely with human sexuality. However, the more sophisticated schools include sensitivity training, techniques and methods of teaching and counseling, and attempt to afford the trainees some practical experience either through clinic or community field work. Several colleges have majors in sex education. They offer courses in personality development, human sexuality, sensitivity training, marital and sex counseling, and field experiences.

Several medical schools have demonstrated outstanding leadership in developing training programs. Mrs. Ethel Nash and Dr. Clark Vincent have been pioneers at Bowman Gray Medical School. Dr. Edward Tyler of Indiana Medical School was one of the first to initiate the use of films as part of his lecture to desensitize his students.

In the course taught at Howard University College of Medicine, the students taking the elective course have the opportunity to gain practical experience in teaching and counseling ward patients in groups or working with adolescent students who attend the District of Columbia schools.

Because human sexuality is fraught with strong emotional content, many of the medical schools are basing the educational experience on the process of desensitization, sensitization and incorporation.

Desensitization as used in human sexuality education refers to a method of teaching. The student, through continuous exposure to an anxiety-producing experience, becomes comfortable with it and no longer has an anxiety reaction. This is often achieved by intensive use of sexual material such as films, slides, pictures, art, sculpture, sexual artifacts, and by the use of sexual expressions in a respectful rather than derogatory frame of reference. Information about variations in sexual practices helps students to become self-aware and assists them in examining and coming to grips with their own values and attitudes.

Sensitization results from this. Once having become desensitized, the student can participate in a more open and trusting manner. His fears and anxieties about sex have been diffused. His readiness for learning is increased. He now can learn the various interdisciplinary facets of human sexuality and particularly its relationship to marital and family life. He can consciously sort out sexual problems and concerns of patients in reviewing a case history, in developing a patient's medical history, and in making a diagnosis and recommending treatment in a specific situation. With experience, the student's sensitivity is enhanced and sharpened.

Incorporation follows. Once the two previous steps have been successfully worked through, the student can integrate the new information and his heightened awareness with his life-style. His clinical experiences enable him to put into practice and check out his sexual learnings, so that he can become more skilled in helping patients.

As the teacher uses the classroom and the counselor uses the clinic or counseling office, so the medical student utilizes the teaching hospital, the schools or clinics in the community whenever he feels his services would be helpful. In the teaching hospital, the maternity wards, pediatric wards, and gynecology wards provide a good laboratory for assisting patients and their families with sex education and sex counseling.

The small group concept appears to be well suited to medical students. Where large classes are necessary for viewing films or listening to a lecture, small-group discussions should follow which allow for ventilation, interaction and the opportunity for participants to check out with each other their feelings and impressions. Much of the success or failure of the small group depends on the skill of the leader. Persons versed in group work who have been comfortable and productive in the process should play the role of leader. Residents, medical staff, social workers, counselors, psychologists or trainers who have successful experience in group work and are familiar with the student body can undertake this role.

At an Institute on Marriage, the Family and Human Sexuality held at Bowman Gray School of Medicine of Wake Forest University, twelve medical educators formulated, during their six weeks together, "materials and personnel relevant to the anticipated needs of some thirty medical schools . . ."

The recommendations outlined here cover a four-year curriculum, although they can be modified to suit the needs of medical schools involved in a three-year experimental program:

The first year is planned with the objective of orienting the student to develop insight into his own behavior and the process of his emotional and social development.

The second year is planned to assist the medical student to deal with the patient as a person in addition to viewing him as a medical problem.

The third year deals with the collection of data and helps with student in learning skills related to *a*) data-gathering, *b*) ability to diagnose, *c*) communication, *d*) patient awareness and his reactions, *e*) sensitivity to patient's psychological and social needs, *f*) awareness of the patient as an individual, *g*) developing a common vocabulary with the patient so that communication between student and patient is facilitated and effective.

The fourth year is concerned with the physician as counselor. In addition to assisting the student to understand counseling functions, technique and scope of problems which he will be involved in, the material is concerned with the physician's limitations and referral choices.

INDIANA UNIVERSITY HUMAN SEXUALITY COURSE

A.M.	Monday	Tuesday	Wednesday	Thursday	Friday
8:00	Physiological and psychological bases of human sexual behavior	Homosexuality	World overpopulation Gynecologist (lecture, films)	The sexually provocative patient Gynecologist (lecture, vignettes)	Effects of pregnancy--wanted and unwanted--on both parents Gynecologist (lecture, patient-demonstration)
9:00		Psychologist (lecture, films)	Contraception I.U.D., Pills, Sterilization, and Family Planning	Sex problems as they present to the G.P.	
	Psychiatrist (lecture, films, slides)	Exhibitionism Sadomasochism		Family physician (lecture)	Premarital sexual examination and counseling
10:00	"Normal" variations and techniques of human sexual behavior	Anthropologist (lecture, slides, films)	Gynecologist (lecture, slides, films) Abortion issues	Therapy of impotence, premature ejaculation and frigidity	Gynecologist (lecture, patient-demonstration)
11:00		Legal aspects of human sexuality			Sex education for children
	Psychologist (lecture, films)	Anthropologist (lecture)	Attorney, Gynecologist, and Minister (panel)	Male-Female Sex Therapy Team (lecture, demonstration)	Educator and Pediatrician (materials and demonstration)

Dr. Edward A. Tyler, Professor of Psychiatry at Indiana University Medical Center, has successfully introduced a one-week required course for students which is outlined above:

Dr. Harvey L. Gochros, Professor of Social Work and Chairman of the Practice Sequence at the School of Social Work, West Virginia University, has pioneered in introducing courses in human sexuality in social-work graduate schools. Due to an absence of such courses, many social workers sidetrack sexual problems and, unrealistically dealing with patients, claim: "It's not within the area of social-work competence." But this appears to be pure rationalization because of the workers' lack of ability to deal with it. It is Dr. Gochros' feeling that "if social workers are to accept the responsibility of working adequately with sexual problems, graduate education must show similar initiative. The first step could be to offer a specific course on human sexuality in graduate social-work programs."

In view of the newness of human sexuality in the social-work curriculum the following format for a course is suggested:

I. Knowledge
   1. Current patterns of formal and informal ways that sexual behavior is learned.
   2. Individual differences and the range of cultural patterns.
   3. Sensitive areas: masturbation, extramarital sexual intercourse, abortion, homosexuality, and sexual dysfunctioning.
   4. Contraception and family planning.
   5. Human sexual responses as enunciated by Masters and Johnson and others.

II. Attitudes
   1. Cultural and family determinants of sexual attitudes.
   2. Individual patterns and life-style coupled with the acceptance of workers to accept and understand clients' needs.

III. Skills
   1. Provide the type of course situation where students can practice testing out their attitudes and feelings through simulated problems and supervised counseling situations. In this way they can develop clinical skills in communication with individuals and groups in various settings where social-work intervention is practiced. This may run the gamut from work in agencies or schools to courts or hospitals.

The following specific outline for a course is suggested by Dr. Gochros:

I. Human sexual behavior and environment influences.
   1. The nature and varieties of sexual expression.
   2. The vocabulary of sex.

3. Social, class, and cultural differences in sexual behavior.
4. Sex and age differences in sexual behavior.
5. Sexual expression in marriage.
6. Rural-urban differences in sexual behavior.
7. The nature of deviance.
8. Pregnancy out of wedlock.
9. Sex offenders and their victims.
10. Physical aspects of sexuality; the anatomy and physiology of sex.
11. Nature of sex-related diseases and dysfunctioning.

II. Social Policy and Sexuality.
1. Sexual rights.
2. The effects of social policy on sexual behavior; the formulation of a national policy.
3. Famliy planning policy.
4. Abortion policy.
5. Pornography and censorship policy.
6. Laws pertaining to sexuality.

III. Social-work practice approaches to sexual problems.
1. Problems.
   a. Unwanted pregnancies.
   b. Deviance.
   c. Common sexual disorders.
   d. Sexual offenders.
   e. The sex offenders' victims.
   f. Sexual aspects of adoption.
2. Approaches.
   a. Prevention: Relevant sex education.
   b. Individual approaches.
   c. Group approaches.
   d. Interviewing techniques.
   e. Planning and conducting research in human sexual behavior.

The above outline is only suggestive of the various topics that could be included in such a course and does not imply a particular sequence. Time limitations and the need to enable students to explore emotionally charged areas adequately require selectivity in content.

Institutes, Seminars, and Workshops

If all colleges and graduate schools had courses of instruction for teachers, counselors, social workers, doctors, nurses, psychologists, ministers, and others involved in sex education there would be no essential need for institutes, seminars, workshops, etc. But at the present time the lack of opportunities for formal training are such that summer courses, workshops and institutes have sprung into being.

The American Association of Sex Educators and Counselors has taken the lead in developing and administering annual, summer and regional Sex Education Institutes. The training consists of concepts, content and techniques. The approach is interdisciplinary and group-centered. Self-understanding of the teacher's sexuality is essential to the process. SIECUS, through its Newsletter, publishes lists of places where sex-education training is available. The Brown Trust associated with the University of Oregon sponsors training programs. New York University, Syracuse University, University of Connecticut, University of North Carolina, University of South Carolina, University of Southern California, Montclair State College, and the University of Maryland all offer courses through the school term.

In spite of the various academic offerings, which teachers, counselors, nurses and other professionals utilize, it appears that they feel the training is inadequate because of the lack of on-the-job supervision and consultation. AASEC encourages its trainees to ask for supervision. The organization is developing a corps of supervisors and consultants who will be available to assist trainees and others throughout the United States. Universities and other organizations dealing with sex-eduaction training are likewise deeply interested in supplying such assistance to the professionals who enroll for sex-education training.

Family-Planning Centers

Family-planning centers traditionally have been medically oriented and usually are part of a hospital, clinic, or planned-parenthood complex. The doctor and nurse customarily rendered medical services which included a) assisting the patient in choosing her contraceptive method, b) explaining the ways in which different methods of contraception work, c) the advantages and disadvantages of each method, d) providing the patient with a pelvic examination and necessary blood and urine tests, including pap smear and sickle-cell analysis and blood pressure, e) taking the patient's medical history, including sexual development, conception history and marital status.

The patient received her contraceptive device, and if she was a teen-ager the chances were, if she didn't receive an I.U.D. (intrauterine device), that she and 50 per cent of her active peers would become pregnant again within eighteen months.

Apparently the average woman needs a more comprehensive service to help her understand her feelings about herself as a sexual person. She wonders about her partner and the differences in their responses. She has a lot of questions about him. A common question that comes up is:

"Why, when he is finished, does he turn over and go to sleep? He doesn't seem to care about me." Many patients, too, have social problems which involve financial and Medicaid registration, housing, along with medical and school concerns of young children.

The National Center for Family Planning, Department of Health, Education and Welfare funds over 500 family-planning centers in the United States. The national goal and policy of this agency reflects the need for local centers to deliver comprehensive services to the poor which go beyond the delivery of contraceptive devices and information about them. In addition to physicians, nurses, social workers and community health aides, the sex-education counselor at the Howard University Family Planning Center performs the following functions:

ACTIVITIES OF HEALTH EDUCATION COUNSELOR

1. Training community workers in sex education, interviewing and able to clarify to patients various facets of sex education and counseling.

2. Meeting with the community workers during two weekly sessions for in-teaching sex education to their patients and discussing cases they are handling.

3. Staff consultant in sex education and counseling to social workers, nurses and others.

4. In-service training for nurses.

5. Individual and group counseling with patients, especially unwed teen-age mothers and fathers.

6. Individual counseling on marital and sex counseling, including abortion, sterilization and sex-related problems which bear upon effective use of family-planning devices.

7. Consulting and training professionals and paraprofessionals in the community in sex and family-life education and counseling.

TYPES OF PROBLEMS SEEN BY
HEALTH EDUCATION COUNSELOR

1. Abortion—from decision to postoperative depression feelings.

2. Sterilization.

3. Frigidity. Woman feels dissatisfied with her own performance or criticism from mate.

4. Inability to have an orgasm.

5. Mixed attitudes concerning her femininity.

6. Premature ejaculation. Attitude of female patient (negative) and anxiety of male toward inability to please.

7. The demasculinizing female—rejects male efforts to please.

8. Overcritical of family-planning devices to the point where apathy exists and none is used.

9. Resistance to use of recommended birth-control device because mate or family is against use.

10. Supersititions and myths about birth control and family planning which prevent effective use of birth control.

11. First out-of-wedlock birth, abortion of teen-ager, 13–20 years of age (group counseling).

12. Second out-of-wedlock pregnancy for all age groups (group counseling).

13. Marital conflicts centered on sexual problems:
    a. extramarital sexual relations,
    b. triangle involving unmarried partners,
    c. family disintegration projected on relationships with children because of dissatisfaction with partners in affectionate roles.

14. Needs assistance in discussing sexual development with children.

15. Premarital counseling involving sexual information and discussion of areas of adjustment in interpersonal relationships:
    a. social,
    b. psychological,
    c. spiritual,
    d. financial,
    e. interaction.

16. Menopause. Need for reassurance of femininity and capacity for sexual pleasure. Other factors involving male.

17. Sex and family-life education when requested.

18. Parent-child conflicts centered on sex play of child, dissatisfaction with companions and dating partners.

19. Insecurities in role of female as partner to mate and in mothering role.

20. Fertility problems. Feelings of inadequacy as a female due to inability to have children.

21. Males seeking assistance concerning impotency, self-image problems, premarital problems concerning foreplay, sexual intercourse.

Church Groups

The three major religious groups in the United States are involved to various degrees in conducting classes, seminars, week-end programs, and retreats for children, youth and parent groups in sex education.

The Unitarian Church has aggressively pursued teaching and counseling in human sexuality for a good number of years. Many programs are conducted within the religious schools which children and youth attend on Sunday mornings. At the present time a package called "About Your Sexuality" which includes texts, film strips, and group-centered discussions is being used nationally by many of the Unitarian churches. Leaders are being trained during week-end sessions to present this material to parents and youth. The emphasis is interdisciplinary with a view toward provoking frank discussions on self-attitudes and values and facilitating using the language of sex. Some of the film strips available for parents and adolescents explicitly depict the act of sexual intercourse. The text deals with the sensitive areas of masturbation, homosexuality, sexual intercourse out of marriage, and the like. The approach is one of understanding and accepting various patterns of sexual behavior in others. Decision-making approaches to learning are incorporated in the methodology.

Many churches use the week-end days of Saturday and Sunday for an intensive experience in family-life and sex education. Many programs originate with a committee composed of parents and youth, the minister and coordinator. The committee explores the needs and readiness of the congregants for a suitable program. Usually the group focuses on the need for information, the need to enhance communication, and the need to learn approaches for problem-solving, as major concerns.

TWO-DAY SESSION

A typical program for a two-day session may follow this format:

Saturday
  9:00   Registration and coffee.
  9:30   Lecture: Why Do We Need Sex Education Today?
10:00   Panel of two parents and two youths respond with "What We Need to Help Us in Today's World."
10:30   Questions from the floor.
11:00   Coffee break
11:30   Small groups: Parents and their children separate into different groups.

        Parents view film on "Boy to Man," and "Girl to Woman," and with a leader discuss the appropriateness of film, explore their attitudes about sexual development and sexual behavior of their children.

        Children are divided in groups according to age levels—primary, junior high school, and high school. They, too, view films.

        The children from grades K–3 view a film on human and animal reproduction, plant reproduction and family life. The 4–6 grades view a film on menstruation or "Girl to Woman" for the girls and "Boy to Man" for the boys. Discussions are led by group leaders. (Boys and girls meet separately.)

        The junior-high-school group are generally concerned with dating patterns or sexual activities which would be received favorably by their peers. The film "Social Sex Attitudes" or

"Phoebe" (teen-age pregnancy) or "A Moral Dilemma for Teenagers" usually provokes a relevant discussion.

The high-school youth is concerned with making appropriate moral judgments and developing his own value system. The need for autonomy and self-direction is often expressed by the young men and women in these discussion groups. "I need to learn on my own even if I make mistakes" . . . "I'm tired of having my parents treat me as though I were a child" . . . "Don't they trust me? After all, they raised me and they should have some confidence that they did their job well" . . . "Didn't they make mistakes while they were growing up, and it didn't kill them?" They enjoy "rapping" and getting a feel of how their peers think. Films are often an intrusion on their desire to talk matters out with each other. Discussions on "How Far Do You Go?" "Contraception Information and Sources of Its Availability," "Parental Attitudes Toward Sexual Activities of Teenagers" are favorite topics.

12:30　Box lunch and informal talk.

 2:00　Entire group meets and representatives from each group present their evaluation of the morning session and share their reactions with each other.

 3:00　Lecture and discussion by a religious leader on "Developing Religious Values of Love, Respect and Trust." (The objective is to reinforce human sexuality with the importance of love and affection in human relationships.)

 4:00　Close of Saturday session. The Committee usually gets together to check out the program for Sunday or to modify Sunday's program, if necessary.

Sunday

 9:30　Sermon in services centered on "What Is Love?" "Human Sexuality Is Part of Healthy Human Relations." "How Does God Feel About Human Sexuality?" "Is the Family Still the Most Important Social Unit?" "Is there a Generation Gap or a Veneration Gap Between Parents and Their Children?" "Is Marriage Old-Fashioned?"

11:30　Mixed (both adults and young people) small-group discussion on the sermon. The leading questions put to the group as a starting point by the leader might be: "How do you feel about the service? Was it relevant to you?"

12:30　Box lunch and informal talk.

2:00   Series of role-playing situations depicting boy-girl conflicts, parent-child conflicts, and husband-wife conflicts. After each dramatization, the general audience breaks up into small groups to discuss the conflict presented and give their reaction to the way in which the conflicts were resolved.

4:00   Evaluation of the two days by general comments from the group. Suggestions for a continuing program.

A Teen-age Series is conducted by many church groups in the form of a Sunday afternoon or evening supper meeting for teen-agers with invited speakers each week to talk and lead a discussion.

Parent Education Seminars may be conducted as "Couples Group," "Young Married Group," "Parent-Child Relations Group" and "One Parent Group." The group decides on its agenda and usually sets the series of weekly meetings for four to six consecutive group meetings. During the last session the group often make plans for continuation when the program is successful.

Parent Education

In a variety of settings groups of adult or teen-age parents may meet in a school, social agency, clinic, church, juvenile court, health center, community mental health clinic, or in any setting which includes parents as part of its educational or counseling program. Group coffee sessions can be organized for the morning, luncheon or after-school periods. It is usually necessary to plan evening sessions if fathers are to attend and there is to be discussion among couples.

Parents may commit themselves to four, six, or eight once-a-week sessions. Often, when a lengthy program stretching over three or four months is planned, parents are reluctant to join. It is better to plan a short program and stretch it when genuine interest to continue is generated within the group.

Parents are interested in learning more about, and gaining a better understanding of, normal sexual development. Many are concerned with alleged "abnormal behavior" and are looking for fast answers to alleviate their anxieties. In a well-led group, they learn the importance of sharing and mutually assisting one another in learning how to approach their concerns in a rational humanistic way. Sharing and caring of group members are important criteria in establishing a good group.

The following topics are usually important to parent groups:

1. Learning to be a boy or a girl (The discovery of sex differences).

2. Preschool and primary child.
   a. When children first ask about birth.
   b. What to do about masturbation.
   c. What to do about sex play, sex talk.
   d. What about parental nudity and privacy?
3. How your child learns to control his impulses.
   a. The development of conscience.
   b. The management of feelings.
   c. The meaning of discipline.
4. Encouraging healthy sex identification in the growing boy and girl.
5. Questions preadolescent children ask.
   a. About their changing bodies and feelings.
   b. About social life and its pressures.
6. Adolescent years. Problems and joys of developing a solid identity as an acceptable male or female.
7. Parent guidance.
   a. Setting limits.
   b. Understanding the social scene.
8. The college period. Preparation for independent living.

Your Growing Child and Sex, a book by Helene S. Arnstein, covers the topics in this outline and was specially written as a parents' guide in consultation with the Child Study Association of America.

Preparing the Community for Sex-Education Programs

Many a well-intentioned teacher, dedicated to her role of fulfilling the learning needs of the children under her care, unwittingly rushes in with a sex-education program. She finds to her dismay that she has irritated and provoked the parents and created a furor over the 45 minutes she spent showing the film "Girl to Woman" to her sixth-grade class of girls and then having the school nurse answer the students' questions. Opposition groups and individual parents have forced the discontinuance of sex-education programs in many communities throughout the country.

A classic situation is the city of Anaheim, California. During the 1960's the John Birch Society and its various satellite groups were most active. The issue so polarized parents and some religious leaders that election to the school board sometimes hinged on the candidate's position on sex education.

During the past five years, the author has traveled throughout the United States and consulted with many citizens who were grappling with the problem of whether or not to initiate a sex-education program in their communities. It is quite clear that, irrespective of the children's needs, the readiness of the community is central to the success of any sex-education program. The following procedures are essential and critical to attaining the goals that well-intentioned professionals seek. The process involves a group-centered approach focused on the community.

Step 1. Any teacher, supervisor, principal or school administrator who is interested in developing a program needs to start with the parent leaders in his school or school district. If a teacher is the initiator she must gain support and approval from her superiors and they in turn must reach to the highest level of school authority.

Step 2. A small committee of key people is then formed to investigate and determine the receptiveness of the parents whose children will be involved. If the group feels that there are many parents who oppose sex education, then these parents will need to meet in small groups with the informed professionals who will patiently answer their questions and help them to overcome their anxieties. Most interested parents have questions which relate to *a*) content of the program, *b*) values to be taught, and *c*) qualifications of the teachers who will be involved in the program. The sympathetic administrator will be sensitive to the parents' concerns and work with them in a continuous dialogue.

On the other hand, when it appears that only a small organized minority is vocal in its opposition, they too should be seen in a small-group setting and be given the opportunity to ventilate their anger and state their position. The professional should patiently answer their prejudices one by one.

Step 3. An Advisory Committee of community leaders who represent the leading components of the community and whose children attend the schools should be organized and chaired by a school administrator. This committee should be composed of representatives from religious groups, parent groups, medical and allied health groups, social-service and psychological groups, and the legal profession.

The function of the Advisory Committee consists generally of advising and supporting the school personnel in over-all policy concerning the nature of the program, its philosophy, concepts and approaches. The committee members cooperate in setting goals for different levels of education. They review films, curriculum and reference materials. Although this may appear to be a tedious task involving a good deal of time, it is well worth the effort to proceed with this educational process for committee members. Once the committee members become familiar with the total approach, they often tend to become ardent supporters and defenders.

Step 4. The Advisory Committee spearheads parent meetings in individual schools. It is recommended that a panel of committee members present their ideas to the group concerning "What is Sex Education?" and "Why the Community Ought to Consider It for Their Children."

It is essential that parents be given an opportunity at the end of the panel and talks to meet in small groups, and discuss their feelings. A member of the Advisory Committee should sit in and lead each of the small groups.

Step 5. After the general meetings a questionnaire should be distributed to all parents asking whether they wish to have sex education for their children and study groups for themselves. They should be asked as to the content they would like to see included, the teacher qualifications they consider necessary, and the approach they would like to see used. If fewer than 80 per cent of those who answer are in favor of sex education, then the administrators need to do more ground work and further education of parents before they proceed.

Step 6. The administrators need to have technical experts to help them in developing a curriculum which is in harmony with the Advisory Committee's recommendation. The curriculum drawn up by this Curriculum Committee should not be put into practice until teachers are adequately trained.

Step 7. Teacher training through in-service courses, institutes, or graduate-school courses needs to be accomplished before any pilot program is introduced.

Step 8. Teachers who are to participate in the program ought to be those who volunteer because of their personal interest in the program. They should then be screened by a professional committee within the school complex as to their attitudes, values, and ability to relate to both students and parents.

Step 9. The initial program should be small, subject to evaluation and considered experimental. During this period of pilot testing, the teachers involved should have ready access to a consultant for assistance and advice. The school administrators should also have frequent meetings with the Advisory Committee during this period to keep them advised and share with them some of the kinks in the program that need to be ironed out.

Step 10. During this step, the Curriculum Committee works on revising and broadening the program where it has been found to be successful. If it has not been successful, alternate approaches and programs are tested. Teacher training continues for those who become part of the teaching corps.

Step 11. Parent education is introduced as parallel education. Realistically parents are the prime educators of their children, and by having them involved, the children in the family are helped, the school and parent become closer and more trusting partners, and the children reap the benefits as well as their parents.

Interpreting Sex Education and Counseling Programs to Parents

In the final analysis, the success or failure of any community program in sex education and counseling will depend in large measure on the adequacy with which such a program is interpreted to the parents of the children who will be involved in the program. This is particularly true when the program is designed to include children in the lower grades. Every community situation is different, and no single method of interpretation will be completely adequate for all. What is suggested here is a model of interpretation whose tone and stance has proven useful in a wide variety of situations. With suitable modification, it will be a useful guide for those who are responsible for this all-important aspect of any successful program.

EDUCATION FOR PARENTS

Parents are becoming increasingly aware of the need for sex education for their children. Finding out, for you, may have been a difficult problem. You want something better for your children.

Sex education for responsible adulthood, for marriage and family relations, is more than teaching the biological facts of reproduction. Human sexuality can be more fully understood if you view and value it as a healthy part of our total personality. Sexuality and your child's growth and development go together from infancy through adulthood. Sexual identity is an important part of your child's self-image and affects every phase of his life. In your home or on trips, your child may see mother or other women pregnant and wonder why their "bellies" are growing. In some homes sex is hush-hush and dirty. From infancy, children are learning attitudes. Later in life, your child's interests, courses in high school and college, and career will be influenced by his sex.

Sexuality also involves the way maturing adolescents and adults satisfy and cope with their sexual needs and urges as responsible and committed human beings.

Human sexuality includes the social and family roles children and adults play. We may be a sister or brother, husband or wife, aunt or uncle, grandmother, grandfather, or just good friend of the family—yet our sexuality gives a distinct character to our relationships in and out of the family. Our friendships and relationships at work are directly affected by our sex. Many young children have difficulty understanding and learning these roles. The parent of children brought up in a one-parent home may have an added chore in helping the children gain confidence in their sexual identity. In recent years, many leading behavioral scientists have stressed the need for young boys and girls to develop strong male and female images early in life.

Your child will acquire sex education not merely from answers to his questions, but also from the kind of life experiences he has within the home. If the family atmosphere is harmonious he will build confidence in himself and marriage. This doesn't mean that parents shouldn't fight or argue in front of the children. On the contrary, arguments and fights that work toward solutions are realistic and healthy. However, the over-all impression that the child has of his parents and home ought to be that of a happy home where family members love one another and cooperate in a helpful way.

Parents may create unintentional difficulties by favoring their boys over their girls, or expecting the children to take sides when they are having problems. If you love and respect each other, and accept and respect your child's sexuality as well, he will probably grow and develop as a healthy sexual person with a feeling of self-worth and self-pride.

You, as parents, may be fearful that new values, standards, and behavior patterns contrary to your own will be taught your child. In a well-developed program, parent representatives will be consulted before a course of study is introduced into the classroom. The sensitive trained teacher is aware of the values and standards in her school community. She refrains from imposing her own values concerning human sexuality, nor does she pass judgment on the values of the families whose children she teaches.

The school can present in an orderly fashion, specific information and concepts that build upon and complete the work of the home. School and parents should participate in an ongoing dialogue that will lead to mutual planning and cooperation in formulating and improving programs of sex education. In the process of cooperating in these programs, educators and parents can learn to trust and understand each other—all to the benefit of the children under their care.

THE SCHOOL'S OBJECTIVES FOR THE PRIMARY CURRICULUM

The child's sex education at school begins in the kindergarten. At this period in his life, he is curious and interested. He may be full of questions. Some children need more time and show an interest at a later period. The child's vocabulary at this age often reflects the names of his sex organs and toilet habits used by his parents or friends.

Goals can be set forth only in general terms. The learning rate and coverage of material described here will vary from class to class. This outline is set forth as an over-all guide for parents.

The objectives during the primary grades (K–3) for the curriculum include the following:

1. To help the child build a healthy attitude toward all parts of his body.

2. To appreciate and be aware of the physical sex differences in girls and boys and develop confidence and pride in being a boy or a girl.

3. To use words for all body parts which are universally understood and accepted (i.e., penis, vagina, urinate, bowel movement, toilet).

4. To learn the meaning of being a cooperating member of a family with specific roles and relationships.

5. To know the elementary facts of human reproduction.

6. To ask questions and participate in class or group discussions without embarrassment.

Of course these goals will vary and the instruction in terms of time and material will also change according to the age and grade of the child.

PROGRAMS FOR THE KINDERGARTEN AND FIRST YEAR

The first important concept taught is that *the family is the basic unit of life*. Affection, health, social, emotional and other basic needs are provided for in the family. Each child belongs to a family. Families differ in size, culture, social economics and religion. Each member in the family has an important role whether he is young or old.

A second concept dealt with is that *all living beings produce their likeness*. Under this concept the children learn first that animals have parents upon whom they depend. Then they understand that all children have a father and mother who are a male and a female. They learn that animals are parents and have babies and that this also applies to human beings. Within each species, the child focuses on the different pattern of development unique for each individual.

A third concept taught suggests that *there are general patterns of growth with variations*. Plants grow according to their species in a certain way, but are affected by soil, climate, moisture and variations in the seed. Animals grow in different sizes, shapes, colors both within and without the species. Children grow at different rates and in different ways, also boys and girls differ in their shape and size.

A fourth concept is that *all parts of the body are healthy and can be described by a name.* Children should be taught words that are universally known.

The first concept is that *the child is a member of a family.* Families are different in many ways but all families have good qualities. Mothers and fathers have responsibilities but each has different tasks. Brothers and sisters are different and have different roles. Their dress, speech and attitude may be different also. The primary-grade child has his responsibilities in the family. The child depends upon an adult for his care. This person may be his parent or someone who takes his parent's place.

The second concept is that *living things grow.* Plants grow, animals grow, and the child also grows physically, emotionally, mentally and socially. Although the types of growth are listed separately, each one depends upon the others. Growth is a continuous process which begins before the actual birth of the child.

SEX ATTITUDES AND KNOWLEDGE FOR PARENTS

With a knowledge of what the teacher and students are sharing in class you can build the values, attitudes and behavior that form the moral judgments for responsible sexual behavior by your child.

Your child's questions concerning sex are originally no different from those asked about food or games. He sees and wonders about pregnancy, where he came from, his body shape and form, and the differences between girls and boys. His questions may appear to be never ending. With patience you can share with your child the joy of discovery and newfound knowledge given in a loving way. A wonderful experience for both parent and child.

A child's personality does not develop by chance. His adult sexual behavior will be determined by the personality he develops as he grows. As an adult he will love or hate not because he was born that way but because he learns to love or to hate from you his parents and other important people in his life.

Sex is fundamentally a healthy powerful drive. A child needs help in accepting himself or herself as a boy or girl. You can help by giving your child the feeling you are pleased with his sexual identification. He needs an understanding of his body. He is curious and will explore and discover, if he is a boy, that playing with his penis is a pleasurable experience. Your daughter will find her vagina a source of pleasure. For the child this is an innocent gesture from which he or she derives pleasure.

Sex information cannot be readily absorbed by your child in one sitting. He can only assimilate one idea at a time. If he is not sure, the chances are that he will ask the same question again and again. This does not necessarily mean that he is preoccupied with sex. It usually shows the struggle he is having in trying to put his ideas together.

The important point for parents is to discover your child's feelings and thoughts at the moment and encourage him to talk about the subject. When he asks where the new baby came from, don't snicker and say that you swallowed a watermelon seed. He will soon discover that you fooled him and he may not come back to you when he has another question. Parents should answer a child's question as openly and simply as possible. Try not to put him off. He trusts and relies on you to help him sort things out. He wants you to understand and respect his desire for knowledge and information.

A mother who accepts her femininity will give her daughter the feeling that to be a woman is great. She does this by example in behavior, clothes, voice, and attitude toward the opposite sex. This education based on the child's observation of the positive attitudes and values expressed by her mother is a dynamic force toward healthy growth. A mother can tenderly teach her daughter with pride that when she grows up she will have breasts and hair on her body similar to mother's and that when she is a grown woman it is possible she will have a husband and babies too, such closeness and warmth can alleviate any anxiety the child may have felt about her own growth and sexuality.

When a child's questions remain unanswered or are evaded because of adult embarrassment, he may investigate in an attempt to satisfy his curiosity. It is not uncommon to observe a little boy pick up a girl's dress. He is not being naughty; he is merely attempting to find answers. Nor is it abnormal for a child to peer under the skirt or look down into the neckline of his mother's dress. When a child experiments or investigates, he is communicating his need for knowledge, reassurance, and pleasure.

The most difficult question for most parents comes from children five to eight years old when they ask, "But how do babies start to grow?" This question can be answered simply, however, by a relaxed parent, along the following lines:

"When mothers and fathers love each other, they want to come close to each other. Fathers have cells called *sperm* which are in a bag behind their penis. The bag is called a *scrotum*. A father's sperm must meet the mother's egg in the mother's body where the baby will grow. The sperm leave the father's body through his penis. He uses his penis to place the sperm in the mother's vagina. The sperm are contained in a fluid called semen. Although the daddy places only a small amount of semen in the mother's vagina, it contains millions of sperm in it. The sperm can move and sometimes one reaches mother's egg and joins it. The egg is then fertilized and a baby begins to grow. It takes nine months before a baby is old enough to be born."

When attitudes, values, and facts are shared between parents and children in an open and trusting way, a fine foundation is laid for healthy sexuality and maturity.

Nearly all children will ask questions about birth by the time they are seven. Some will do this at a much earlier time. Those who never ask at all are probably not as trusting of the answer given. Without doubt, "Where did I come from?" is sure to be on the mind of normal children. It is a question full of wonder and curiosity. As a matter of fact, mothers and fathers expect the question, hoping that when it comes they will be able to answer it to the satisfaction of themselves and their child.

Please bear in mind that where answers are not given at home, healthy curious children with eager minds will seek answers elsewhere. Hopefully the classroom will become the forum for accurate and understandable facts which the child can comfortably comprehend. Otherwise, the child will set about exchanging tidbits of information with school friends who are equally confused and uninformed. Much of this friend-to-friend information is shared in an atmosphere of conspiracy. They appear to be involved in "forbidden talk" which they were made to believe is only proper conversation for older brothers and sisters or adults.

Parents often wonder what to do about *nudity* and *modesty* both in and outside the home in helping their children toward a healthy adjustment. Concerns about nudity and modesty are very closely tied together. Many parents are apprehensive lest their children grow up being immodest and too casual about nudity. Children from infancy on enjoy their nudity in the bath, romping with very little on at the beach, and running about the house naked. Small children are naturally curious and not at all self-conscious about their bodies, but the thought that they will behave this way always creates tensions and anxieties in some parents.

Somehow, when parents are comfortable with their bodies and respect each other's need for privacy, the children sail into their school years with attitudes and behavior that wears well both in and outside the home.

Children are basically imitators, and parents serve as models during the early years. A child soon learns to close the door when he is going to the toilet or taking his bath if his parents do. When he arrives at school age he usually enjoys dressing and undressing in private. However, if others are sharing the room or happen to come upon him while he is in the process, he accepts this as part of family life. He carries a healthy attitude toward nudity when he uses a public shower, changes clothing for gym classes or camps out with a group his age.

Sex talk is not unusual among children between the ages of four and ten. They may giggle together when they urinate or may laugh about "dirty words." They may touch each other's genitals or buttocks, and indulge in self-stimulation. The latter is less frequent than during the preschool years. Sometimes various types of body play involving the genitals comes about through playing "doctor" or "hospital."

Where children appear so absorbed in sex play that they lose interest in other activities usually enjoyed by children at this age, parents ought to take a second look. "Are they feeling guilty and withdrawing from other experiences?" "Are they developing patterns of sex play at times where they are drawing attention to themselves?"

Obviously, where excessive sex play seems to get in the way of friendship and various other experiences, parents ought to pay closer attention to supervision of the child's free time and to help him broaden his range of interests.

Many parents fear that masturbation is a bad habit which will prevent the child from developing into a healthy adult who will enjoy lovemaking and mating with a member of the opposite sex. The truth is, however, that masturbation is normal behavior and does not necessarily interfere with healthy heterosexual relationships. Parents should learn to see masturbation as a part of the growth and learning process of a boy or girl. Punishing the child or making threats involving castration for the boy or inability to have children for the girl is senseless and can even be damaging. The situation is best ignored when possible. If practised in public, it is well to tell the child in a warm accepting manner his parents accept and understand why he masturbates, but would prefer, for his sake, that he do it in private. The only real harm connected with masturbation is the worry and tension that go with it when parents and child believe it is wrong. As with sex play, children who masturbate in the extreme so that it interferes with their usual routine and activities are perhaps lacking proper supervision. Maybe they are using masturbation as a substitute for pleasures which other children receive from their round of activities. When parents are aware of the child's overwhelming preoccupation with sex play or masturbation, professional advice should be sought.

Sex education has a language all its own. Somehow because of the emotional feelings of parents involving the teaching of the vocabulary, many children are deprived from learning the appropriate vocabulary. Children will learn some kind of vocabulary whether or not their parents teach it to them. Unfortunately many parents are embarrassed and inhibited from helping their children develop an adequate vocabulary. In spite of the handicaps these parents bring to their role as sex educators, they should attempt to teach their children the correct and commonly accepted terms.

Teaching the correct words early saves a lot of relearning later. The right word properly taught also carries with it the right attitude. When a child starts school his baby talk and nicknames may be embarrassing to him when the other children in class use the correct terms. Furthermore, parents and their children are usually more comfortable and less emotional about the sex vocabulary if the correct words are learned before children form an emotional attitude toward sex. With many parents, the most comfortable choice varies with the child's age and with whom he is talking. They prefer to use the baby terms when their children are under five and the scientific terms when their children start school. There is no rigid rule about all this, however. The outcome is what matters. Again, the child's use of sex words and his attitude when he uses them is the important issue.

Experimental and innovative programs have been sparked by public and private financial support. The opportunity for evaluation of the behavioral objectives in sex-education demonstration programs came about through Federal-funded Pacemaker grants.

The introduction of mass media through films, records, charts, plastic models, pamphlets and well-researched textbooks has helped to improve teaching and counseling. However, the need to train more competent educators and counselors is compelling and immediate. Training programs are available for elementary, secondary and college level teaching, and in an increasing number of professional schools. The number and effectiveness of such programs will almost certainly increase in the future.

10

Curricula for Sex Education

Before any curriculum content is planned, those responsible need to spend time sorting out the objectives they seek in sex education. Whether or not a full-scale program is undertaken, a skeletal developmental program should be projected for the future, so that in planning specifically for any particular grade the curriculum planners will be aware of what areas have been or should be learned beforehand and also have a knowledge of what would logically follow. This overview is essential to planning the most effective program for the individual child.

Team teaching appears to be a most effective approach to sex education and ought to be considered in the curriculum planning. In urban centers opportunities abound for enlisting the help of experts from the community. Since a comprehensive school program in sex education should be multidimensional, it will need to involve teachers in all subject areas as well as staff members such as the counselor, school nurse, doctor and psychologist or social worker.

Sex and sexuality ought to be dealt with in many courses in the curriculum rather than be confined to one course labeled "Sex Education," "Personal and Family Living" or the like. It can be introduced in courses in biology, sociology, health, history, literature, economics, and psychology, and at the elementary level in science, social studies, English or at the teachable moment when it occurs.

The following seven objectives will serve as guides in working out realistic goals for specific schools, community groups and health centers. It is essential that the programs be consumer-oriented, with the consumer in this case being the child and his family.

OBJECTIVES OF SEX EDUCATION

1. To provide whatever factual information the individual desires on all aspects of sex and family planning.
2. To increase sexual self-understanding so that individuals may become self-confident members of their own sex.

3. To increase understanding of the opposite sex in order to promote positive relationships between the sexes.

4. To understand other patterns of sex behavior among peers, within the youth and adult generation, and in various cultures, so as to prepare individuals to accept various sexual life-styles.

5. To open up communication and promote understanding between adults and youth.

6. To develop an appreciation of sex as an integral part of a healthy life.

7. To enable each individual to work towards improving the quality of his life through family planning.

Preschool Through Third Grade

By the time a child is three years old he has developed a sense of his maleness or, if a girl, a sense of her femaleness. The degrading factors involved in sexism and stereotyping of sex roles can be dealt with and corrected from the time a child is born. However, the preschool-third grade teaching team are afforded an excellent opportunity to teach pride and understanding of self.

The Glen Cove (N.Y.) public schools and Mrs. Rose Daniel, consultant, have set up curriculum objectives which reflect the essence of a well-thought-out guide. These curriculum objectives are outlined below:

KINDERGARTEN

1. Know sex differences between girls' and boys' bodies.
2. Give direction toward male or female role in adult life.
3. Learn correct names for body parts and terms concerned with elimination.
4. Understand that human baby develops inside body of mother in uterus.
5. Understand baby gets milk from mother's breast by nursing.
6. Appreciate that there are good body feelings.
7. Learn to recognize signs of love and devotion within family.
8. Develop idea of continuity of living things—incubate hen's eggs.

FIRST YEAR

1. Understand egg cell is basic to new life.
2. Learn that some animals hatch from eggs and others develop inside body of mother until birth.
3. Appreciate wonder of human body.
4. Develop sense of responsibility for own body.
5. Appreciate efforts of mother and father for family members.
6. Recognize influence of emotions on body health.

SECOND YEAR

1. Learn that different animals need different amounts of time to get ready to be born.
2. Understand that the egg cell does not develop into a baby by itself—role of father.
3. Understand the process of internal fertilization.
4. Learn that some animals are born alive through a special opening in the mother's body.
5. Recognize that growing up brings responsibility.
6. Appreciate importance of mutual love and consideration in family.
7. Understand composition of family does not necessarily determine happiness of family.

THIRD YEAR

1. Know that growing up means more than just getting bigger.
2. Appreciate the amazing structure and function of major body organs.
3. Develop increasing sense of responsibility to self, peer group and family.
4. Understand that each person's unique heredity is determined at moment of fertilization.
5. Understand function of gonads and process of menstruation in human productive cycle.
6. Study life cycles of various animals, including humans.

A team of four District of Columbia teachers of preschool and elementary-school children, working in a Title III program, developed and administered the following fine program:

PRE-KINDERGARTEN AND KINDERGARTEN PROJECT

Title　　　—My Family and Me
Population —Teachers)
　　　　　　Parents　)　　　Pre-Kindergarten
　　　　　　Aides　　)　　　Kindergarten
　　　　　　Counselor
　　　　　　Nurse
How Long—9 Weeks
How Often—1 Day per Week
A. Concepts to be developed each week
　　1. Child belongs to a family
　　2. Families are different
　　3. Everybody is important
　　4. Animals have families
　　5. Family health and cleanliness (doctor or nurse)
　　6. Roles of each family member
　　7. Child belongs to a family (self-image)—second week
　　8. Animals have families (second week)
　　9. Exhibit and assembly program

B. Activities
   1. Books: *Everybody Has a House; Grandmother and I; Grandfather and I,* etc.
   2. Songs: *How Many People Live in Your House?* and others
   3. Paintings and drawings of families
   4. Bringing in pictures of our families
   5. Finger plays
   6. Poems
   7. Clay modeling—human and animal families
   8. Papier-mâché—human and animal families
   9. Dramatizing family life (projecting ourselves as future family members)
C. Culminating activity
   Counselor will invite parents and grandparents to school to see our exhibit on families—human and animal. Refreshments will be served and a short play will be presented by the children. This will be a spontaneous expression of family activities as they are played in our playhouse.

BIBLIOGRAPHY

BOOKS

Animal Families—Weil
Daddy Is Home—Blomquist
Our Family—Burkhardt
Daddies-Mommies—Carton
You and Your Family—Experimental Development Program
We Want a Little Sister—Matmuller
Mommies are for Loving—Ruth Penn
Sorely Trying Day—Russell Hoban
Big Brother—Zolotow
Love Is a Special Way of Feeling—Anglund
The New Pet—Flack

SONGS

"How Many People Live in Your House?" from *Singing Fun*—Webster
"Old MacDonald's Farm," from *Sharing Music*—American Book Co.
"Cows in The Pasture," from *Sharing Music*—American Book Co.
"Daddy's Lullaby," from *Magic of Music*—Ginn & Co.
"Everybody Loves Baby," from *Magic of Music*—Ginn & Co.
"My Dog Jack," from *Magic of Music*—Ginn & Co.
"Barn Yard Song," from *Growing With Music*—Prentice Hall

VISUAL AIDS
Filmstrips
"Animal Life"
"Learning About Animals"
Movies
"A Happy Family"
"Kittens—Birth and Growth"
"Mother Hen's Family"
"Miss Brown's Class Goes to the Zoo"
"Make Way for Ducklings"
"Story of Ping"
POEMS
"Ten Fingers," *Time for Poetry*—Arbuthnot
"Boy's Names," *Time for Poetry*—Arbuthnot
"This is the Mother," *Let's Do Finger Plays*—Grayson
"The Family," *Let's Do Finger Plays*—Grayson
"Little," *Time for Poetry*—Arbuthnot
"My Brother," *Time for Poetry*—Arbuthnot

Fourth Through Sixth Grade

Goals for the older elementary child should include:

1. Learn that certain glands regulate each person's unique pattern of body growth and development.
2. Appreciate wonders of circulatory, respiratory, and digestive systems and realize their functional potential is influenced by habits being developed.
3. Understand importance of protecting vital body parts from injury, i.e., during sports.
4. Appreciate miracle of reproduction and maternal care among various animals, including humans.
5. Learn to evaluate responsible and irresponsible behavior in peer and family group relationships.
6. Understand menstruation occurs as a natural part of a girl's growing up.
7. Understand seminal emissions occur as a natural part of a boy's growing up.
8. Learn that although nature readies our bodies for reproduction at puberty, several more years are needed to prepare for marriage and responsibility of parenthood.
9. Understanding one's emotions—feelings of love, anger, aggression—and how anxiety and guilt affect relationships between family members and friends.

As boys and girl approach puberty, there is need for an assessment of their feelings about themselves and others. They need help in how to build a confident self-image about themselves and their bodies.

A lesson starting with a drawing of self doing something they enjoy and then writing a composition on "Why I Enjoy Being a Girl/Why I Enjoy Being a Boy" brings out much feeling of pride and also uncertainty which they share with their peers. The drawings are then exchanged and shared by all the students. This can be followed with a "Put Yourself in Her Place" approach. Pre-puberty youngsters enjoy giving advice and counseling each other, and a game of this kind gives them ample opportunity.

CASE STUDY

Mary, an eleven-year-old only child, had learned to read even before she went to kindergarten. Mary's mother was often critical of Mary. She felt that Mary "always had her nose buried in a book" and that she was truly an "ugly duckling."

Before long, Mary began to believe that her mother's criticisms were true. In school, nobody had ever wanted Mary on any team. Because of her shyness and lack of confidence, her timing was off in every game, and she was convinced that she had no coordination at all.

Mary also had no doubt that she was homelier than almost every other girl. Years of being called "ugly duckling" had seen to that. As a matter of fact, Mary was not homely, but since she thought she was, she gave that appearance.

The situation reached a climax the day of the class picnic. Mary did not have a partner for the square dance. When she reported the incident at home, her mother's response was, "You brought this on yourself!"

Questions

What would you do if you were Mary?

Was this situation entirely Mary's fault?

What could have been done in the past to avoid this problem?

SUGGESTED ACTIVITIES

1. A panel discussion might consider permissive parents versus firm, disciplinarian parents.

2. The quest for independence begins in childhood and is essential for growing into adulthood. The intensity of the quest increases and reaches its peak around fifteen, sixteen, or seventeen years of age. It is interesting to have the students chart the steps of the quest beginning with self-feeding until pre-puberty.

3. An authority on "Growing Up Emotionally" would be an appropriate outside speaker for this chapter.

4. If possible, arrange for groups of students to visit another elementary school and a playground to observe the behavior of the children.

FURTHER READING

Levine, M. I., and Jean H. Seligmann, *The Wonder of Life*. Golden Press, 1952. A book for older children about the creation of life in animals and humans. Good glossary and diagrams.

AUDIO-VISUAL AIDS

Frustrating Fours and Fascinating Fives, 22 minutes.
From Sociable Six to Noisy Nine, 22 minutes.
From Ten to Twelve, 26 minutes.

All three are Ages and Stages Films, National Film Board of Canada.

Junior High School

The junior-high-school curriculum goes more in depth than the sixth-grade course of study on the reproductive system and body changes and their influence on interests, attitudes and feelings. The curriculum can deal with customs, values and standards in dating and in boy-girl relationships. Emphasis can be laid here on the developing aspects of maleness and femaleness and the various creative roles young people play. Because for many young people this is a time for sexual experimentation, the curriculum needs to deal with venereal disease, pregnancy that is unwanted, and the economic, social, legal and psychological factors involved in carrying on the responsibilities of adulthood.

The Family Life Education Program of the Flint Community Schools, Flint, Mich., coordinated by Dr. George C. Chamis, suggests the following four-session outline for eighth grade. This illustration of lesson content can be modified for seventh- and ninth-grade students:

SEX EDUCATION FOR EARLY ADOLESCENCE
EIGHTH GRADE CLASSES (4 sessions)

Specific Objectives
1. To interpret pubertal development, reproduction, fetal development, and birth.
2. To prepare boys and girls for healthy heterosexual relationships.

Suggested Vocabulary

1. Abortion	4. Conception	7. Fallopian tubes
2. Caesarean	5. Contraction	8. Fertilization
3. Chromosomes	6. Erection	9. Genes

10. Genitals	17. Nocturnal emissions	24. Seminal vesicles
11. Homosexual	18. Ovulation	25. Spinal column
12. Hymen	19. Pelvis	26. Syphilis
13. Intercourse	20. Pituitary	27. Urethra
14. Labor	21. Puberty	28. Vagina
15. Menopause	22. Pubic bone	29. Venereal
16. Menstruation	23. Rectum	

Introduction

Feel free to ask questions as we go along with our discussion. We are interested in three aspects of the subject, the facts, and the feelings and the attitudes that you have.

Materials

Dickinson Belskie models

Charts of male and female reproductive systems

Chart "Health Habits" for girls

Chart of vocabulary

Blackboard and chalk

Projector and films to be shown to both boys and girls: (1) "Boy to Man"; (2) "Girl to Woman."

Swartz, Wm., *Teacher's Handbook on Venereal Disease Education*, NEA Publication, 1965.

Suggested Outline for Four or More Sessions

I. Female reproductive system.

    A. Pelvic bones.

    B. Bladder and urethra.

    C. Rectum and anus.

    D. Uterus and vagina.

    E. Ovaries.

        (1) Hormone production.

            (a) Skin changes.

            (b) Shiny hair.

            (c) Breasts.

            (d) Wider hips.

        (2) Egg production.

    F. Ova.

        (1) 300,000 to 500,000 immature cells at birth.

        (2) 1/200 in length.

        (3) 300 to 400 released in lifetime.

        (4) Mature production beginning at 9 to 16 in age.

        (5) Fertilized egg.

        (6) Nonfertilized egg.

II. Growth and development.
   A. Fertilization.
   B. Heredity.
   C. Implantation.
   D. Describe development of embryo-fetus at 4 weeks, 6 weeks, 7 weeks, 2½ months, 3½ months, 4½ months, 5½ months and 7 months.
   E. Discuss function of placenta.
III. Labor and delivery.
   A. Signs of labor.
   B. Describe how uterine muscles contract resulting in child's birth.
   C. Return of uterus to usual size.
IV. Male reproductive system.
   A. Description of external organs.
      (1) Penis.
         (a) Circumcision.
         (b) Erection.
      (2) Scrotum.
         (a) Protection of testicles.
         (b) Temperature regulator.
      (3) Testicles.
         (a) Size.
         (b) Number.
         (c) Undescended.
         (d) When they descend.
      (4) Function of testicles.
         (a) Hormone production, pubic hair, beard, active oil production, lowering of voice.
         (b) Sperm production.
            1. Hereditary contribution.
            2. Size—1/500″ in length.
            3. Location of testicle.
   B. Description of internal organs.
      (1) Vas deferens.
      (2) Seminal vesicles.
      (3) Prostate gland.
   C. Nocturnal emissions.
      (1) Age of starting.
      (2) When it occurs.
      (3) Meaning.
   D. Masturbation.
      (1) Superstitions.
      (2) Psychological meanings.

    E. Attitudes to be promoted.
       (1) Respect for body.
       (2) Pride in becoming a man.
    F. Homosexuality.
  V. Simplified discussion of mating.
    A. Way of starting a family.
    B. Husbands' and wives' love for each other.
  VI. Menstruation.
    A. Time of puberty.
    B. Ovulation.
    C. Preparation of uterus.
    D. Flow from 5 to 7 days. Use of napkins.
    E. Good health habits (use chart).
       (1) Plenty of rest.
       (2) Good posture.
       (3) Proper exercise.
       (4) Three properly balanced meals each day.
       (5) Avoid fatigue.
       (6) Do not get chilled.
       (7) Keep happy.
    F. Attitudes to be promoted.
       (1) Pride in becoming a woman.
       (2) Pleasure in being healthy.
    G. Homosexuality.
    H. Menopause.
       (1) Meaning of term.
       (2) Age.
       (3) Symptoms.
       (4) Treatment if necessary.
  VII. Responsible Parenthood.
    A. Who is responsible for newborn child?
    B. Mother's role—What is a good mother?
    C. Father's role—What is a good father?
    D. Needs of infant.
    E. Contribution of other family members.
  VIII. Venereal Disease Education—What is it? How contacted?
  How it affects body? How cured?

Senior High School

During the high-school years, students are interested in interpersonal relationships. Many are dating on a steady basis, a few are planning to marry, and some are parents and living together as a married couple or just partners.

Key concepts to be explored are love, human sexuality, equality and responsibility. Leading content areas should include consideration of marriage, family planning, infant care, vocational choices and opportunities, divorce, unwed motherhood and fatherhood, masturbation, homosexuality, and conflicts confronting young men and women in their social and personal relationships.

A lesson or two on family planning is essential at this grade level. It should be taught in the frame of reference that the quality of life is the inherent right of each individual and that the potential for reaching this goal is best exemplified by planning parenthood and rearing wanted children.

The *American School Health Journal* issue of May 1967 in an article entitled "Growth Patterns and Sex Education" published an excellent suggested outline for teaching family planning to high-school students:

FAMILY PLANNING

A. Teachable material
1. Family planning means the development of a family according to a purposeful design, hopefully having children when they are wanted.
2. Factors to consider in planning a family
   a. finances
   b. educational goals for children
   c. the number of children wanted
   d. the need of husband and wife to adjust to each other in a marital relationship before a third party enters the relationship
   e. the acceptance of personal responsibility for controlling the population explosion
   f. the effects of planning on parents' attitudes toward the arrival of each child and upon his being accepted
3. Spacing children
   a. child-spacing is an aspect of family planning that involves having children at appropriate intervals
   b. reasons for spacing children
      (1) mother's health; spacing allows mother to recuperate physiologically and psychologically from each pregnancy before having another child
      (2) the long-range health and welfare of the children
         (a) the importance of an affectional maternal-infant re-

lationship to all aspects of the baby's growth and development

(b) spacing allows each child ample time to develop a feeling of security within the family unit before he is displaced from his role as "the baby" by a younger child

4. Procedures involved in family planning

Discuss the fact that there are family planning procedures available to and considered acceptable by persons of any social, religious and ethnic group. Description of family-planning devices or methods need be given; this information is also available from physicians, religious advisors and perhaps parents at the time a person is ready for marriage. Many young people will accept from members of their peer group advice and information about contraceptive measures that are either ineffective or dangerous to their health. Letting them know that there are appropriate methods, that families do use them, and that the subject may be one they will wish to discuss in greater detail with their families or religious or medical advisors or to explore further as a research project can help to counteract the problems of unwise experimentation, misunderstandings, and unanswered questions. Depending upon local circumstances, the teacher may wish to mention specific sources of reliable family planning information. Invite a family-planning consultant.

B. Profitable activities

1. Prepare reports on several different aspects of the "population explosion." Discuss the following topics:

a. the effects that value systems of persons in various cultures have upon the relative success of efforts to control the population explosion

b. the ways in which the population explosion is in turn affecting people's values

c. the role of the individual in controlling the population explosion

d. the right of an individual couple to determine the size of their family versus the right of a government to control family size in the interest of the total populace

e. the impact of the population explosion on such matters as the nation's economic development, family living, the individual's opportunity to realize his potential.

2. Develop a debate on the pros and cons of family planning.

3. Have each student in the class find out what it costs to rear one child in his particular family setting. Multiply this amount by the various numbers found in different families to determine the estimated minimum financial responsibility involved in rearing children.

4. List the problems that might develop as a result of attempting to maintain too large a family on too small an income.

5. Discuss whether children like to be members of a large family or of a small family. Point out the advantages and the disadvantages of each situation.

6. Discuss the changing patterns (as pointed out in the unit on Family Living) and the influence of family living in our culture upon family size.

7. Debate the advantages and the disadvantages of having a working mother.

8. A committee might be appointed to visit a Planned Parenthood clinic to talk to its director about the work done by this agency.

Sex Education and Counseling for Adults

To attempt to interpret to parents the needs of their children for sex education and counseling is to discover that these needs do not end with the years of formal academic training. The years after adolescence, as a matter of fact, include several periods during which sex-related problems can become acute:

1. The period during the early marital years.

2. The first pregnancy and arrival of the new family member.

3. The time when the children take flight from the home and build new relationships.

4. The sexual concerns of the "geriatric set."

Ironically in our western culture, body beauty and physique are still equated with sexual desire and potency. As physical aging takes place in face and form, and the many pressures of daily and family living surround us, the anxieties of aging adults increase. Often the psychological reaction to these multiple pressures is a desire for greater intimacy, identity and the personal reassurance of continuing sexually attractiveness and sexual competency.

In many instances when couples or parents seek help for their young, the presenting problem is often a cover for the relief they desire for themselves. The ability and sensitivity of the professional to respond and to view adults as sexual people is paramount to effective professional performance.

In spite of the increase in sexual communication through the mass media and personal dialogue, about 60 per cent of our adult population are concerned about some form of sexual dysfunctioning.

Irrespective of the specific needs of those seeking help and information, the sex educator and counselor might deem it wise to communicate some of the following essential facts to those adults who request help.

1. Partners need the reassurance from each other that it takes time to work out a satisfying sexual relationship. The fantasy wish in a new relationship says: "This sexual union will be complete and more beautiful than any other." On the other hand, both bring to this experience all their hangups, and self-doubts. Reassuring couples that it takes time —for some as long as a year—can be beneficial. But both need to be frank about their feelings. They need to express their likes and dislikes toward particular techniques, positions, and foreplay approaches so that through intimate sharing they learn together about each other's feelings and sexual needs.

2. During a first pregnancy the joy of expectant parenthood for husband and wife is euphoric. Yet women invariably turn to their mothers and intimate women friends to share their feelings about their new roles and expectancies. The expectant father may well revert to discussing his new state of bliss with his boss and colleagues. Obviously they both need to encourage the sharing of their feelings with each other. The sharing and delight and sometimes the disappointment of the woman in her physical appearance, awkward movements in bed, and fatigue in participating in sex play are often not openly and freely shared with her partner. A new sexual position which would be more comfortable can result in a delightful experience for both. Experimentation which pleases both can add new excitement during the pregnancy.

With the birth of the first child, the family tends to form a magic circle around the baby. Talk, activity, and an abundance of energy are concentrated on the precious being in the crib. Feeding time, bathing time, diaper-changing time become grandiose events in the household. Frustration time increases as well. The need to remain lovers who sexually excite each other and devoted parents as well is not an easy task, though it is one that has been surmounted by many caring adults. Questions like "Is it normal to have less desire after the children come?" "Orgasm is harder to come by now—why?" are frequently asked.

The sex educator knows that the questions are symptomatic of frustrations, fatigue, and communication failures that interfere with and impede continued satisfying coitus. It is important for couples to be reminded that although they are now parents, they are not each other's mother or father too, but adults who can continue to be lovers. They need to remind each other that they enjoy each other as woman and man both in and out of bed. If they can openly handle their hostility out of bed, it will leave them more time and pleasure for sex in bed.

3. The onset of menopause in the woman and the climacteric in the male brings into focus the need for sex educators to remind adults that they are growing older instead of growing old. Sexual activity and pleasure is based on hormones and habit—"the two H's" as it is often called. And habit is an important factor in continuing pleasurable sexual activity. However, many complicated and mixed feelings are involved because of the aging process. Related to physical aging is the feeling of loss of self-esteem in enacting physical sex activities.

To both partners, the onset of menopause reflects a sign of passing years and increased age. Rationally, couples learn that menopause starts somewhere between the early forties and mid-fifties. They also know that with good health, they can enjoy life into the seventies, so that menopause comes at a time where adults have many good years ahead for living and loving.

Today menopause need not be a time of deep emotional disturbance. The glandular disturbances can be corrected by competent medical care. Besides the process of menopause lasts for only several years for most women. Hot flushes and perspiration are related to the lack of sex hormones, which is correctable.

For the male, his sex aging process is not similar to the menopause. For him the process is gradual. Cessation of ovulation never takes place. His sperm count may diminish, but the dramatic event for the woman is evidence that she can no longer have children. For many women this is a blessing. She can exercise greater freedom and spontaneity in enjoying coitus. Males frequently fear the loss of power to have and maintain an erection. And when the anxiety is great, it may set off a spiral of sexual dysfunctioning.

Many sex counselors find that premature ejaculation and other degrees of impotency have a strong psychological component resulting from negative expectations that he, the male, will not be able to make it, and will fail both himself and his partner.

Statistically more than 25 million adults in the United States have reached the age of sixty. Out of this large population, a substantial percentage are involved in sexual expectations and disappointments. Our professional people can hardly manage to ignore the concerns that beset our senior citizens concerning their alleged sexless years. It is also interesting to note that in the early 1960's over 35,000 marriages a year took place wherein one of the partners was age 65 or older.

The following facts concerning sexual competency are supported by credible research findings, and ought to be shared by educators and counselors with those seeking assistance.

1. Masters and Johnson report that "the aging human female is fully capable of sexual performance at orgasmic response levels, particularly if she is exposed to regularity of effective sexual stimulation." This appears to carry over into the years after the menopause.

Similar to the female, the team of Masters and Johnson learned that in men after fifty the intensity and duration of the physical responses are lessened during the orgasmic cycle. This occurs in the main for men over 60 years of age. During these years, erection takes longer, ejaculation is less forceful and shorter in duration. They state "the human male's sexual responsiveness wanes as he ages" but "when regularity of sexual expression is maintained in a sexually stimulative climate within the marriage, a healthy male's capacity for sexual expression could extend beyond the seventies and into the eighty-year age level."

2. Regularity of sexual activity is the central factor to sexual responsiveness in both the aging male and female. It has been reported by Masters and Johnson that "those men [geriatric sample] currently interested in relatively high levels of sexual expression report similar activity levels from their formative years." Kinsey in his research supports these findings.

These conclusions help to eradicate the myth that one can use oneself up sexually in one's youth and therefore it is best to be less active during the formative years in order to save one's sexual potency for later on in life. Actually semen, like saliva, is quickly replaced by the body.

3. Lack of hormone production in the body during the post-menopausal years can be corrected with hormone-replacement therapy. When women complain of pain during contraction of the uterus possibly due to steroid imbalance, medical care can lessen this discomfort.

It is also possible medically to deal with problems where women complain of pain during penetration, or of a burning on urination which may develop from the thrusting movement of the penis because the vagina may have become tissue-paper-thin. Some medical doctors prescribe estrogen creams or suppositories which are applied locally to relieve and restore the vulva and vaginal tissues to their normal layers and correct the discomfort and complaints within several weeks.

Masters and Johnson sorted out six areas which they felt contributed to male sexual dysfunctioning:

1) monotony of a repetitious sexual relationship,
2) preoccupation with career or economic pursuits,
3) mental or physical fatigue,
4) overindulgence in food or drink,
5) physical and mental infirmities of either the man or his wife,
6) fear of failure.

Obviously all of these six factors are likely to occur during the maturing years. The sex counselor will need to be alert for early signs of these significant factors which contribute to sexual dysfunctioning.

Boredom and ennui which may settle in through repetitious sexual activity with a single partner is often precipitated and aggravated by sloppiness, careless personal hygiene which results in unattractive body odors, physical characteristics including obesity.

Variety in sex play can add much spice to a relationship which both partners enjoy. Participating in outdoor activities can help aging couples maintain their physical fitness and share in a pleasant pastime. Bird watching, nature walks, and so on, are still possible for city dwellers who live near parks and public gardens and walking trails. The Kinsey investigators maintain that "good health, sufficient exercise, and plenty of sleep still remain the most effective aphrodisiacs known to man."

4. For those aging people who are separated from their partners either by death or divorce, and who suffer from sexual tension because they have not found new partners with whom to share their sexual needs, leading sex counselors feel that masturbation should be encouraged as a legitimate source for sexual gratification. Many studies concerning the sexual activities of older people support the fact that large numbers engage in masturbation as a source for gaining sexual release from sexual tension.

It should be obvious to all sex counselors and educators that their obligation to their aging counselees who seek guidance is to offer the reassurance that irrespective of the limitations imposed by physical aging, the pleasure and need for sexual expression can continue to be a source of satisfaction. This is especially valid where both partners continue to enjoy relatively good health and an enthusiasm for life and each other.

Regardless of the age group involved in the learning process, it is clear that the effectiveness of any curriculum must be seen in relationship to the ability of the teacher to teach and the readiness of the student to learn. Once we find a teacher who can humanize the learning experience through her warm, trusting and accepting disposition, we can then anticipate her ability to motivate learners. Where the curriculum in sex education or counseling is planned on an interdisciplinary basis and encompasses a variety of interesting experiences for the learner, then the learning process is accelerated. The need for a creative approach is requisite in view of the various attitudes and values that exist in our society today. The most successful curricula seem to be those that mirror the flexibility of effective teachers and learners.

APPENDIXES

I. SEX-ATTITUDE SAMPLE INVENTORY FOR ADOLESCENTS

The following statements are designed to find out what your attitudes are toward *Sex, Dating, Marriage, Love,* and *Yourself.* You will notice that there are no statements which call for factual answers, instead they seek out your personal attitude. Also, since there are no factual answers, your answers are not graded as on a regular type of test. This sex-attitude sample is used in the Webster Girls' School, D.C., as a research tool to determine the extent of attitude change.

Please fill in the following information:
Today's date_____
Age_____
Code No._____
Grade_____

Some statements below can be answered with "A" for *yes* or "D" for *no.* If you are uncertain, mark the statement "U" for *uncertain.*

$$A = yes \quad \text{(I agree with the statement)}$$
$$D = no \quad \text{(I disagree with the statement)}$$
$$U = ? \quad \text{(I am uncertain)}$$

To answer a statement use the letter identifying the answer you choose by writing it in the underlined portion in the blank space to the left of the statement.

Section A—DATING

_____ 1. The more experience one has in dating different people, the easier it will be to know the kind of person you would like to marry.

_____ 2. When a boy goes out on a date with a girl, it is both the girl's and boy's job to see that they both have a good time.

_____ 3. Joining a group with boys and girls in it is a good way to learn how to act with the opposite sex.

4. The purpose of going to group events on a date, or dating many different boys is to:
_____ a. have fun
_____ b. get to know what kind of person you like
_____ c. find out how to conduct yourself on a date

5. "Going steady" with a boy or a girl:
_____ a. is a convenient way of being sure of a date
_____ b. means you like the person very much
_____ c. means you are doing it because you don't want to be left out
_____ d. means you plan to get married
_____ e. comes before being engaged
_____ f. is the same thing as being engaged

6. If you are out with a date the first time is it all right to:
_____ a. hold hands
_____ b. have a goodnight kiss
_____ c. kiss a lot
_____ d. neck
_____ e. pet
_____ f. have sexual intercourse

7. If you find you like each other on the first date, it is all right to:
_____ a. hold hands
_____ b. have a goodnight kiss
_____ c. kiss a lot
_____ d. neck
_____ e. pet
_____ f. have sexual intercourse

8. If you have dated each other a number of times and are still dating other people, it is all right to:
_____ a. hold hands
_____ b. have a goodnight kiss
_____ c. kiss a lot
_____ d. neck
_____ e. pet
_____ f. have sexual intercourse

9. If you are going steady with a person it is all right to:
_____ a. hold hands
_____ b. have a goodnight kiss
_____ c. kiss a lot
_____ d. neck
_____ e. pet
_____ f. have sexual intercourse

10. When you are engaged it is all right to:
_____ a. hold hands
_____ b. have a goodnight kiss
_____ c. kiss a lot
_____ d. neck
_____ e. pet
_____ f. have sexual intercourse

———11. "Going steady" with a boy is the same thing as being engaged.

———12. An unmarried girl should not have premarital sexual relations because a baby could be born and it isn't fair to the baby.

———13. I know how to control my sex urges when with some one of the opposite sex.

———14. Most girls don't realize how easy it is to become pregnant.

Section B—MARRIAGE

——— 1. It is best to finish your education before you get married.

——— 2. I know the kind of person with whom I could be very happy in marriage.

——— 3. Married people who stop loving each other should separate or get a divorce.

——— 4. It is best for a young couple not to marry.

——— 5. When there are personality clashes or other problems, it is wise to visit a marriage counselor to discuss them.

——— 6. A young couple should consider whether they can financially afford to marry and have a family.

——— 7. Both husband and wife should agree on how the family budget is made, even when the husband is the sole worker.

8. Planning to have children when married should depend upon:
——— a. the couple's financial standing
——— b. strength of couple's desire to assume the personal responsibilities of parenthood
——— c. emotional and social maturity of couple.

9. You are ready for marriage when:
——— a. you can stand on your own feet and live your own life comfortably without being dependent on your parents.
——— b. you can give and accept mature love, understanding, and respect between you.

———10. Companionship and love are the real basis for marriage and there should be no children if you don't have this first.

———11. It is best not to marry because you might "fall out of love" and be stuck with someone you no longer care for.

Section C—CHILD REARING

——— 1. Parents should agree upon the method of raising their children.

——— 2. Same kind of discipline is better than discipline which is first easy and then harsh.

——— 3. The child's basic security is all wrapped up in the way parents feel about the child.

_____ 4. It is best to wait a year or so after marriage before having your first child.

_____ 5. When I become a parent I will give my child all the freedom of action he wants.

_____ 6. Disciplining a child is a sign that parents care for the child.

_____ 7. Patience and understanding should be shown to children when they are naughty.

_____ 8. Some married couples should have no children at all.

9. The child born out of wedlock:
_____ a. is just like any other child born to married parents
_____ b. has a social handicap because it has no father
_____ c. does not need a father to grow up properly
_____ d. should be put up for adoption so that it will have both a father and mother
_____ e. is the reason its parents should get married if they love each other
_____ f. is the reason they get married even though they don't love each other

_____10. It is all right for an unmarried girl to become pregnant and have a baby if she loves it and takes care of it.

_____11. It is all right for an unmarried girl to have a second baby if she loves it and takes care of it.

_____12. It is all right for a boy to get a girl pregnant if he helps to support the baby.

Section D—SEX ATTITUDES AND PRACTICES

_____ 1. It is all right to have sexual relations before marriage if you are in love.

_____ 2. Sex is necessary, but it is a dirty thing which should not be talked about.

_____ 3. Sexual intercourse is an appropriate way of telling a date, "I like you, and want to go steady with you".

_____ 4. One of the important reasons for sex in marriage, as important as having children, is for companionship and expression of love.

5. I learned about sex at:
_____ a. school
_____ b. home
_____ c. friends

_____ 6. It is all right to have sexual relations before marriage if you use a safe form of birth control.

_____ 7. Even when a young couple are not in love, they should get married for the sake of the child.

_____ 8. Safe birth control can add to the security and love of a marriage by helping couples to have children when they want them.

9. As an unmarried girl who is going to have a baby, do you feel:
_____ a. sorry for yourself
_____ b. happy
_____ c. it is your own business
_____ d. ashamed of it
_____ e. serves you right for playing around
_____ f. you should marry him
_____ g. you should stop school if necessary and support the baby
_____ h. you have proved that your are a *real* woman

10. Since you know an unmarried boy who is soon to be a father, do you feel:
_____ a. sorry for him
_____ b. happy for him
_____ c. it is his own business
_____ d. he should be ashamed of it
_____ e. serves him right for playing around
_____ f. he should marry
_____ g. he should stop school if necessary to support the baby
_____ h. he has proved himself a *real* man

_____11. One good way of getting parents' consent to marry when you are under age is for the girl to become pregnant.

_____12. Sex relations are disgusting and disillusioning.

_____13. Sex is fun and one takes one's chances.

_____14. Sex is love and self-fulfillment.

15. My mother told me that:
_____ a. men use women for sex
_____ b. men are out for what they can get
_____ c. men should never be trusted

_____16. A person can become ill if he holds back sex urges.

_____17. When you are not attractive physically, you have to take second best or do without.

_____18. Telling unwed mothers about birth control will encourage them to have sex relations.

_____19. Telling single school-age girls about birth control will encourage them to have sex relations.

_____20. There are ways of satisfying your sexual desires in ways other than sexual intercourse.

_____21. The child born out of wedlock does not need a father to grow up properly.

_____22. When you are below the legal age for marriage and parents will not give permission to marry, then it is all right to have sexual intercourse.

_____23. It is none of my parents' business that I became pregnant.

_____24. A good way for me to get my parents' consent to marry when I am still under age, is to become pregnant.

_____25. A young couple should have premarital sexual relations in order to find out if they are sexually suitable for each other.

_____26. It is impossible for a girl to stop wanting sex relations once she has become pregnant.

Section E—LOVE & MEANING

_____ 1. Love is sweet and tender.

_____ 2. Love is cruel and hurtful.

_____ 3. Love is romantic.

_____ 4. Love is helping the loved one when needed.

_____ 5. Love is assuming responsibility for the loved one's health and welfare.

_____ 6. Love is being concerned about the loved one's security and satisfaction.

_____ 7. Love means enjoying the loved one's companionship.

Section F—EGO STRENGTH

_____ 1. Sex relations help a girl who feels loneliness and emptiness.

_____ 2. Sex relations help a girl feel that she is wanted and needed, even when she doesn't feel love.

_____ 3. Sex relations help a girl who feels unappreciated.

4. I think of myself as being:
_____   a. above average in looks
_____   b. average in looks
_____   c. below average in looks

5. I think that my personality is:
_____   a. more attractive than most girls'
_____   b. average
_____   c. below average

_____ 6. I wish that I had been born a boy rather than a girl.

7. My parent(s) are:
_____   a. proud of me
_____   b. disappointed in me
_____   c. indifferent to me

_____ 8. I think that I am popular with boys

_____ 9. I think that I am unpopular with boys.

10. I think of myself as:
_____   a. an above average student

————   b. an average student
————   c. a below average student

11. The boys I go around with are:
————   a. good students
————   b. average students
————   c. below average students

————12. I like my home and neighborhood.

————13. I am ashamed of my home and neighborhood.

14. I think that my future looks:
————   a. bright
————   b. dark
————   c. hopeless

————15. My mother does not understand me.

————16. My father does not understand me.

17. My closest friend or person in whom I confide is: ————————

————18. My parent(s) do not approve of my boy friend(s).

————19. My parent(s) do not approve of my girl friend(s).

————20. I could be happy without a single friend.

————21. If my parents are divorced, I probably will be divorced too, if I get married.

————22. If a person will take responsibility for his action, it is all right for him to do anything he wants.

————23. If I have not had enough love as a child, I will not be able to have a successful marriage.

————24. It is none of my parents' business what I do outside of the house.

————25. First impressions can be deceiving, therefore, love at first sight can be a mistake.

————26. A high-school diploma is necessary today for decent job opportunities.

————27. An unmarried mother has as good an opportunity to advance herself on a job as any other person with equal ability.

II. THE TRAINING OF SEX EDUCATORS *

When human beings are interacting with each other, sex education is going on nearly all the time. Everyone is a sex educator, whether he recognizes it or not; and everyone is receiving sex education, whether he recognizes it or not. From infancy to maturity, our self-concept as men and women is continually changing and developing, becoming damaged or being enhanced. Probably the most powerful influences that shape this image are our parents, our religious upbringing, and our association with our peers.

Although much of this cannot be controlled by the individual or by society, there are particular situations and circumstances in which more formal sex education can be offered. Most of us would agree that the home and the church have a duty in this regard, although that duty is often neglected or avoided. We would have to agree, also, that the school is undoubtedly the best medium for reaching all children, for the simple reason that all children go to school, and that the greatest impact on their learning comes from the peer group.

In our time, sexuality is gaining increasing recognition and acceptance as a major component of human personality, and this recognition makes us increasingly aware of the duty of society to provide good sex education. In the past, programs of sex education have been seen as remedies for such social evils as venereal disease and unwanted pregnancy. Today, we see it more clearly as a vital positive contribution to the full development of the personality; and, as this concept becomes more widely accepted, we become aware of the great need for organized programs in this area and for the special training of these men and women whose responsibility it will be to implement these programs.

Discussion about training for sex educators can be traced back to the last quarter of the nineteenth century, when groups such as the American Purity Alliance, the Child Study Association, the YMCA and YWCA sponsored discussion groups and panels dealing with sex-related topics. As early as 1912, the National Education

---

* Report of Training and Standards Committee of the American Association of Sex Educators and Counselors. Published as a booklet by AASEC. Members of the committee were:

David R. Mace, *chairman*

Michael A. Carrera	Vera C. Mace
George C. Chamis	Patricia Schiller
LeRoy Graham	Murray Vincent
Gerald T. Guerinot	Alan J. Wabrek

Association passed a resolution emphasizing the need for special training for those who would be involved in the field of "sex hygiene." In taking up this task, therefore, we are addressing ourselves to business that has been too long unfinished and to one of the major purposes for which AASEC exists.

What Is Sex Education?

This question needs some further elaboration. Fortunately, the excellent statement of Dr. Lester Kirkendall, published as a SIECUS Study Guide, provides a definition so adequate and so comprehensive that it can be taken as representing the view AASEC would adopt. We are concerned here only to emphasize one or two points.

We have referred to parental and religious influences in the formation of the child's concept of his sexuality. Often these early concepts are later outgrown or even repudiated as part of the normal life adjustment process. It is not, however, the task of the sex educator to undermine or discredit such early influences, but rather to broaden the understanding of the growing child, to extend his knowledge, and thus to enable him to come to terms, responsibly and maturely, with the wider range of opinions and options available to him as he learns to live in our pluralistic society.

As already indicated, we are concerned here with the more formal types of sex education which can in some measure be planned and controlled. We are also concerned primarily with such education provided on a group basis, although we recognize the value of person-to-person discussion with the student, particularly in a counseling setting. It is our purpose, however to prepare later a separate statement on sex counseling, so we shall refer to it only incidentally here.

Formal sex education for organized groups can be provided through schools, churches, and many other social agencies. The patterns of such education will vary naturally with the age group concerned, and with other factors representing differences which distinguish groups of persons from each other. Whatever the sex educator is taught to do, therefore, must not be seen as a rigid stereotype, but rather as a set of general principles which must be interpreted in terms of his own unique personality and gifts, and adapted flexibly to the particular group of students with whom he is working.

We recognize also that organized sex education is at the present time generally provided within a wider context rather than as a subject complete in itself. Frequently it is incorporated in courses on marriage preparation, on family-life education, on personality development, or on some similar subject. We are not sure whether this is based on pedagogical principles or on expediency; and this does not seem to us to be important, so long as the task of sex education, which is of vital importance, is carried out.

Desirable Qualities in the Sex Educator

Since sex education is a delicate task, all too easily mismanaged, it is in our opinion advisable to sketch a profile of the good sex educator. This may differ little from the profile of the good teacher, but it does enable us to emphasize certain qualities which we consider to be important in those who propose to equip themselves for this particular task.

We would emphasize the following qualities in the good sex educator:

1. He has achieved a healthy attitude to his own sexuality.

2. He has the quality of empathy, which we interpret as sensitivity to the attitudes, values, and feelings of other persons.

3. He has sufficient intelligence to understand clearly material about human personality which comes from a variety of fields of knowledge, and to coordinate it coherently in his teaching.

4. He can communicate warmly and effectively, both verbally and nonverbally, with his students.

5. He has an inherent respect and concern for other persons, whether they be children, youth, or adults, and regardless of their particular race, socioeconomic status, or other characteristics that distinguish them from the particular segment of society to which he personally belongs.

6. He finds life satisfying and rewarding, particularly when he can contribute to the happiness and well-being of others.

7. He is able to safeguard, with strict confidentiality, private and personal material communicated to him.

8. He is able to relate to his students in an open and trusting manner, while maintaining an appropriate professional attitude in his relationship with them.

9. He can create a supportive climate in the classroom which can enable his students to express their true feelings and honest opinions without fear of rejection or censure.

10. He has the ability and willingness to cooperate fully and easily with his professional colleagues.

We recognize that some of these qualities are innate while others can be developed with training and experience. We consider, however, that a candidate for training in sex education should from the beginning be generously endowed with these particular personality characteristics; and we would consider it ideal if candidates for training in this field could undergo some process of selection and screening at the outset.

Training in General

We believe that the time must come when the training of the sex educator will be perceived and defined very much as is the training of any other specialist in the human relations field. The lack of such defined and recognized training at the moment is, as we see it, perhaps the greatest barrier to the effective development of this professional specialty.

We will attempt to define below the areas which should be included in this training. We consider that enough material is involved to make it appropriate for such a corpus of training to be expressed in terms of the requirements for a master's degree, or as a major for a doctorate. We hope that colleges and universities will give serious consideration to the experimental initiation of such programs of graduate training. Meanwhile, we recommend that workshops now being offered in this field, which vary greatly in both quantity and quality, might usefully seek to provide sections of the corpus of training, in the form of defined units, offering academic credit wherever possible and convenient. We believe that AASEC itself should seek to foster and facilitate this process by organizing workshops, particularly in the areas of attitudes and skills needed for sex education.

We see the task of training sex educators as comprising three sections—content, attitudes and professional behavior—and educational and counseling skills. What all this might involve is elaborated in the following.

Training as Content

The sex educator must not only be able to provide selected information in the form of statements and lectures, but must also be able in his role to answer questions, lead discussions, correct misconceptions, and provide accurate facts as a basis for sound attitudes. To fulfill these roles effectively, he must be able to draw upon a considerable store of information. The extent of the fields of knowledge which he needs to study (and in most of them the body of knowledge is increasing rapidly today) can be fully realized only when seen in broad prospective.

Our purpose here is not to provide a curriculum in detail, but simply to outine the areas in which the sex educator must be knowledgeable if he is to win and hold the respect of his students. The list of topics is illustrative rather than exhaustive.

1. *The process of reproduction.* Reproductive Biology—Heredity—Sex Determination—Menstruation—Conception—Pregnancy—Embryology—Childbirth—Multiple Births—Infertility and Sterility—Contraception—Abortion—Population Control.

2. *Sexual development.* Sexual Components of Physical, Mental, and Emotional Growth During Infancy, the Prepuberty Period, Puberty, Early Adolescence, Late Adolescence to Adulthood—Fixation and Arrested Development—Sexual Responsiveness in Early Adulthood, Middle Age, and Old Age—Menopause and Climacteric.

3. *Sexual functioning.* Male and Female Anatomy and Physiology—Masturbation in Infancy, Childhood, Adolescence and Maturity—Nocturnal Emissions—Sex Dreams and Fantasies—Male and Female Homosexuality—Sexual Deviations (Sadism, Masochism, Fetishism, Exhibitionism, etc.)—Male and Female Coital Response—Coital Inadequacy (Premature Ejaculation, Impotence, Vaginismus, Dyspareunia, Orgasmic Dysfunction), Myths and Fallacies Relating to Sexual Functioning.

4. *Sexual behavior.* Cultural Values Relating to Sex—Views of Various Religious Groups—Sexual Restraint—Chastity—Fidelity—Celibacy—Sex Ethics—Sexual Guilt—Laws Relating to Sexual Behavior—Premarital Petting—Premarital Coitus (Fornication)—Extramarital Coitus (Adultery)—Out-of-Wedlock Pregnancy—Prostitution—Cultural Attitudes to Sexual Varietism.

5. *Sex and gender.* Male and Female Sexual Characteristics (primary and secondary)—Hermaphroditism and Transsexualism—Masculinity and Femininity—Gender Roles and Stereotypes—Male Dominance—Women's Liberation.

6. *Marriage, family, and interpersonal relationships.* Courtship and Mate Selection—Sex Adjustment in Marriage—Sexual Communication in the Family—Oedipus and Electra Conflicts—Incest—Sexual Inhibition—Sex Education in the Home—Parents as Gender Models—Psychology of Family Relations—Sex in Changing Marriage Patterns—Mate-Swapping—Group Sex.

7. *Sex and health.* Sex-related Biological Anomalies and Anatomical Malformations—Sex and Hormones—Venereal Disease—Sex and Mental Health—Sexual Anxiety and Conflict—Sex and Neurosis.

8. *The study of sex.* History of Sex Beliefs and Attitudes in Western Culture—Sex in Other Cultures—Sex Among Primitive Peoples—Sex in Subhuman Species—The Scientific Study of Sex (Havelock Ellis, Freud, Kinsey, Masters and Johnson)—Findings of Major Sex Studies—Ongoing Sex Research.

A careful perusal of the above outline will reveal clearly that a year of intensive study could do little more than provide an introductory acquaintance with so many fields of knowledge. It seems to us that the case for setting up programs of graduate studies in this area needs no further demonstration. We hope that in the not too distant future such opportunities of study will be widely provided by centers of higher education.

Training in Attitudes and Professional Behavior

We have already seen that the good sex educator must be able to relate comfortably and flexibly to others. Such capacity derives, in part at least, from the possession of inherent personality qualities. Many of the needed skills in relationships can, however, be learned; and existing capacities can be further developed through learning. Such learning is the objective of this second part of the sex educator's training. The training would seek to achieve three specific objectives:

1. *A healthy and mature attitude on the part of the sex educator to himself, to his own sexuality, and to his role.*

2. *A comfortable, flexible, and outgoing attitude of the sex educator to his students.* Essentially this means an attitude that is nonjudgmental, acceptive, and tolerant. His attitude to others, of course, derives very largely from his self-acceptance and assurance.

3. *A clear understanding of proper professional behavior in the sex educator.* This means a readiness to take full responsibility for the teaching process; to give leadership when this is appropriate; to be firm or gentle as the occasion requires; neither to overestimate nor to underestimate his own ability and competence; and to be able maturely to cope with any crisis situation that is likely to arise.

Again, it is not our purpose to elaborate in detail how this kind of training can best be given. Part of it would no doubt involve individual counselng interviews with instructors. Part of it would be achieved through growth groups providing experiences in self-awareness. Some of it could come through role-playing and subsequent discussion. Observation of highly qualified sex educators in action could provide valuable insights. And, when the trainee is ready, actual experience of being involved in sex education, with interpretation from fellow trainees and supervisors, would be particularly valuable. Training of this type is being more and more widely used now in the preparation of persons entering the helping professions; and a detailed program could easily be worked out for any given group of trainees.

Training in Educational and Counseling Skills

The first two parts of the training process are intended to give the sex educator the equipment that is essential for his task. The third part of training is designed to teach him to perform that task. The following are some of the procedures likely to be involved:

1. *Learning to prepare the way for a sex education program.* Public attitudes to sex education are often ambivalent, so that the success of a program may require a good deal of preliminary work. In a school situation, it is important to explain the program to parents and secure their support; to convince community leaders, and especially religious leaders, that the project is being carried out responsibly

and competently; and to secure in advance the support of the school administration. Many otherwise sound programs in sex education have failed because this preliminary work had not been adequately done.

2. *Learning to involve students in cooperative planning and full participation in the teaching process.* Authoritarian and rigidly didactic approaches to this kind of education are invariably self-defeating, because the imparting of information is less important than the freeing of the student to express his own views and attitudes on highly controversial questions. The achievement of the necessary *rapport* between teacher and students is never easy, but it is essential to success.

3. *Learning to select and use the right materials as teaching aids.* A considerable variety of materials is now available to the sex education teacher—textbooks, wall pictures, tape recordings, films, slides, etc. In his training the student should gain acquaintance with these teaching aids, learn their proper use, and develop discrimination in selecting them for various purposes and various groups.

4. *Understanding methodolgies of classroom teaching.* This would include the choice and prepartion of an appropriate curriculum, the setting of suitable assignments, recognition of the comparative values of the lecture approach, class discussion, small-group discussion, role-playing, field trips, etc. The student should not only learn about these various procedures, but also have the opportunities of observing them carried out by experienced teachers, and of attempting them himself.

5. *Learning techniques of evaluation.* In a field like sex education, it is important not only to judge what is happening by direct observation, but also to provide for the anonymous opinions of the students to be freely expressed. The preparation of appropriate questionnaires and other instruments of evaluation should be part of the teacher's training.

6. *Learning techniques of group leadership and counseling.* Because of the dynamic nature of this kind of teaching, the trainee should have some understanding of the basic principles of group dynamics and should have enough understanding of group counseling procedures to be able to handle confidently situations in which the students go beyond the point of asking for information and begin to ask for personal help. Experience of personal participation in competently conducted growth groups is a valuable asset.

7. *Learning basic counseling and referral skills.* This kind of teaching often awakens in the student personal needs that must be met in face-to-face communication with the teacher. A good teacher will not shrink from this aspect of his task. He will not embark upon counseling that requires professional aid, but will do such basic counseling as is necessary, and then make wise and appropriate referral. He will require training to do this effectively.

8. *Learning to work with parent groups.* Sex education programs for children and young people should ideally be accompanied by collateral programs for their parents, so that communication and mutual understanding can be improved simultaneously from both ends. It may not always be practicable to set up such a parents' seminar, but it should be attempted wherever possible. The sex educator will be better motivated to make this attempt if he has ben trained to work with parents and is confident of his ability to do so.

We have outlined some of the skills which the sex educator needs to be taught. Although they have been described with a school classroom in mind, they are equally applicable to a variety of other situations in which sex education can be undertaken—some examples are church youth and adult groups; a YMCA or

YWCA course; a clinic course taught by a physician or nurse; a formal undergraduate or graduate college course or less formal campus student group.

The Sex Education Coordinator

We wish to refer to a special role which may increasingly be made available to some sex educators, and preparation for which should be included in future training. The college campus will furnish a good illustration of this role.

On many campuses today a good deal of sex education, of various types and qualities, is going on. It may be offered through the student health service, at the student counseling center, by the campus chaplains, by dormitory counselors (often graduate students), by course instructors, by student association lectures, or by student leaders of student groups. Many of these activities may overlap or even compete with one another, and the several approaches may be uncoordinated and even contradictory. Moreover, the continuity of these programs often depends on persons who are voluntarily going beyond the call of duty and whose efforts may be abruptly discontinued. In such a situation, we recommend the appointment of a campus coordinator who is himself a trained sex educator who can give quality and continuity to the entire project, and who can make the best use of all the individuals concerned, and give their efforts support, encouragement, and skilled supervision.

The use of a coordinator can likewise facilitate the entire effort of sex education in a school system, for a group of churches or clinics, or in any other large grouping of persons for whom the provision of sex education is a desirable service. The skilled coordinator will involve as many others as possible in the program, rather than carrying it out himself, and thus make sex education a widely shared community concern. In fact, since we know that most sex education is done through conversations among peers, such a skilled coordinator can, by enlisting the cooperation of those who exercise natural leadership in the peer group, do much to provide accurate information and to develop responsible attitudes.

A similar process of coordination would be particularly applicable to the graduate schools which train the members of the helping professions. We strongly urge that medical and nursing schools, law schools and theological seminaries, schools of social work and teacher training institutions, should appoint to their faculties professors who have had the kind of training we are advocating here and whose primary function would be to act as sex education coordinators.

Further Learning through Experience and Supervision

Completion of the training program we have outlined would normally be followed by the taking up of the task of sex education, and the skills already learned would be progressively sharpened as more and more experience was gained. However, while there is much truth in this statement, it can also be challenged. There is a good deal of evidence that persons trained in the helping professions, as they then go to work, are in danger of developing stereotyped rule-of-thumb patterns of functioning, which tend to be reinforced by accumulating experience, and thus the stimulus for improvement is gradually lost. The sovereign remedy for this has been found in systems of ongoing supervision; and in a field like sex education, which is growing and developing all the time, we feel that such supervision is essential if experience is truly to lead to growth.

It is essential that the sex educator should be continuously open to constructive criticism from his colleagues. Probaby the best way to provide this is to secure the services of a mature and experienced sex educator with whom regular sessions for report and evaluation can be held and who can even sit in and observe the beginner in action. Failing this, however, there are other means by which growth and improvement can be fostered. One way is for several sex educators to team up together and meet periodically to discuss their experiences with each other. Another way is to attend workshops and conferences when these are available. In each individual situation, the best available methods can be sought out and put to use. The aim is to insure that continuous growth, through constructive criticism, should be taking place.

The American Association of Sex Educators and Counselors (AASEC) hopes that the time may come in the near future when it will have a roster of approved supervisors throughout the country, whose professional assistance will be available, in terms to be appropriately defined, when requested.

Accreditation and Professional Ethics

At the present time, there are compartively few people who spend their whole time doing sex education and for whom "sex educator" represents their primary professional title. Most of those presently active in the field perform this task during part of their time, their main preoccupation being in some other area; or, even if most of their time is given to sex education, they do not carry this as their primary title.

It seems likely, however, that the time is approaching when an increasing number of persons will be known and recognized as "sex educators and counselors" and will spend all or most of their time in this work. It will then become important, as in other professions, for them to receive some formal recognition which identifies them as specialists and distinguishes them from persons performing the same task but without comparable training and skill. It will probably become necessary for AASEC to establish a special membership category for such persons. In that event it will also be necessary to set up a committee on accreditation to investigate their credentials, examine their knowledge and skill, and, if they meet the standards that have been set, admit them to the new category of membership. Along with such accreditation normally goes the formulation of a code of professional ethics defining standards to which the accredited person undertakes to conform, and an ethics committee to see that the code is honored. These professional committees of AASEC would serve the double function of recognizing and commending its members to the public, and at the same time disciplining them if and when serious complaints about their competence or behavior are preferred. AASEC believes that it should assume these responsibilities but also recognizes the importance of joining with other organizations in the establishment of such a system of accreditation to insure coordination of effort. The precise direction in which we will move in the future is not yet clear; but it seems certain that, in one way or another, a system of accreditation must ultimately develop.

Training the Sex Counselor

As indicated earlier, it is our hope that AASEC will follow up this memorandum on the training of sex educators with a similar one on the training of sex counselors. We considered at first attempting to fulfill these two tasks together, but decided that this was not practicable. It is our view, however, that the training of sex counselors should cover, in almost identical terms, the first two parts of the training of sex educators which we have outlined. In the third part, however, there would clearly be a dividing of the ways. Sex counselors require advanced clinical skills that sex educators do not need nor possess.

We have indicated that the sex educator should receive some basic training in counseling skills, and should be equipped to deal with a student who comes for personal help by scheduling an exploratory interview in order to identify the problem. If the problem should prove to be relatively simple, based mainly on misinformation, the sex educator will probably be equipped to do all all that is necessary. But we would strongly urge that, where the matter is in doubt, the sex educator should be fully aware of the danger of exceeding his powers, and should normally make an appropriate referral.

We see the sex counselor as a person who has had sufficient recognized clinical training to meet fully the requirements of one of the established clinical specialties. That is not to say, however, that a qualified member of any one of these specialties may necessarily claim to be a qualified sex counselor. Just as the student who has covered the training in sex education outlined in this document must, in addition, in order to become a recognized sex counselor, qualify in the counseling field; so someone already qualified in a counseling field must, in order to meet requirements as a sex counselor, provide evidence that he has covered also the equivalent of the first two parts of the training we have designated for the sex educator.

Although the sex educator and the sex counselor can be said to represent two distinct professional specialties, it is likely that many persons who plan to work with people in the field of human sexuality will want to possess both qualifications; and this is certainly desirable, for each role complements and enhances the other.

Summary and Conclusions

The ground which we have covered in this statement may be summarized as follows:

1. We believe the time has come to recognize sex education as a professional specialty in the field of education; education being defined in the broadest terms as the facilitation of the fullest possible development of individual human potential.

2. We believe that this recognition can come only when some clearly defined standards for the training of sex educators have been established and have become generally accepted.

3. We have attempted to outline such training standards in terms of at least one full year of graduate study, covering three parts—content, atitudes and professional behavior, and operational skills.

4. We would encourage colleges and universities to embody this training in a graduate program for a master's degree, or as partial fulfillment of the requirements for a doctorate.

5. In addition to the completion of this training or its equivalent, we would urge sex educators to subject themselves to an ongoing process of supervision, designed to insure their continuing growth.

6. We foresee the time when the trained sex educator will be recognized as a professional specialist, and when a system of accreditation, involving acceptance of a code of professional ethics, will be set up as a regulatory mechanism.

7. We believe that AASEC should commit itself, as one of its major goals, to the attainment of these objectives; and, in so doing, should cooperate closely with other organizations and professional groups working with the same ends in view.

III. BUILDING A CORE LIBRARY IN SEX EDUCATION *

Before a teacher or school district family-planning center or medical school attempts to build a core library with a reserved shelf for teachers, counselors, or students, the following essential materials ought to be reviewed by a competent curriculum or course designer or a representative committee. These contain agency references, school references, and commercial references as well.

ANNOTATED BIBLIOGRAPHY

Agency Bibliographies

American Association for Health, Physical Education and Recreation (NEA), 1201 Sixteenth St., N.W., Washington, D.C. 20036.

> *Catalog of Publications 1969–1970.* Includes references in sex education.

> *Sex Education Resource Units: Grades K–4, 5–7, 1969.* 71 student references, 126 teacher references, 63 other general references. Well annotated section on supplementary teaching aids, films, filmstrips and slides, transparencies, charts, catalogs, teaching lists. All primarily commercially produced.

American Medical Association, for Joint Committee on Health Problems in Education of the National Education Association and the American Medical Association, 535 North Dearborn St., Chicago, Ill. 60610.

> *Miracle of Life and Sex Education Series.* Seven booklets specifically relevant to sex education. Four are for parents, the other three for children. About 20 more about related areas of health care. Also a health education materials catalog. Two booklets on physiology included.

American School Health Association, Committee on Health Guidance in Sex Education, 515 East Main St., Kent, Ohio 44240.

---

* From Volume V, Technical Report of the Commission on Obscenity and Pornography. Quality Education Development, Inc. Washington, D.C., 1972.

Growth Patterns and Sex Education. 1967. An extensive bibliography emphasizing texts and audiovisuals along with other materials.

Cleveland Health Museum, Euclid at 89th St., Cleveland, Ohio 44106.

Teacher's Guide for Instructed Classes, 1968–1969. Given to teachers planning to accompany classes to the museum. Comprehensive program of long standing. Includes series of films on "Sex in American Culture." No bibliography, but list of above films and several others.

Family Life Publications, Moorhead, Minn. 56560.

Family Life and Sex Education: A Graded Program, 1967. J. Mark Perrin Ed.D., and Thomas E. Smith, Ed.D. Contains over 100 references, noted as to "student" or "adult" sources.

Family Service Association of America, 44 East 23rd Street, New York, N.Y. 10010.

Agency Sources for Material on Sex Education: B-22F. 1969. A list of agencies or associations which prepare accepted information on sex education. Also a list of publications.

Marriage, Parenthood and Family Relationships. (Reading references on). A list of 68 books and over 100 pamphlets on family life.

Minnesota Council on Family Relations, 1219 University Avenue, S.E., Minneapolis, Minn. 55414.

Family Life—Literature and Films. 1970. This 189-page bibliography of books, pamphlets, films, and tapes is carefully categorized into sections such as the American Family, Perspectives, Human Sexuality and Sex Education, etc. Each section has its own appropriately annotated bibliography.

National Council of the Churches of Christ in the U.S.A., 475 Riverside Drive, New York, N.Y. 10027.

Sex Education in Major Protestant Denominations. John H. Phillips, Ph.D. This does not have a separate bibliography, but cites volumes used by each denomination; relies heavily on publications of Concordia Press.

National Council on Family Relations, 1219 University Avenue, S.E., Minneapolis, Minn. 55414.

Journal of Marriage and the Family, Vol. 32, No. 1, February 1970. Of the 22 articles at least 16 are directly connected with some form of sex education. References to many other articles. Book reviews.

The Family Coordinator: Journal of Education, Counseling, and Services, Vol. 19, No. 1, January 1970. 17 articles devoted to family living; some have extensive reference lists, mostly to other articles. Final article is of particular interest: "Community Experiences with the 1969 Attack on Sex Education."

National Education Association of the United States, 1201 Sixteenth Street, N.W., Washington, D.C. 20036.

Family Life and Sex Education in the Elementary School. 1968. Helen Manley. Bibliography by grade levels; 66 items, some prepared for students, some for teacher training.

National School Public Relations Association, 1201 Sixteenth Street, N.W., Washington, D.C. 20036.

Sex Education in Schools. 1969. EDUCATION U.S.A. Special Report. A general discussion of what has been and might be done in public schools; surveys current status of states and communities. Bibliography of 67 items; about half are curriculum guides of various public schools. Also books, pamphlets, journals and magazine articles, agency aids, and audiovisuals.

New England School Development Council, 55 Chapel Street, Newton, Mass. 02158.

Sex Education Programs for Public Schools. 1968. A booklet of four articles, two appendixes which are bibliographies of books and audiovisual teaching aids.

Planned Parenthood Publications, 515 Madison Avenue, New York, N.Y. 10022.

Planned Parenthood Publications. 1970. This is a catalog of literature offered by Planned Parenthood—World Population. A variety of reprints and current publications pertinent to their own purposes are available from PPP.

Sex Information and Education Council of the United States (SIECUS), 1855 Broadway, New York, N.Y. 10023.

Sexuality and Man. 1970. Charles Scribner's Sons, 597 Fifth Avenue, New York, N.Y. 10017. A complete chapter devoted to resources used and a bibliography.

State and local curriculum guide biblographies

Alaska

Guidelines to Human Sexuality Education. 1967. Withdrawn from circulation; new guidelines being prepared for 1970 curriculum. Clifford R. Hartman, Commissioner of Education, Juneau, Alaska 99801. A very good guide with bibliographies at each grade level unit. Approximately 100 films, books, pamphlets listed, many with excellent annotations. Commercial, government and agency sources included, plus an appendix of organizations with additional materials available.

California

Contra Costa County, 75 Santa Barbara Road, Pleasant Hill, Calif. 94523. *Family Life Education.* 1969. Three sections: K–6, 7–8, 9–12. Extensive bibliographies at end of each section.

San Diego City Schools, Health Services Department, San Diego, Calif. 92101. *Overview of Social Health Program in the San Diego Schools.* 1969. The overview states quite clearly that this is designed and intended to be "A voluntary program designed to supplement the teaching of the home and church." Brief discussion of program offered at 6th, 9th, 11th, and 12th grades. Program appears spotty; teachers appear very well prepared. Each grade level contains bibliography; also accompanied by pamphlet containing 38 references.

San Mateo County Division of Education, Curriculum Department, San Mateo, Calif. 94402. *Family Life Education—Teacher Resource Guide.* 1969. A two-volume (K–8, 9–12), very extensive report with a vast list of resource materials, with appropriate pages of books, films, etc., correlated with exact grade-level content. Appendix includes a reproduction of a sound track on "Human Reproduction."

Colorado

An Outline Guide for Family Life Education (For Parents, Schools, and Other Community Groups). 1967. John C. Thompson, Ph.D., Colorado Department of Education, Colfax and Sherman, Denver, Colo. 80203. A two-page outline of attitudes, information, content goals, at each level. About 40 references in bibliography. Also cites associations which might be helpful.

K–12 Health Instruction Guide for Colorado Schools. 1969. Leo P. Black, Assistant Commissioner, Colorado Department of Education, Colfax and Sherman, Denver, Colo. 80203. Routine outline form. Chapter XV contains bibliography including textbooks, resource books and pamphlets, films; commercial, government and agency sources are identified.

Illinois

School District 65, Evanston, Ill. 60204. *Family Living Curriculum Guide.* Extensive bibliography.

Kansas

Unified School District No. 501, Topeka, Kan. 66603. *Health Concepts and Their Development: A Teacher's Guide for Health and Safety Instruction in the Junior High School.* Dixie L. Barb and Richard S. Mossman. Unit IX: Human Growth and Development is of special interest. The general bibliography does not appear to have many items concerning sex education.

Kentucky

Fayette County Public Schools, 400 Lafayette Parkway, Lexington, Ky. 40503. *Sex Education Curriculum Guide.* 1969. Bibliographies scattered throughout two volumes (grades 1–6, grades 7–8); approximately 60 books, articles, films, tapes.

Maryland

Anne Arundel County Public Schools, Annapolis, Md. 21404. *Pilot Unit on Human Reproduction: Evolution Report of Grade Six.* 1969. Eva M. Pumphrey, Director of Curriculum. A clear-cut text dealing only with human reproduction. Brief bibliography lists one basic text, with two supplementary texts, two transparencies, five films.

Massachusetts

Lexington, Mass. 02173. A Summary Report—1969 Summer Workshop. *Human Development and Human Relations: A program including Family Living, Sex Education and Interpersonal Relations.* Committee of parents and teachers developed a general outline of a model for a curriculum; studied different approaches, developed a questionnaire for parents. Contains bibliography of 16 books and a materials bibliography, including books, films, records of 42 items annotated.

Newton, Mass. 02158. *Family Life and Sex Education per Grade Level.* This is a broad concept guideline with an attached bibliography of 150 titles, indexed by authors.

Michigan

Report on the Advisory Committee on Sex Education. 1969. State Department of Education, Lansing, Mich. 48924. A fairly comprehensive set of guidelines for Sex Education and Family Planning Information Programs in schools, citing numerous governmental, religious, and professional agencies. The 10-page bibliography includes books, films, records, charts, slides, and transparencies.

Minnesota

Family Living and Modern Sex Education, St. Paul Public Schools, Elementary Resource Units, Curriculum Bulletin No. 349, Secondary, Resource Units, Curriculum Bulletin No. 350, Fall 1969 (and 1968 No. 332). Independent School District 625, St. Paul, Minn. 55102. Detailed curriculum by grade from K–12. Concepts in detail with questions and discussion and specific activities outlined; bibliography, equipment, books, films, etc., all annotated. Actual classroom units developed from the 1968 curriculum guide are recorded. Children's questions are recorded along with suggested teacher "pivotal questions."

Bloomington Public Schools, Minneapolis, Minn. 55420. *Family Life Education,* 1969–1970, a summary of the curriculum (K–12). Collection of committee reports, with bibliographies in each. "Summary and Report of Family Life Meetings," 27 schools surveyed materials, as to number of schools using specific and general categories of transparencies, filmstrips, books, tapes, charts. Number of schools and grades using titled materials are reported. Concerns of parents as stated at meetings are recorded.

Missouri

Ferguson-Florissant School District, 655 January Avenue, Ferguson, Mo. 63135. *Education for Family Living: A Guide for Elementary Teachers.* 1969. Bibliography cites six charts, films, books, transparencies.

New Jersey

Public Schools, Department of Health and Physical Education, Montclair, N.J. 07042. *Education in Human Growth and Development.* 1968. A working copy only. This appears to be a thorough parent-teacher-student program. Extensive resource material lists for each grade level, with suggested texts and films for parents.

North Carolina

Family Life and Sex Education. 1970. Health and Physical Education Section, State Department of Public Instruction, Raleigh, N.C. 27603. A straight bibliography, evaluated as appropriate for use at specific grade levels. No annotations. 18 books, 19 films, 14 filmstrips with recordings, four records, one set of charts. Broad approach.

Winston-Salem/Forsyth County Schools, Winston-Salem, N.C. 27102. *About You.* Eighth-grade health-class curriculum guide; teacher's guide; extensive bibliography. All Science Research Associates; films and other audiovisuals list. *The Miracle of Me.* Fifth-grade program; teacher's manual; bibliography of 27 books and pamphlets, three films.

Ohio

The School and Sex Education. 1969. P. C. Bethel, Ohio State Department of Education, Division of Elementary and Secondary Education, Columbus, Ohio 43215. Discussion of various points, citing programs in other public schools. Two bibliographies; bibliography of seven guides, six resources of audiovisual materials, 11 resource agencies.

Bexley City Schools, Bexley, Ohio 43209. *The Study of Family Living and Sex Education: A Curriculum Guide for the Addendum-Health Curriculum.* 1969. There is a fairly extensive bibliography at end of this publication. Deals with all phases of health, and items pertaining to sex education are scattered throughout; probably two or three references per grade.

Columbus, Ohio, Public Schools, Columbus, Ohio 43215. *Guidelines for Sex Education.* 1967. A mimeographed 6-page brochure; essentially a bibliography for each grade level. 15 books, 12 films, four tapes, about one dozen articles and pamphlets listed.

Pennsylvania

Conceptual Guidelines for School Health Programs in Pennsylvania—A program continuum for total school health. 1970. Section 3, Human Sexuality. Outline format, brief bibliography.

Lower Merion School District, Ardmore, Penna. 19003. *Health Education Curriculum Guide.* 1969. Chapter on human sexuality is particularly good. Developed by Department of Health Education of Lankenau Hospital for Main Line Project Learning of Lower Merion School District (Haverford, Lower Merion, Radnor). Four pages of bibliography.

Commercial sources

Association Press, 291 Broadway, New York, N.Y. 10007.

Sex and Family Life Education. Three books by Dr. Evelyn Millis Duvall:
1. *About Sex and Growing Up.* 4–6 grade text about sexuality. $1.50 paperback.
2. *Love and the Facts of Life.* For teenagers. $.95, paperback.
3. *Today's Teenagers.* Guide for educators and parents. $4.95.

Sex in the Adolescent Years: New directions in guiding and teaching youth. By Isadore Rubin and Lester Kirkendall. $4.95. (Includes "What parents should do about pornography.")

Sex in the Childhood Years. By Isadore Rubin and Lester Kirkendall. $4.95.

ACI Productions, 16 West 46th Street, New York, N.Y. 10036.

For Better, For Worse. A film concerned with teenage marriage and its accompanying problems. Upper grades, 25 minutes, B&W, price $160.

Addison-Wesley, 2725 Sand Hill Road, Menlo Park, Calif. 94025.

Biology—Introduction to Life, 1969. High-school biology text, with teacher's guide and laboratory manual.

American Library and Educational Service Company (ALESCO), 404 Sietta Drive, Paramus, N.J. 07652.

The Teenager and His World, 1969. A collection of materials concerning teenagers' needs and interests. 90 books, annotated. Covers the spectrum of sex education. Sound filmstrips, cost $35 to $40. Books from $2.00 to 6.00.

Bantam Books, Inc., 666 Fifth Avenue, New York, N.Y. 10019.

Love and Sex in Plain Language. By Dr. Eric Johnson. Paperback. Wide distribution. An excellent brief text or reference book.

Barron's Educational Series, Inc., 113 Crossways Park Drive, Woodbury, N.Y. 11797.

Teenage Sex Counselor. Paperback written for perplexed teenager seeking advice. $1.50.

CCM School Materials, Inc., 342 Western Avenue, Boston, Mass. 02135.

Sex Education and Family Living Series, 1970. Transparencies, models, etc. A graphic and factual set of materials. Comprehensive. Basic set, $265. Models available from $12.50 to $124. All available individually or in sets with cor-related transparencies.

Channing L. Bete Co., Inc., 45 Federal Street, Greenfield, Mass. 01301.

Him 'n' Her (ABC's of sex). One of series of booklets on drugs, V.D., health, etc. Basic anatomy, biology, psychology of sexuality. Transparencies available.

Creative Educational Society, Inc., Mankato, Minn. 56001.

Creative Life Science Series, March 1970. By Julian May. A set of eight titles, the first three of which are especially appropriate. Grades K–4, $3.95 per book.

Creative Visuals, Box 1911, Big Spring, Texas 79720.

Human Living and Sex Education, 1970. Transparencies covering four levels from primary through senior high school; six areas of concern, including Family

Relations and Dating Relations. 30 to 70 transparencies in each series covering social attitudes and emotional and physical growth. Cost is $6.00 individual transparency or $117 to $275 for each set with teacher's manual.

Don Bosco Films, New Rochelle, N.Y. 10802.

Concordia Sex Education Series. A coordinated set of six books, four filmstrips, and record sets for grades 5–8, 9–11, 12–14, 15 and over, and for parents and pastors. Prepared for Christian educators. Books $1.95; film strip and record set $10.00.

Doubleday & Company, Inc., Garden City, N.Y. 11530 (School Library Division).

Family Living and Sex Education. Categorized list, elementary, junior and senior high school, and adult. 21 books, annotated, noting recommendations from book lists, journals, etc.

Educational Progress Corp., 8538 East St., Tulsa, Okla. 74145.

Human Growth and Development, 1970. Recordings, filmstrips, and printed materials for K–6 (30 filmstrips and tapes) and 7–9 (10 filmstrips and tapes) with teacher's guide covering basics of family living—biology, physical growth, dating, etc. Cost: K–6, $360; 7–9, $132. Some levels available separately.

Friendship Press, 475 Riverside Drive, New York, N.Y. 10027.

Questions for Christians: What About Sex? Booklet by Frank and Leslie Wier, with reading list, secular instruction. Cost $0.65.

George F. Cram Co., Inc., School and Library Division, 301 S. LaSalle Street, Indianapolis, Ind. 46206.

Materials for Sex Education and Human Development, 1970. Plastic, dissectible models of male and female torsos, with sex organs. 16 models of development of embryo, etc. Prices: organic-muscular torso with interchangeable sex organs $399; embryo $90.

Guidance Associates, Pleasantville, N.Y. 10570.

Who Am I? 1970. Four sets of sound filmstrips at about $40 per set. "Masculinity and Feminity," "Dare to be Different," "Your Personality," "Sexual Values in Society."

Henk Newenhouse, 1825 Willow Road, Northfield, Ill. 60093.

Family Living, Human Growth and Human Development Materials. 16mm. films, filmstrips, tapes, records. Contributions by: E. C. Brown, National Film Board of Canada; Margolis-Fleming, Portafilms; Hillar-Harris, Audio Productions; Wexler, National Council on Family Relations; Churchill, McGraw-Hill; Brigham Young University; Medical Arts Productions; Granada-British. Costs $80 to $300, rentals $10 to $30. Some B&W; some color.

Holt, Rinehart and Winston, 383 Madison Ave., New York, N.Y. 10017.

Modern Sex Education. A text at the secondary school level, science.

Imperial International Learning, Box 548, Rt. 54, South Kanakee, Ill. 60901.

Human Growth and Understanding. Audio-tape series.

Instructional Aids, Inc., P.O. Box 191, Mankato, Minn. 56001.

Reproduction and Human Development, 1970. Six sets of study prints with text on reverse side of illustrations and diagrams, for use in the teaching of reproduction and human development. Grades 4 and up. Each set, $14.95; series of six sets, $25.

Jayark Corp., Educational Programs Division, 10 E. 49th St., New York, N.Y. 10017.

Lessons in Living and Education for Sexuality, 1969. Three phases: "I Am Me" (K–5), "You Are You" (6–8), "Mind of Your Own" (9–12). Cartridge films, transparencies, charts. 120-page teacher's manual, five illustrated units. Coordinated multimedia comprehensive K–12 program.

Kensorthy Educational Service, Inc., P.O. Box 3031, 138 Allen St., Buffalo, N.Y. 14205.

How to Tell Teenagers About Growing Up. Two records.

Kimberly-Clark Corp., Box 551-CK, Neenah, Wis. 54956.

Life Cycle Center. Diagrams, films, and series of booklets on menstruation and personal relationships. Fourth grade through college. All printed material free. Film, $3.00.

Laidlaw Brothers, Educational Publishers, Thatcher and Madison, River Forest, Ill. 60305.

The Laidlaw Health Series. Limited coverage of sex education materials. One booklet "Human Growth and Reproduction," price $0.84.

Life (Magazine) Education Program, Box 834, Radio City Post Office, New York, N.Y. 10019.

The Human Body, 1970. Three lecture booklets and correlated filmstrips "Life Before Birth," biology of birth. Filmstrips $6.00, reprints $0.75; bulk rates available.

J. B. Lippincott Co., Educational Publishing Div., East Washington Square, Philadelphia, Pa. 19105.

Toward Adulthood and *Love and Sex in Plain Language.* For use in sex education classes as text or reference.

NASCO, Fort Atkinson, Wis. 53538.

The Human Reproduction System. A set of 10 overhead transparencies with accompanying lecture guide. Also as 2 x 2 color slides. Aims at a straightforward, biological approach to the teaching of human reproduction for high schools and colleges.

National Instructional Television, Inc., Box A, Bloomington, Ind. 47401.

A Time of Your Life, 1970. Series of 20-minute video-tape lessons in family-life education for grades 5 and 6. Also 10-lesson course. Lessons on sex education also available on film. Previews available, and teacher's manual. Also grades 1 and 2 program, "All About You"; high-school series, "Health: Your Decision."

Population Dynamics, 13201 9th Ave., N.W., Seattle, Wash. 98177.

Beyond Conception. Sound film for junior and senior high school and junior college grades. 35 minutes, color, population ecology, contraception. Cost $275; $15 rental fee.

Pyramid Films, Box 1048, Santa Monica, Calif. 90406.

Breath of Life, Pulse of Life, Cautious Twins, Sound Off. Safety and Health Series; range of 10- to 27-minute films. Cost $100 to $250; rental $10.

Q & ED Productions (A Division of Cathedral Films, Inc.), 2921 West Almeda Ave., Burbank, Calif. 91505.

Filmstrips for Education, 1969–1970. Four series of filmstrips, records, and study guides. First two include basic book for series. Grades through senior high and college, parents and teachers. "About Sex and Growing Up" (by Dr. Duvall) $36.50; "Love and the Facts of Life," (by Dr. Duvall) $46.00; "A Base for Morality," $45.90. Others now in production.

Scholastic Book Series, Division of Scholastic Magazines, Englewood, N.J. 07632.

What You Should Know About Sex and Sexuality. 64-page booklet with teacher's guide. Discussion of sexuality, all aspects. Separate booklet on V.D.

Scott-Foresman, 99 Bauer Drive, Oakland, N.J. 07436.

The New Basic Health and Safety Program. Includes "The Human Story: Facts of Birth, Growth, and Reproduction." For grades 5–8. Cited in public-school curriculum guides. 48-page set and cover book with teacher's handbook. School price for both, $1.08.

Stephen Bosustrow Productions, Malibu, Calif. 90265.

A Basis for Sex Morality. Study guide and six filmstrip series. Comprehensive discussions with moral emphasis.

Sterling Educational Films, 241 East 34th St., New York, N.Y. 10016.

Family Life Education and Human Growth, 1969. 33 16-mm. films covering grades K–12. Sex, family life, physical, emotional, moral concepts. Primarily sex education, but some films on drugs, child development. Total cost $4,870; total Sex and Family Life Series costs $3,910. Three levels: K–6, 12 titles; grades 7–9, 12 titles; grades 10–12, 15 titles.

Teachers College Press, 1234 Amsterdam Ave., New York, N.Y. 100277.

Family Insights Through the Use of Short Story: A Guide for Teachers and Workshop Leaders. Use of short stories in "Marriage and the Family" adult classes. Paperback, $1.95. Booklet, *Teaching Family Life Education, 1970. The Toms River Program: an example of community involvement,* paperback, $1.00.

Universal Education and Visual Arts, A Division of Universal City Studios, Inc., 221 Park Ave. South, New York, N.Y. 10003.

Where Does Love Begin? 1970. An 8-minute movie of a natural childbirth. For sex education courses, senior high school level, college; and adult. B&W, sale price $60 (16 mm.); $48 (Super 8).

Warren Schloat Productions, Inc., (Prentice-Hall Company), Pleasantville, N.Y. 10570.

Human Birth, Growth, and Development; Facts and Feelings. Six sound filmstrips, teacher's guide with narration and bibliography for preparation and follow-up. Senior high and college.

SCREENING

(Once having obtained a comprehensive overview of the available content material and teaching resources, the pruning-down process begins:

1. Select three or four books rich in concepts, theory and content.
2. Select curriculum guides that are tailored to the grade levels and special interests of your group.
3. Select essential audiovisual materials. These are expensive and new films, filmstrips, overhead projectuals are becoming available.
4. Subscribe to essential journals and newsletters in order to keep up with new books, pamphlets and issues in sex education.
5. Select several books dealing with skills and attitude modification in working in a group-centered approach.)

Organizations and Agencies

These organizations publish journals, newsletters and reading lists of immediate interest to sex educators.

American Association for Health, Physical Education and Recreation
1201 Sixteenth Street
Washington, D.C. 20036

American Association of Sex Educators and Counselors
815 Fifteenth Street, N.W.
Washington, D.C. 20005

The American Institute of Family Relations
5287 Sunset Boulevard
Los Angeles, Calif. 90027

American Medical Association
Department of Community Health and Health Education
535 North Dearborn Street
Chicago, Ill. 60610

American Psychological Association
Task Force on Psychology, Family Planning and Population Policy
1200 Seventeenth Street, NW.
Washington, D.C. 20036

American Social Health Association
1790 Broadway
New York, N.Y. 10019

Association for the Study of Abortion, Inc.
120 West 57th Street
New York, N.Y. 10019

Association for Voluntary Sterilization
14 West 40th Street
New York, N.Y. 10018

Child Study Association of America
9 East 89th Street
New York, N.Y. 10028

E. C. Brown Center for Family Studies
1802 Moss Street
Eugene, Ore. 97463

Educational Foundation for Human Sexuality
Montclair State College
Upper Montclair, N.J. 07043

Erickson Educational Foundation
4047 Hundred Oaks Avenue
Baton Rouge, La. 70808

Institute for Sex Education
18 South Michigan Avenue
Chicago, Ill. 60603

Institute for Sex Research, Inc.
Indiana University
Bloomington, Ind. 47401

International Planned Parenthood Federation
18-20 Lower Regent Street
London, S.W. 1, England

National Alliance Concerned With School-Age Parents
Room 705, Board of Education
Parkway at 21st Street
Philadelphia, Penna. 19103

National Association for Repeal of Abortion Laws
250 West 57th Street, Room 2428
New York, N.Y. 10019

The National Council on Family Relations
1219 University Avenue, Southeast
Minneapolis, Minn. 55414

National Council on Illegitimacy
44 East 23rd Street
New York, N.Y. 10010

Planned Parenthood—World Population
810 Seventh Avenue
New York, N.Y. 10019

Sex Information and Education Council of the U.S. (SIECUS)
1855 Broadway
New York, N.Y. 10028

The Society for the Scientific Study of Sex, Inc.
12 East 41st Street
New York, N.Y. 10017

Transnational Research in Family Planning Behavior
American Institutes for Research
8555 Sixteenth Street
Silver Spring, Md. 20910

Religious Organizations

National Council of Churches
Commission on Marriage and the Family
475 Riverside Drive
New York, N.Y. 10027

Synagogue Council of America
Committee on the Family
235 Fifth Avenue
New York, N.Y. 10016

United States Catholic Conference
Family Life Bureau
1312 Massachusetts Avenue, N.W.
Washington, D.C. 20005

Federal Programs

A complete list of federal agencies supporting research and service programs
appears in the April 1971 issue of *Family Planning Perspectives* (Vol. 3, No. 2).

The U.S. Department of Health, Education and Welfare published an inventory
of population research supported by Federal agencies in 1970. It is entitled, "The
Federal Program in Population Research" (For sale by the Superintendent of

Documents, U.S. Government Printing Office, Washington, D.C. 20402. Price 70¢).

Publications

Newsletter. American Association of Sex Educators and Counselors. Quarterly notice of meetings, articles, books. Mailed to members.

Family Planning Perspectives. Available free of charge from the Center for Family Planning Program Development, 515 Madison Ave., New York, N.Y. 10022.

Emko Newsletter. A monthly digest of sex information available free from Emko Newsletter, 7912 Manchester Avenue, St. Louis, Mo. 63143.

Perspectives in Maternal and Child Health. Available from Dept. of Hygiene and Public Health, Johns Hopkins Univ., Room 1511, 615 North Wolfe St., Baltimore, Md. 21205.

Journal of Marriage and the Family. Available from the National Council on Family Relations, 1219 University Avenue, S.E., Minneapolis, Minn. 55414.

Studies in Family Planning. Available from The Population Council, 245 Park Ave., New York, N.Y. 10017.

Medical Aspects of Human Sexuality. Available from Clinical Communications, Inc., 18 East 48th St., New York, N.Y. 10017.

Sexology. Available from Sexology Corp., 200 Park Ave., South, New York, N.Y. 10003.

School Health Review. Published by the American Association for Health, Physical Education and Recreation, 1201 Sixteenth St., N.W., Washington, D.C. 20036.

Sexual Behavior. Available from Interpersonal Publications, Inc., 299 Park Avenue, New York, N.Y. 10017.

The Journal of Sex Research. Available from the Society for the Scientific Study of Sex, Inc., 12 East 41st St., New York, N.Y. 10017.

IV. GLOSSARY

Whether or not the educator or counselor feels it wise to interpret this vocabulary to the pupil or client, it is imperative that the professional be able to use this core vocabulary easily and with a sense of comfort. Here are a few basic and specific words selected from the glossary in *Human Sexuality* by James L. McCary.*

Abortion. Premature expulsion from the uterus of the product of conception—a fertilized ovum, embryo, or nonviable fetus.

Adolescence. The period of life between puberty (appearance of secondary sex characteristics) and adulthood (cessation of major body growth).

Adultery. Sexual intercourse between a married person and an individual other than his or her legal spouse.

Afterbirth. The placenta and fetal membranes expelled from the uterus following the birth of a child.

Anal eroticism. Pleasurable sensations in the region of the anus.

Androgen. A steroid hormone producing masculine sex characteristics and having an influence on body and bone growth and on the sex drive.

Autoerotic. Pertaining to self-stimulation or erotic behavior directed toward one's self; frequently equated with masturbation.

Bartholin's glands. Two tiny glands in a female, located at either side of the entrance to the vagina.

Birth control. Deliberate limitation of the number of children born—through such means as contraceptives, abstinence, the rhythm method, *coitus interruptus,* and the like.

Castration. Removal of the gonads (sex glands)—the testicles in men, the ovaries in women.

Celibacy. The state of being unmarried; abstention from sexual activity.

Cervix. Neck; in the female, the narrow portion of the uterus or womb that forms its lower end and opens into the vagina.

Climacteric. The syndrome of physical and psychologic changes that occur at the termination of menstrual function (i.e., reproductive capability) in the woman and reduction in sex-steroid production in both sexes; menopause; change of life.

Clitoris (adj. clitoral). A small, highly sensitive nipple of flesh in the female, located just above the urethral opening in the upper triangle of the vulva.

Coitus. Sexual intercourse between male and female, in which the male penis is inserted into the female vagina.

Coitus interruptus (also called "premature withdrawal"). The practice of withdrawing the penis from the vagina just before ejaculation.

Conception. The beginning of a new life, when an ovum (egg) is penetrated by a sperm, resulting in the development of an embryo; impregnation.

Condom. A contraceptive used by males consisting of a rubber or gut sheath that is drawn over the erect penis before coitus.

Contraception. The use of devices or drugs to prevent conception in sexual intercourse.

Cowper's glands. Two glands in the male, one on each side of the uretha near the prostate, which secrete a mucoid material as part of the seminal fluid.

Cunnilingus. The act of using the tongue or mouth in erotic play with the external female genitalia (vulva).

Diaphragm. A rubber contraceptive, used by women, that is hemispherical in shape and fits like a cap over the neck of the uterus (cervix).

Dysmenorrhea. Painful menstruation.

Dyspareunia. Coitus that is difficult or painful, especially for a woman.

Embryo. The unborn young in its early stage of development—in man, from one week following conception to the end of the second month.

Erection. The stiffening and enlargement of the penis (or clitoris), usually as a result of sexual excitement.

Erogenous zone. A sexually sensitive area of the body, such as the mouth, lips, breasts, nipples, buttocks, genitals, or anus.

Estrogen. A steroid hormone producing female sex characteristics and effecting the functioning of the menstrual cycle.

Fallopian tube. The oviduct or egg-conducting tube that extends from each ovary to the uterus in the female.

Fellatio. The act of taking the penis into the mouth and sucking it for erotic purposes.

Fertilization. The union of egg (ovum) and sperm (spermatozoon), which results in conception.

Fetus. In humans, the unborn child from the third month after conception until birth.

Foreplay. The preliminary stages of sexual intercourse, in which the partners usually stimulate each other by kissing, touching, and caressing.

Frigidity. Coldness, indifference, or insensitivity on the part of a woman to sexual intercourse or sexual stimulation; inability to experience sexual pleasure or gratification.

Genital organs (or genitals or genitalia). The sex or reproductive organs.

Gestation. Pregnancy; the period from conception to birth.

Gonad. A sex gland; a testicle (male) or ovary (female).

Homosexuality. Sexual attraction to, or sexual activity with, members of one's own sex; the opposite of heterosexuality.

Hymen. The membranous fold that partly covers the external opening of the vagina in most virgin females; the maidenhead.

Hysterectomy. Surgical removal of the female uterus, either through the abdominal wall or through the vagina.

Impotence. Disturbance of sexual function in the male that precludes satisfactory coitus; more specifically, inability to achieve or maintain an erection sufficient for purposes of sexual intercourse.

Incest. Sexual relations between close relatives, such as father and daughter, mother and son, or brother and sister.

Labia majora. (sing. labium majus). The outer and larger pair of lips of the female external genitals (vulva).

Labia minora (sing. labium minus). The inner and smaller pair of lips of the female vulva.

Lesbian. A female homosexual.

Libido. Sexual drive or urge.

Masturbation. Stimulation of the genitals through manipulation; autoeroticism.

Menopause. The period of cessation of menstruation in the human female, occurring usually between the ages of 45 and 55; climacteric; change of life.

Menstruation. The discharge of blood from the uterus through the vagina that normally recurs at approximately four-week intervals in women between the ages of puberty and menopause.

Nocturnal emission. An involuntary male orgasm and ejaculation of semen during sleep; a "wet dream."

Orgasm. The peak or climax of sexual excitement in sexual activity.

Ovary. The female sex gland, in which the ova are formed.

Ovulation. The release of a mature unimpregnated ovum from one of the Graafian follicles of an ovary.

Ovum (pl. ova). An egg; the female reproductive cell, corresponding to the male spermatozoon, that after fertilization develops into a new member of the same species.

Penis. The male organ of copulation and urination.

Premature ejaculation. Ejaculation prior to, just at, or immediately after intromission; *ejaculatio praecox*.

Prophylactic. A drug or device used for the prevention of disease, often specifically venereal disease—often used to describe a condom.

Puberty (or pubescence). The stage of life at which a child turns into a young man or young woman: i.e., the reproductive organs become functionally operative and secondary sex characteristics develop.

Scrotum. The pouch suspended from the groin that contains the male testicles and their accessory organs.

Semen. The secretion of the male reproductive organs that is ejaculated from the penis at orgasm and contains, in the fertile male, sperm cells.

Seminal vesicles. Two pouches in the male, one on each side of the prostate, behind the bladder, that are attached to and open into the sperm ducts.

Sex hormone. A substance secreted by the sex glands directly into the bloodstream, e.g., androgens (male) and estrogens (female).

Sexual intercourse. Coitus; the union of the male and female genitals.

Sodomy. A form of paraphilia, variously defined by law to include sexual intercourse with animals and mouth-genital or anal contact between humans.

Spermatozoon (pl. spermatozia). A mature male germ cell.

Sterilization. Any procedure (usually surgical) by which an individual is made incapable of reproduction.

Syphilis. Probably the most serious venereal disease, it is usually acquired by sexual intercourse with a person in the infectious stage of the disease and is caused by invasion of the spirochete Treponema pallidum.

Testis (pl. testes). The male sex gland or gonad, which produces spermatozoa.

Umbilical cord. The flexible structure connecting the fetus and the placenta; naval cord.

Urethra. The duct through which the urine passes from the bladder and is excreted outside the body.

Uterus. The hollow, pear-shaped organ in females within which the fetus develops; the womb.

Vagina. The canal in the female, extending from the vulva to the cervix, that receives the penis during coitus and through which an infant passes at birth.

Vas deferens (or ductus deferens). The sperm duct(s) in males, leading from the epididymis to the seminal vesicles and the urethra.

Vasectomy. A surgical procedure for sterilizing the male involving removal of the vas deferens, or a portion of it.

Venereal disease. A contagious disease communicated mainly by sexual intercourse, such as syphillis or gonorrhea.

Vulva. The external sex organs of the female, including the mons veneris, the labia majora, the labia minora, the clitoris, and the vestibule.

Womb. The uterus in the female.

Zygote. The single cell resulting from the union of two germ cells (sperm and egg) at conception; the fertilized egg (ovum).

BIBLIOGRAPHY

Abortion—The Agonizing Decision. David R. Mace, Abingdon Press, 1972.

Analysis of Human Sexual Response. Ruth and Edward Brecher, eds. New American Library, 1966.

And the Poor Get Children. Lee Rainwater, Quadrangle Books, 1960.

Black Rage. William Grier and Price Cobbs, Basic Books, Inc., 1968.

Child Psychology. 6th ed. Arthur T. Jersild, Prentice-Hall, 1968.

Clinical Approach to Marital Problems. Bernard L. Greene, Charles C Thomas, 1970.

"Clinical Child Psychology Newsletter" (publication dealing with sex education), Vol. X, Summer and Fall, 1971, article by Robert Pickett, sociologist. The American Psychological Association.

Comprehensive Group Psychotherapy. Harold I. Kaplan and Benjamin J. Sadock, eds. Williams & Wilkins Co., 1971.

Counseling and Psychotherapy. Carl R. Rogers, Houghton Mifflin Company (Riverside Press, Cambridge, Mass.), 1942.

"Effects of Mass Media on the Sexual Behavior of Adolescent Females," Patricia Schiller. Study published in Vol. I, Technical Reports of the Commission on Obscenity and Pornography, 1972. Supt. of Documents, U.S. Government Printing Office, Washington, D.C. 20402.

Fundamentals of Human Sexuality. Herant A. Katchadourian and Donald T. Lunde, Holt Rinehart and Winston, Inc., 1972.

Growth through Reason. Albert Ellis, ed. Science & Behavior Books, Palo Alto, California, 1971.

Gynecology and Obstetrics, Davis. Vol. II, Chapter 51. "Premarital and Marital Counseling," Harper and Row, 1971.

Helping the Handicapped Teenager Mature. Evelyn West Ayrault, Association Press, 1971.

Human Relations and the Family, Rose M. Sommerville, Teachers College, Columbia University, 1964.

Human Sexual Behavior and Sex Education. 2nd ed. Warren R. Johnson, Lea & Febiger, 1968.

Human Sexual Development. Edited by Donald L. Taylor, F. H. Davis Company, 1970.

Human Sexuality and Social Work. Edited by Harvey L. Gochros and LeRoy G. Schultz, Association Press, 1972.

249

Human Sexual Inadequacy. William H. Masters & Virginia E. Johnson, Little, Brown & Company, 1970.

Human Sexual Response. William H. Masters & Virginia E. Johnson, Little, Brown & Company, 1966.

Human Sexuality. James L. McCary, Van Nostrand-Reinhold, 1967.

Human Sexuality in Medical Education and Practice. Edited by Clark E. Vincent, Charles C Thomas, 1968.

Human Teaching for Human Learning. George I. Brown, Viking Press, 1971.

"Introducing Human Sexuality into the Graduate Social Work Curriculum," Harvey L. Gochros, *Social Work Education Reporter,* Vol. XVIII, No. 3., Sept.–Oct. 1970.

Listening With the Third Ear. Theodor Reik, Pyramid Publications, 1972.

Manual for Group Premarital Counseling, Lyle B. Gangsei, Association Press, 1971.

Marital Therapy. Edited by Hirsch L. Silverman, Charles C Thomas, 1972.

Marriage Counseling—Theory and Practice. Dean Johnson, Prentice-Hall, 1961.

Modern Woman. Edited by George D. Goldman and Donald S. Milman, Charles C Thomas, 1969.

Nature and Evolution of Female Sexuality. Mary J. Sherfey, Random House, 1972.

Patterns of Life. Dolloff and Resnick, Charles E. Merrill, 1972.

"Pilot Training Project for Professionals in a Model Interdisciplinary Approach for Counseling," Patricia Schiller. Published in the *Family Coordinator,* Vol. 18, No. 4, Oct. 1969.

Psychodrama and Sociodrama in American Education. Edited by B. D. Haas, Beacon House.

Readings in Marriage Counseling. Edited by Clark E. Vincent, Thomas Y. Crowell Company, 1957.

Report to the President, White House Conference on Children, 1970. Supt. of Documents, U.S. Government Printing Office, Washington, D.C. 20402, 1971.

"Sex Education: Who Is Teaching the Teachers?" *Teachers College Record,* No. 2, December 1967, 69:214.

"Sex Education for the Handicapped," Medorn S. Bass. *Family Life Coordinator,* Vol. XIII, No. 3., July 1964, pp. 59–68.

Sex in the Adolescent Years. Edited by Isadore Rubin and Lester Kirkendall, Association Press, 1968.

Sex in the Childhood Years. Edited by Isadore Rubin and Lester Kirkendall, Association Press, 1970.

Sex in Marriage. Dorothy W. Baruch, and Hyman Miller, Hart Publishing Co., 1970.

Sexual Myths and Fallacies. James L. McCary. Van Nostrand–Reinhold Company, 1971.

Sexuality: A Search for Perspective. Edited by Donald Grummon. Van Nostrand–Reinhold Company, 1971.

Technical Report of the Commission on Obscenity and Pornography, Vol. V. Supt. of Documents, U.S. Government Printing Office, Washington, D.C. 20402, 1972.

"Webster School—A District of Columbia Program for Pregnant Girls," Children's Bureau, U.S. Dept. of H.E.W.

Woman's Choice: A Guide to Contraception, Fertility, Abortion, and Menopause. Robert H. Glass and Nathan G. Kase, Basic Books, Inc., 1970.

Your Growing Child and Sex. Helene S. Arnstein, Bobbs-Merrill Company, 1967.

INDEX

abortion, 57–58, 99, 138
 counseling in adolescent pregnancies,
  79–80, 138
 liberalization of laws regarding, 29
adolescent pregnancies:
 abortion counseling in, 79–80, 99,
  138
 counseling programs for, 75–79, 138–
  139
 and educational system, 73–74
 group approach to counseling of, 108–
  109
 problems of, 72–73
 problems of fathers, 74
 statistics relating to, 29, 72
 surveys of, 104–105
adoption, 129–130
adultery, 24
American Association of Marriage and
 Family Counselors, 96
American Association of Pastoral Counselors, 133
American Association of School Administrators, 135
American Association of Sex Educators and Counselors (AASEC), 27,
 34, 85, 96, 133, 134, 136, 137, 172,
 180
American School Health Journal, 207
Augustine, St., 21

Bass, Medora S., 81, 82
Bible as influence on sexual attitudes,
 20–21

birth control, 28, 57, 65, 76,
 advisability for handicapped, 83
 rhythm method, 47
 see also contraceptives, use of; family planning
blind man's walk, *see* trust walk
Bloom, Jean L., Dr., 82
Brown, George I., 95

Calderwood, Deryck, Dr., 133
Calvin, John, 21
celibacy, 21
Center for the Study of Sex Education
 in Medicine, 140
Chamis, George C., Dr., 203
Christenson, Cornelia V., 37
churches:
 and sex education, 27, 133–134, 182–
  183
 training programs offered by, 183–
  185
coeducation, 44–45
college training programs, *see* sex educator, college training programs for
communication, 3-part exercise in, 95–
  96
community preparation for sex education, 186–188
 outline of procedures, 187–189
Comstock Laws, 21–22
contraceptives:
 as factor in sex revolution, 24–25
 influence of religion on, 65–66
 surveys relating to, 28

251

contraceptives (*cont.*)
  use by handicapped, 83
  use of, 25, 26, 28, 57, 65–66, 138
  see also birth control; family plan-
    ning
Coombs, Robert H., Dr., 39

day care for children, 29
decision-making, teaching of, 126–127
desensitization, use of, 175–176
deviant sexual behavior, 37
double standard, 20
  absence in black community, 41
  Luther's rejection of, 21
  medieval Christianity as root of, 21
  Puritans and, 21
  see also single standard

Elementary and Secondary Education
    Act, 27
elementary school training programs,
    see under sex educator
Ellis, Havelock, 23
Encounter Sessions, 95–96, 130
extramarital intercourse, *see* sexual in-
    tercourse

family life:
  disorganization in, 28–29
  influence of poverty on, 41–42
family planning, 57, 65
  education and counseling in, 26, 100–
    101
  for handicapped, 83
  outline for teaching of, 207–209
  problems most frequently discussed
    in, 138–139
  role of Federal Government in, 27–
    28, 72, 137
  role of sex educator in, 101–102
  see also birth control; contraceptives
Family Planning Service and Popula-
    tion Research Act, 28
family-planning movement, 25
finger dancing, 92
Freud, Sigmund, 23
frigidity, *see* human sexuality, psycho-
    logical aspects of

Genné, William, Rev., 133
Gochros, Harvey L., Dr., 178

Gordon, Sol, Dr., 134
Gorham, Peggy, 166
graduate and professional school train-
    ing programs, *see under* sex edu-
    cator
Graffiti Board, use of in counseling,
    99–100
group-centered approach, 51, 104–106,
    127
  case discussion in, 110–111
  as a growth experience, 106
  and parents, 109
  reactions of students, 108–109
  relation of group to teacher, 106–107,
    127–128
  responsibilities of leader, 107–108
  use of role-playing in, 113–115

handicapped, the:
  sex counseling of, 80–82
  techniques in teaching, 81
homosexuality, 29, 37, 71, 98, 115–116
human sexuality, biological aspects of,
    35–36, 211–213
  discussion with children, 68–69
  importance of accurate knowledge of,
    46
  infertility, 139
  language of, 48–50, 85–88, 99, 195–
    196
  menopause, 139, 211
  menstruation, 68
  nocturnal emission, 69
  orgasm, 46, 60–61,
  teaching of, 36, 193–194
human sexuality, psychological aspects
    of, 33, 36–37, 138
  frigidity, 58–59, 61–62, 138
  premature ejaculation, 61, 138, 211
  see also sexual identity, development
    of
human sexuality, social aspects of, 37–
    41, 101, 138, 189–90
  dating, 118–119
  during adolescence, 103, 107, 117
  during post-adolescence, 118
  and group counseling, 104–105, 107–
    108
  in marriage, 66–67

incorporation, use of, 176
Interfaith Council for Sex Education, 133
Israel, home life in, 40

Johnson, Dean, 89
Johnson, Virginia, 52
Johnson, Warren K., 49
Johnson, Warren P., 60

Kinsey, Alfred, 23
Kirkendall, Lester A., 34

Levy, Ronald B., 115
Lief, Harold I., Dr., 86, 141
life-line approach, 97–98
Luther, Martin, 21
Lynd, Robert S. and Helen Merrell, 23

Mace, David R., 79
McHugh, James, Father, 133
Malfetti, James L., 25
marriage problems, 66–67
    limitations on the retarded, 81
Marriage Council of Philadelphia, 133, 141
mass media, and sexual identity development, *see* sexual identity, development of
Masters, William, Dr., 52
Masters and Johnson sex studies, 23, 212
masturbation, 37, 48, 59–60, 80, 97, 195
Mattachine Society, 140
"me as a kid," 94–95
Menninger Foundation, 133, 141
modeling, 50
modesty in the home, 194–195
    see also nudity
Mussero, P., 39

Nash, Ethel, 175
National Association for Retarded Children, 81
National Council of Churches, 133
National Education Association, 135
nonverbal communication, 50–51
nudity, 69–70, 97–99, 194–195

orgasm, *see* sexual intercourse; human sexuality, biological aspects of

parents, training of, 185–186, 189–90, 192–193, 209–211
peer group, *see* sexual identity, development of; human sexuality, social aspects of
Pomeroy, Wardell B., Dr., 37
population problem in U.S., 29
pornography, 34, 48, 134
    President's Commission on Pornography and Obscenity, 122, 134
pregnancies, adolescent, *see* adolescent pregnancies
premarital intercourse, *see* sexual intercourse
premature ejaculation, *see* human sexuality, psychological aspects of
preschool training programs, *see under* sex educator
primary schools; sex education in:
    bibliography for, 200–201
    outline of goals, 191, 198–199, 201–202
    outline of program, 191–192, 199–200, 202–203
public schools, sex education in, 32–33, 73–74, 135
Puritans and sex, 21

Rainwater, Lee, Dr., 41
Reed, David M., 86
reflective exercise, 90–91
Reik, Theodor, 88
retarded, sex counseling and education of, 81–83
Rogers, Carl R., 106
role-playing, 113–115
    sample situations, 117–119
    use with elementary-school children, 116
Rutherford, E., 39

Sanger, Margaret, 22
Schiller, Patricia, Dr., 166, 173
secondary schools, sex education in:
    outline for teaching of family planning, 207–209
    sample program for, 203–205

sensitivity development, 127
  exercises, for, 90–92
sensitization, use of, 176
sex counselor:
  abortion counseling, 79–80
  activities of, 30–31, 181
  in clinics, 136
  in college health services, 137, 139–
    140
  counseling for adolescent pregnancies,
    76–78
  counseling of elderly, 209, 211–213
  counseling of handicapped, 80–82
  features of effective training program
    for, 143–144
  group counseling, 62–63, 104–106
  initial interviews, 53
  needed to work in different settings,
    142
  premarital counseling, 62–63, 138
  questionnaire for trainees, 145–146
  role of, as opposed to sex educator,
    29–31
  sterilization counseling, 138
  techniques employed by, 88, 96, 107–
    108, 113–115
  training in listening, 88–89
  training of ministers as, 133, 141
  types of problems seen by, 181–182
  use of films by, 111–112
  use of joint interviews, 55
  use of lecture and discussion groups,
    124–125
  use of reflective questions, 89–90
  use of tapes, 112–113
sex counselor, training programs for,
    see under sex educator
sex education in community, 186–189
sex educator:
  activities of, 30
  art and music as teaching aids, 121–
    122
  in clinics, 136
  in college health services, 137, 139–
    140
  in education of handicapped, 81–83
  effective training programs for, 143–
    144
  literature as teaching aid, 119–120

objectives of teaching programs, 197–
    198
  preparation of community for sex ed-
    ucation, 186–188
  preparation of parents for sex edu-
    cation, 185–186
  questionnaire for trainees, 145–146
  and sex counselor differentiated, 29–
    31
  students' perception of, 96–97, 105,
    108–109
  techniques employed by, 87–88, 89–
    90, 96, 107–108, 113–115, 122–
    124, 126–128
  training in listening, 88–89
  training of ministers as, 133, 141
  use of lecture and discussion groups,
    125
  working in different settings, 142
sex educator, college training programs
    for:
  course outline, 173–175
  type of programs, 172
sex educator, elementary and secondary
    school training programs for:
  concepts behind, 156
  evaluation by trainees, 161–162, 168–
    170
  plan of, 155
  problems presented in, 157
  projects completed in, 166–168
  teaching methods used, 157, 161,
    164–165
  topics covered, 160
  trainee comments on, 158–159
sex educator, graduate and professional
    training programs for:
  outline of curriculum, 177–179
  summer courses and workshops, 179–
    180
  techniques used in, 175–177
sex educator, preschool training pro-
    grams for:
  conclusions reached by trainees, 151–
    153
  evaluation of, by trainees, 153–155
  goals of, 144
  outline of contents, 147–148
  practicum projects in, 148–150
  problems presented in, 147

self-awareness training, 151
supervision of trainees, 150–151
Sex Information and Educational Council of the United States (SIECUS), 27
Sex Knowledge and Attitude Test (SKAT), 86
sex-education movement, 25
sex-role development, 38–39, 67–68, 71, 79, 193
sexual conflicts, 71
  in marriage, 66–67, 138
sexual identity, development of, 33–34 36, 38–40, 42, 56, 79, 85, 189, 192–194
  in adolescence, 44, 103
  influence of home life, 34, 56, 103, 132
  influence of mass media, 34–35, 51
  parental influence, 39, 42–44, 67–69, 71, 139, 193–194
  see also sex-role development; human sexuality
sexual intercourse:
  during pregnancy, 47
  extramarital, 63–64, 97
  foreplay, 61
  oral-genital, 47–48, 61
  and orgasm, 46–47, 60–62
sexual mores, 19–20, 45
  among black Americans, 40–41
  in lower socio-economic groups, 64–65
  influence of Bible on, 20
  influence of minority groups on, 24
  of ancient Greeks, 21
sexual myths, 46–48, 138
sexual self-image:
  development of, 85–86

during childhood, 94–95
use of sensitivity training in, 90–91
sexual stimuli:
  alcohol, 47
  male and female reactions to, 36–37, 119
  pornography, 48
sin, sex as, 20–21
single standard, 45
  see also double standard
Social-Sex Attitude Inventory, 75–77
  use of by sex educators and counselors, 85
socialization of children, 38–39, 44–45
socio-drama, see role-playing
Somerville, Rose, 119
Staples, Robert, Dr., 40, 41
Sullivan, Harry Stack, Dr., 38
survey of teacher-preparation institutions, 25

team-teaching:
  justification for, 123, 131
  lecture and discussion groups, 124–125
  use, of 122–124
therapeutic relationship, 106–107
trust walk, 93–95
Tyler, Edward A., Dr., 175, 178

venereal disease, 22

Webster School, 75–77, 104, 124
wet dreams, see human sexuality, biological aspects of
White House Conference for Children:
  identity exercise developed, 94
  report quoted, 25